Wind and Shadow

Chrissie Parker

Copyright
Wind Across the Nile © Chrissie Parker 2018
First published by Fossend Publishing 2018
Devon, England

Cover Design © Rachel Lawston Designs 2018

This novel is a work of fiction. Names, characters and events are fictitious and a product of the author's imagination and any resemblance to actual persons, living or dead, is entirely coincidental.

All rights reserved. No part of this publication may be reproduced, stored in a retrieval system, or transmitted in any form or by any other means, electronic, mechanical, photocopying, recording or otherwise, without the prior permission of the copyright owner.
ISBN-13: 978-1916402508
ISBN-10: 191640250X

Also by the Author

Integrate (Book one of the Moon Series)

Temperance (Book two of the Moon Series)

Among the Olive Groves

The Secrets (A collection of poems and short stories)

Dedication

To my amazing cousin Jessica Betts,
who loves Egypt as much as I do.
Love you loads JB.

CHAPTER ONE

Southampton, England, 1909

The night was still. The damp chill of late autumn seeped its way through the small ramshackle dwelling. The night seemed darker than normal, as though a thick swathe of tar had been painted across the sky. Candles flickered throughout the gloomy room, casting an eerie yellow glow. Wax pooled and dripped off the side, mixing with other detritus that littered the floor. It was an unwelcome, seedy and dirty place that the family was forced to call home.

Albert MacKenzie's weak and frail body was racked with excruciating pain. He lay on the uncomfortable bed, tangled in a damp, threadbare sheet, and his mind drifted back and forth between stark reality and dream-like hallucinations. His eyes occasionally flicked open to take in his squalid surroundings, before closing as he drifted off again; in and out of consciousness. The stench of stale alcohol surrounded him, seeping from every pore, permeating the bed, spreading loathsome tentacles across the room. Thousands of memories flew through his confused mind, taking him away from his current hell and, as they finally faded, he would find himself back in the same place: the small, cramped cesspit he called home, staring at the one constant in his life.

The person he loved above all else.

The person he would gladly die for.

His beloved wife, Randa.

He saw her again now. Her beautiful flawless face. Raven locks that tumbled long and straight around her shoulders. Beautiful dark chestnut eyes; pools of deep liquid that pulled you in and seemed to go on forever. Her dainty delicate frame, so small and precious, that he always felt a need to protect, just as he would a fragile piece of ancient pottery. Looking at Randa, Albert could see she had been weeping for him. Her cheeks were stained with remnants of salty tears, her expression a mixture of love and utter despair. She looked exhausted as though she hadn't slept for days.

Albert didn't want her to cry for him. He was undeserving.

This moment called death was a testament to his thoughtlessness. His complete self-absorption. Of putting himself and his own sinful needs above those of his wife and child. It made him angry but, more than that, he was ashamed. His body was failing through abuse and neglect, and he only had himself to blame.

Albert's eyes rolled and flickered once more, to another hallucination that he was unable to stop. It dragged him under, transporting him to a different, happier time.

Egypt, it was a land far removed from the cold, miserable, polluted climes of England. Distant memories stirred within him and he found himself standing in the dry heat, wearing his best suit and favourite hat. The sun shone brightly upon him and dust swirled at his feet, coating the hem of his trousers in a light brown film. Looking around, he smiled.

He was in Thebes.

He was home.

This is where it had all begun. This was where he had first met Randa, his beautiful Egyptian wife. He had been happy, living in a country he adored. They had fallen in love and conceived a child, and he had loved them both dearly, but it wasn't to be.

His aristocratic English family was furious. He had disgraced them, and Randa had shamed her Egyptian family. Both had been cut off. With little money and only a few meagre possessions to their name, they left Egypt, humiliated and disavowed.

~

Albert's daydream abruptly ended and he was brought back to stark reality: the stinking Victorian slum, to the stench, the pain and the depression that was now his everyday existence. Randa was still loyally sitting by his bedside, cradling the young child — their daughter. She was as pretty as her mother and just as loving. He tried in vain to reach out to her but his body refused. He no longer had the strength, the pain of it all was unbearable, and unforgiving.

It was time. As suddenly as the flame of a candle can be extinguished by a whisper of breath, Albert's body failed. Intense pain ripped through him, wrenching him from his family. He was barely able to say '*I love you*' as his heart finally shattered and withered, forcing him into the bleak never-ending darkness that was death.

CHAPTER TWO

London, England, 2002

The familiar chaotic soundtrack of London awoke Cora Thomas. She turned onto her back and lay there, staring at the ceiling, listening. An occasional siren screamed down the road, planes circled overhead, people shouted and called to each other on the street outside and her neighbour's radio played just a little too loudly.

She was home, back in her London flat with the squeaky floorboards, erratic boiler and views of cluttered urbanism. She had returned home the previous night after saying a tearful farewell to the wilds of Scotland and her Great Aunt Mary. She had spent the last few weeks in her old family home, Craigloch Manor. It had been the most upsetting and traumatic time of her life.

Her parents' house had been so familiar and yet alien. Since moving to London six years previously, in her early twenties, she had only managed to visit them once a year and Scotland was far removed from the bright lights, hustle and bustle of London. She felt isolated there, the nearest neighbour being almost a mile away, with nothing but a vast expanse of trees and rolling countryside between. It truly was the definition of remote.

Even though the feeling of isolation had weighed heavily upon her, the manor had been peaceful and was, after all, her family home. It had provided the solitude she'd needed before being subjected to the public outpouring of grief that had inevitably taken place. On the day of the funeral, the house had come to life, filling to the brim with distant relatives and family friends, all wanting to pay their respects, all wanting to pass on cherished memories of her family.

Stretching, Cora sat up and got out of bed, she shuffled into the kitchen and made herself a pot of coffee; after pouring herself a large cup, she walked into the living room and sat down. Sipping the hot liquid, Cora stared out onto the dull London street, her mind flashed back to that fateful night two weeks ago. She had been getting ready for bed when the phone rang. Answering the call, she had listened to the voice at the other end as though it were a dream. Once the call was over, she had been sick, her body reacting violently to the tragic news, forcing her to lie down on the cold bathroom floor in case she passed out. Waves of nausea had continued to plague her throughout the following few hours, making her feel as though she were being tossed about on a storm-ridden ship.

That phone call had completely changed her life.

Her parents and brother were dead, all killed in a car accident. It was then that the dizziness and nausea had subsided and her brain kicked in. There had been a frantic rush to get to Scotland, driving northwards at breakneck speed. In a daze, her mind had worked overtime, as street lamps and headlights flashed past in a hazy blur.

Maybe the police and doctors were wrong?

Maybe it was someone else's family and not hers?

Cora had desperately tried to hold on to some hope. Everything would be okay, it wasn't her family, it was all a huge mistake. But, upon reaching the hospital, her worst fears had been confirmed, and her hope fizzled away to nothing.

The hospital confirmed that her family had died and were never coming back. Her mum and dad were gone; her younger brother Alastair, lost far too early.

Exhausted, Cora had collapsed into the arms of the doctor as the grief enveloped her. She was unable to stop crying, and the dizziness and nausea returned in great crashing waves. The sympathetic hospital staff sat her in a quiet, clean, but clinical, relative's room where her shaking hands clutched a cup of lukewarm, stewed tea. She had tried her best to listen, to take it all in as the doctors explained everything, but she found it hard. The journey to Scotland had exhausted her and she was so tired from lack of sleep and stress. She was also weak from not eating and it was all she could do not to pass out, but she had to listen. She needed to know what had happened.

A kindly police officer informed her that it had been a stupid senseless accident caused by bad weather and an unsafe road surface; there was nothing anyone could have done. He assured Cora that her family hadn't suffered, death had been instantaneous and they wouldn't have felt a thing, but it didn't make it any easier. If anything, it made it worse. How could she blame weather and tarmac? If it had been a drunk driver or someone driving without a license, she would have had someone to blame, somewhere to vent her grief-tainted anger, but she couldn't and she was forced to accept that it was an accident.

Cora asked if she could see her family one last time — she needed to see them — but the doctor refused. They were too badly injured. The hospital had tracked down the family's dentist so that identification could be confirmed from dental records; their remaining belongings, like their bodies, were too damaged.

Cora had sunk back into the uncomfortable seat in the relative's room and the awful reality of the situation hit her. They were gone and she had never been given the chance to say goodbye.

~

Grief bubbled to the surface again, and tears pricked her eyes, but she defiantly swiped at them with the back of her hand. Draining the last of her morning coffee, Cora knew she couldn't spend another day crying, but it was hard and she never knew when the anguish would creep up on her. She settled her gaze upon the outside world. London. The weather had turned miserable, an overcast day with darkening sky, which littered everything with rain. Rivulets of silvery water ran down the windows as another cloud passed overhead, shedding its load on the house and deluging everything in sight.

Cora turned her back on the elements. It was time to unpack and sort out a new normal. She was feeling ungrounded. Normally when things went wrong in her life, she would call her mum and talk things through. Her mum was very supportive and always seemed to have the right answer. She would give anything to be able to pick up the phone and talk to her mum but it just wasn't possible.

~

Later that day the rain still fell heavily, but at least London was warmer than Scotland. As Cora wiped down the side in the kitchen, she caught sight of the engagement ring on her finger. It was a shock to still see it there. Forcefully, she yanked it off and threw it onto the floor. She was still so angry with Damon, her ex-fiancé. He had hurt her so deeply, just when she reached her lowest point.

Cora had met Damon Warner three years before, when she had taken a new job in the financial heart of the city. He had walked into the office one sunny day and immediately struck a chord with her. They got to know each other as work colleagues and it wasn't long before she found herself sitting across a table from him at one of the city's most romantic restaurants. They had grown closer over the next year, sharing a love of good food and regular visits to the cinema. It helped them wind down after a long day at the office, and they both loved watching the latest films. A year later, he had proposed and everything in Cora's life had seemed perfect.

Then the accident happened and she lost her family. Just when she needed Damon the most, he failed to turn up for the funeral. He had arrived late in the afternoon, after the mourners had departed, and they had argued, leaving her tense and on edge for the rest of the day. Later that night, she had learned the reason for Damon's tardiness. An unexpected text message arriving on his phone revealed to Cora that he had been unfaithful to her with a work colleague. He had told Cora his late arrival at her family's funeral had been due to having to work, when he'd actually been with another woman all along. She couldn't forgive his betrayal and insensitivity. It was just too much to take in and her world completely fell to pieces. In a fit of anger, she had banished him from the house, telling him that she never wanted to see him again.

Turning her back on the ring, and the heartache it brought, Cora walked into the small living room and shook thoughts of the past from her head. She turned on the lamp and caught sight of a carrier bag on the sofa. She had completely forgotten about it. Figuring it would be a good distraction, she sat down, opened it and removed the contents. Her mind instantly flew back to Craigloch Manor.

After the funeral Cora had gone through her parents' house in great detail, cleaning, tidying, and sorting personal items into bags for the charity shop and landfill, whilst taking a few keepsakes for herself. It had been a mammoth and unwelcome job but it had to be done. So many memories surfaced. Whilst going through her parents' wardrobe she had come across her dad's favourite suit. The one he had worn to every wedding, funeral and event. The last time she had seen him wear it was at Alastair's graduation. Her parents had been so proud of her brother that day. She had held the suit closely and inhaled, breathing in the unmistakable scent of her dad's aftershave and cigars. It had been so upsetting to put it in the charity bag but she also knew she had no use for it.

The hardest thing had been clearing out her mum's craft room. Mum had collected so many things over the years: yarn for knitting, material for patchworking and making clothes, and multi-coloured threads for cross stitch, all skills she had, and had tried to teach Cora over the years. But it wasn't until she opened the bottom drawer of the dresser that Cora really broke down. Buried inside was every drawing, and card that Cora and Alastair had ever made as children and presented lovingly to their parents. Cora hadn't known that her mum had kept them all, or that they had meant so much to her. Despite knowing she should be clearing the house, Cora had sat there and read and looked at every single one of them, sometimes laughing, sometimes crying. Once finished, she had carefully packed them into a box to go back to London with her.

Clearing the house had taken days, and she had ended up in parts of the house she'd rarely been, including the attic. After opening the small door at the end of the landing, and climbing narrow steps, Cora had found herself in the cramped confines of the eaves. Stepping gingerly in the darkness. Under dim electric light she had battled with dust, cobwebs and gloom, surprised at the amount of stuff her parents owned.

After hours of sorting, Cora had spied an old wooden trunk, hidden away, barely in sight. It had been locked but, after a lengthy search with no key to be found, she pried it open with an old iron drapery rod that she found. After dropping the rod, she pulled out the items. There were three old cotton shawls, worn with age and full of holes, the colour sadly faded. In addition, there were some old photographs, two small stone statues, and two old maps. One was labelled 'Cairo, Egypt' and one was of a place called 'Thebes'. Finally, she uncovered an old battered, leather-bound book. She'd never seen these items before and her interest piqued.

Sitting in the murky attic, as dust motes danced around her in twinkling shafts of yellow electric glow, Cora slowly unwound the cord that was wrapped around the book. Carefully, she opened it and perused the aged, yellowing pages.

The writing was indecipherable.

Who had it belonged to? Her parents?

Even as she thought about it, she knew the items were much older than that. They were before her parents' time. Reaching for the maps, she unfolded one. There were no airports on it and the writing was a swirling, old-fashioned script.

Intrigued, she had stood and dusted down her clothes, before gathering up the items, deciding to take them to London so that she could study them further. After hauling down everything, she had left the small cramped space, and shut off the light leaving the attic to its forgotten darkness.

Now, here she was, back in her own home, with the contents of the trunk on her lap. She stared again at the photographs, faded, sepia-coloured images, printed on thick card rather than paper. Over the years they had become ragged at the edges and spotted with mildew. Despite the damage, the images were still visible: portraits of a couple. The man looked English but the woman was foreign, yet Cora couldn't work out where she was from. One photograph showed the couple seated and holding a baby. In another they were older and the baby was now a young girl of around three years of age, although she couldn't be sure. She wished she knew who they were, but the damage to the photos made it difficult to see their faces properly, and nothing was written on them.

Placing the photos aside, Cora lifted the book and unravelled the length of leather cord. Flicking through the delicate aging pages, one thing stood out. Each leaf was covered with the same unrecognisable script. Perhaps a life's work recorded for posterity? Buried within the pages was another aged, sepia-coloured photograph of the couple, this time a wedding portrait. They looked so young and happy, the bride exotically beautiful.

Cora's mind filled with questions. Who were they and what did they have to do with her family? She knew next to nothing about her family history and what little she did know related to her dad's side. Her mum's side was a complete mystery, a subject that hadn't been discussed. Cora didn't even know the names of her maternal grandparents. They had died when she and her brother were very young and they were never mentioned.

Leaning over to the coffee table, she reached for the phone and dialled her great aunt, then waited for the line to connect.

"Aunt Mary. It's Cora."

"Cora my darling, it's lovely to hear from you. How are you?"

"I'm bearing up, Mary. How are you?"

"I'm okay. I still can't believe that William and Elizabeth are gone. It's so hard coming to terms with what's happened. The weather's getting colder so I can't go so far, but I'm okay otherwise. What can I do for you?"

"I found some old stuff of mum and dad's. Photos of a couple I've never seen before, some statues and a book written in what looks to be a foreign language. They were locked in a trunk in the attic at the manor. Do you know anything about them?"

The line was silent and the pause a little too lengthy.

"No, my dear, I don't." Swiftly she changed the subject. "When are you going back to work, my dear?"

"I'm not sure I am." Cora steered the conversation back, certain that Mary was hiding something. She pushed her again.

"Are you sure you don't know something, Mary? Anything at all would help."

"I'm sorry, my dear, I really don't. I have to go, but look after yourself. I'll be in touch soon."

All that remained was a dead line. She was no further forward and it was unlike Mary not to talk to her at length on the phone, normally she was so chatty. Cora was unsettled. She was sure by her reaction that Mary was leaving something unsaid, but it would keep. For now.

~

Cora's best friend Erica sat opposite her in the small kitchen. The sun had long set, street lights were glowing and a large dish of half eaten lasagna sat on the table between them. The two women had been best friends since school, and enjoyed spending time together.

It had been a warm spring day when a young Cora had arrived at school as the new girl. She had stood in the playground at lunchtime, shy and unsure of what to do next. Two boys, who had been following her all morning, sneaked up and began to tease her again. One had pulled her hair hard, making her head snap back. Her neck seared, and tears stung her eyes. The other had laughed whilst trying to grab her bag from her, but she clung on tightly, refusing to let it go. As she struggled with them, kicking out blindly in the hope of making contact, she had slipped and fallen, grazing her hands and knees as she went down. A trickle of blood sprang from her knee and slid down her leg, staining her fresh white sock. Resigned, Cora had sat on the ground giving into the tears as boyish taunts circled her head.

Erica Johnson had appeared from nowhere and stepped in. She had seen what the boys were up to and it made her mad. After marching across the playground, she had grabbed one of them by his collar, then kicked him smartly in the shin, making him cry out. Erica then turned and held up her fists to the other boy, threatening to fight him if he didn't back off. The boys fled, knowing better than to mess with her. For a girl, Erica had a fierce reputation and a temper to match and won every battle she fought. Erica bent down, immediately taking control. She had wiped the blood from Cora's knee before helping her to her feet and giving her a consolatory hug.

It was the start of a friendship that would last a lifetime.

As she ate her pasta, Cora knew Erica was staring at her, she sighed as she pushed food around her plate. She was glad Erica had come to visit her but she wasn't in the mood for company. All she wanted to do was sit on the sofa and watch TV. She still couldn't work out why her life had gone so wrong.

Two months ago, life had been good. Her family had made regular trips down to see her, her dad and Alastair loving London because they could visit Lord's and the Oval to watch the cricket. But it was the time she spent with her mum that was most important to her. Every time her family visited, Cora and her Mum would choose another part of London to explore. One month they were traipsing around the shops in Knightsbridge, visiting Harrods and trying on ridiculously expensive clothes that neither of them could afford, for the fun of it. Another time they had got on the Underground and headed out to Kew, dragging her dad and Alastair with them. They had explored the gardens and that included a huge variety of plants and trees. It didn't matter where they went or what they did, the Thomas family always enjoyed spending time together. They had been a close and integral part of her life. She had a good job in London, one that she had fought hard to get, with fairly good prospects and she had shared her life with a man she loved.

Now it was all gone: her family dead, her cheating fiancé dumped and her job on the brink of resignation. She was left with nothing. How could she start again? What was she supposed to do without her family, the people who had always supported her, through good times, bad times and everything in between? Cora was well aware that they hadn't been happy about her move to London. They had been worried about their daughter heading to the capital but, despite their reservations, they had still supported her. Her dad had driven her to the city to flat hunt and paid her first month's deposit so that her mum wouldn't worry about her too much. Mum had phoned her every few days to check that she was eating, and that she hadn't got lost or mugged. Cora loved that they cared so much. Their loss now left a gaping hole in her life as well as her heart, and she really wasn't sure if she would recover. She would give anything to be able to phone home and hear her Mum say, "Hello my love!" once more.

"How are you?"

Cora looked up at Erica and shook her head, "Not good. I don't know how to deal with all of this. How do I come back from what's happened? How do I live again?"

WIND ACROSS THE NILE

Erica reached across the table and took hold of her best friend's hand. "By taking one step and one day at a time. I know that sounds trite, but that's all you can do."

"But I have no one."

"You have me."

"I know. And I'm so grateful for your friendship, and I know that you'll always be here for me, but how do I recover from the loss of my family? They were my whole life, every birthday, Christmas, every time I was ill. You know Mum taught me to make my first roast dinner? I'd be completely lost in the kitchen if it wasn't for her, she was so patient and I was so lucky to have her as a mum."

Cora paused and took a deep but shaky breath. "And Dad, he taught me how to drive, admittedly when I was fourteen, but I used to love it when we went out on the estate and he let me and Alastair get behind the wheel and drive across the fields and along the old tracks. I remember one summer we took Mum with us. We were heading out for a picnic by one of the lochs, but Al and I pestered dad to go driving, so much so, that on the way he relented. Mum was horrified, but by the time we finally got to the loch she was laughing as much as we were."

"That was such a great day. The four of us sat on an old ragged blanket eating cheese and pickle sandwiches, Al and Dad playing catch with an old rugby ball, Mum and I reading our favourite books as we watched them. I'd give anything to see them again, just one last time." Cora wiped away the stray tears that had spilled onto her cheeks. "How am I supposed to live without them? How am I supposed to move on?"

Erica shook her head. "I don't know. I've been part of your life for so long, but even I can't begin to imagine how you feel. I know you were close to them Cora. You had a family that most of us envied. I have no idea what the answer is, but you do need to try and keep on living. You don't have to let their memory die, they'll always be with you. Just take it a day at a time, and you know you can always call me anytime, anywhere."

"Thank you. I do appreciate having you in my life, Erica, and you know I will call you. Probably often," Cora said with a sad chuckle.

They fell silent and Erica continued to hold her best friend's hand. Cora could see the worry on Erica's face, probably because things were likely to get worse before they got better.

CHAPTER THREE

Oxford, England, 2002

He sat upright in the uncomfortable wingback chair. He hated these chairs, and always had. He had no idea why his father still kept them in the house. They were barely used; just another showy taste of his false grandeur.

His father's pacing was driving him mad, but he knew he couldn't interrupt. It was his father's way of thinking; how his mind worked. He would pace back and forth, slowly wearing out the carpet until, abruptly, he would stop, as all the thoughts that had been flying about his head finally settled into some kind of rational order.

This time, the pacing had lasted for fifteen minutes and he was still waiting for his father to stop and speak. He was tired and bored and, even worse, he hated being at his father's beck and call.

When he had been told that the mantle had finally been handed to him, he had rejoiced. He already knew the story. His father had been telling it to him since he was a child. Two families pitted against each other. One the master of the other. The other left with nothing but death and destruction in its wake. He'd always had a mean streak and was looking forward to taking over from his father and causing a little death and destruction of his own, but he was becoming impatient for it to begin.

His father suddenly stopped and rounded upon him.

"Take the job. Go to Egypt."

"But won't that take me away from the pursuit?"

"No."

"But..."

"Don't question me. Just go."

He sighed. His father had spoken. He wished *he* were fully in control, but his father had always kept a tight grip of the reins and was still reluctant to fully let go.

"Yes, Father."

The meeting was over.

He and his father barely spoke on a normal day, so there wasn't much love lost between them. It was the excuse he needed and he couldn't get out of the house quickly enough. Egypt it was, then. On his way out, he swiftly kissed his mother goodbye and climbed into his car. Reaching over to the glove box, he opened it and pulled out a large envelope. Dropping the papers into his lap, he scoured them. He could finally close another chapter of his life and begin again. This time he would make it count.

~

As each day dawned, Cora began to relax a little more. The recent traumatic events understandably turned her world upside down. She needed to figure out what she was going to do with the rest of her life. She needed a change of direction, but the direction itself eluded her. Or maybe she needed things to stay the same for a while, until she properly mourned. Ugh. It was hard to know what to do. One thing the death of her family *had* done was make her realise life was too short, which was why she had made the decision to leave her job. She hated it anyway. A soulless institution that left her bored and feeling as though she was stuck in a rut. If she were to make a new start, then why continue doing something unfulfilling?

The family solicitor had contacted her to tell her that the legal side of the estate was in hand and not to worry about anything. It was a relief to know it was being handled sensitively, but she didn't want any of it. All she wanted was her family back. She missed them terribly and their loss left an ache that wouldn't subside.

Cora lifted the mysterious leather bound book and turned it over and over in her hands, trying to make sense of why her parents had it and where it came from. She couldn't read the contents and had no idea how to even begin getting them translated. The more she thought about it, the more confused she became, and wished she knew more about her family history. She had even phoned Mary again, but her aunt was insistent that she didn't know anything. It was a complete mystery, one that made her more and more determined to find out what the items were and why they were in her parents' attic. Finally she realised she had something to focus on besides her turmoil.

~

A few days later, Cora awoke feeling a little brighter. The sun was shining, a welcome change from the continuous rain that had fallen lately. Perusing a newspaper, she caught up on the usual world events, celebrity gossip and sports headlines. As she half-heartedly skimmed the remaining pages, an advert for the latest exhibit at the British Museum caught her eye.

"I wonder...," she thought out loud, a plan forming in her mind. Glancing at the clock, she decided there was no time like the present. She needed to get out of the house anyway. Cabin fever was setting in. Pushing back her chair, Cora grabbed her coat and bag, and paused in the living

WIND ACROSS THE NILE

room to put the diary, photos, maps and statues into her bag.

A little over an hour later, she was standing in the courtyard of the British Museum staring up at the imposing stone columns of its main entrance. Making her way through a heaving mix of school parties and tourists, she climbed the stone steps, passed under the columns and entered the building through heavy glass doors. Once inside the atrium, she stopped in surprise. The size of it was astonishing. She'd only been there once before as a young child, and the beauty of the sweeping shiny marble staircases, vast gleaming floor space and enormous glass ceiling left her awestruck. She didn't remember it being so big and architecturally beautiful. Cora caught sight of the information desk, she remembered why she was there, and walked over to it.

"Can I talk to someone about these?" Cora asked, showing the statues to the man at the desk.

"I'm not sure, Miss." The man took a closer look at the statues. "They look like Shabti, but I can't be sure. Let's start with someone from the Middle East Department."

Whilst she waited, Cora watched the comings and goings in the atrium. The space was light, bright and airy and filled with tourists from many nations, interspersed with crocodile lines of smart, uniformed school children. Gazing upwards, her view filled with the enormous diamond-leaded glass roof. Through it was the most breath-taking view of delphinium blue sky laced with fluffy white clouds. It was as though someone had dropped her inside a huge bubble, and she marvelled at the heavenly view.

"Excuse me, Miss." The man interrupted her daydream and she turned her attention back to him. "Someone will be down in a few minutes."

Cora thanked him as he turned to assist the next person. She moved to the end of the desk, and picked up an information leaflet to read whilst she waited. It seemed the museum housed collections from all over the world, relating to a variety of ancient histories that included Egyptian, Roman, Greek and Persian, as well as many modern collections. Cora decided she would come back another day and explore properly. It was time she got out a bit more instead of being stuck at home watching TV all day.

A voice broke her concentration, and she placed the leaflet back in its holder. Looking up, she was greeted by man she didn't know. He had a friendly face, grey hair and beard and bright sparkling eyes.

"I understand you wanted to talk to someone about some statues?"

"Yes. I'm Cora." She held out her hand and he shook it.

"Professor Harry James. Let's take a seat in the library and you can tell me more."

Cora followed him across the atrium, through the gift shop and into the small library. Once seated, she pulled the items from her bag, set them on the table, and explained how they had come into her possession. The professor picked them up, and studied them carefully, before finally turning his full attention to the photographs.

"I can't really tell you much about the photos, other than the woman looks as though she could possibly be of Middle Eastern or North African origin. The man looks very aristocratic and, at a guess, I would say they lived about a hundred years ago, maybe more."

He placed them back on the table before picking up the statues.

"These are Egyptian. Unfortunately, I'm not an expert in that field. That would be my colleague, Professor Foster. We have some in the museum, they're called Shabti. If you turn them over you can just make out some hieroglyphs on the rear."

He showed her the unusual symbols on the reverse. She hadn't noticed them before and she gently traced her finger along the ancient writing. She felt a small flutter through her body as realisation set in that she was touching something that was probably thousands of years old.

Why on earth had they been in her parents' attic?

Mum and Dad had been normal people with relatively normal jobs; they never talked about history, let alone collected ancient artefacts. Her mum had been happiest knitting, sewing or in the kitchen baking, and her dad had loved his sport. Those were their true passions. It was puzzling.

Finally, Professor James turned his attention to the book. He opened it, and gently turned the delicate pages as if they were the most precious thing in the world to him.

"This is quite old, maybe eighty to a hundred years, but that's just an estimate. It could well be older. I think the writing is Egyptian Arabic, but again it's not really my area. It's a shame Professor Foster isn't here. He'd be able to confirm it for you, but he's in Egypt on an excavation. In fact, you've only just missed him as he flew out to Cairo yesterday. Whatever it is, I would take great care of it. The pages are really quite delicate."

"Thank you for being able to tell me as much as you have, Professor James."

"I'm sorry I couldn't be of more help. If you do want to speak to Professor Foster, he'll be back in a few months, or you could reach him at the Egyptian Museum in Cairo."

"Thanks again. I really appreciate it."

"You're welcome. I'm just sorry I couldn't be of more help."

Cora gathered the items, and safely stored them in her bag. They left the quiet solitude of the library and walked back out into the bright and noisy atrium. Professor James shook her hand one last time before leaving her standing in the swirling midst of museum visitors, contemplating her next move.

CHAPTER FOUR

Cairo, Egypt, 2002

The heat of the midday sun blazed upon the world below. It baked the earth, making it uncomfortable for both man and beast, neither shade nor breeze giving respite from its intensity. He pulled his hat farther down his forehead to protect his eyes from a glare that rendered his sunglasses nearly useless.

It was always an adjustment.

The dry burning heat of Egypt was always so different to the topsy-turvy inclement climate of England. Fanning himself in a futile attempt to keep cool, he crossed the bridge towards Tahrir Square. A brief breeze rising from the swirling rushing waters of the Nile below refreshed him. The phone in his pocket vibrated and he pulled it out. He'd been ignoring all of his father's calls since landing at the airport but, glancing at the screen, he smiled, recognising the number. This was definitely a call he wanted to take. Pressing the green button, he placed the phone to his ear.

"Yes."

Staring out across the shimmering waters, he listened to the voice. The conversation was brief and, once he had heard the essentials, he ended it and placed the device back in his pocket. So. She had turned up at the museum seeking help. His contact told him that she had uncovered information that his family had so far been unable to find. This was good news. He had been worried about leaving England and coming to Egypt, but his network of spies were doing their jobs well.

Keeping an eye on her was essential to his plan. He knew everything there was to know about Cora Thomas and her family. *His* family had been keeping tabs on *hers* for generations now, and the job had now fallen to him. It had become both an obligation and an obsession, but one he was more than willing to accept. It was his destiny, as much as it was hers. A desperate hope had continued to run through his family, down through the generations, a hope that the information they so desperately sought would one day finally surface.

So far, his family had been left disappointed. Ancestors had fallen into their graves, empty-handed. Until now. He didn't have finite proof as yet but, if his source was correct, new information had finally surfaced. A diary *did* exist. A diary that was key to *his* future. All he had to do was work out how to get his hands on it. It was time for the game to begin and, if the bitch got in his way, she, like many of her ancestors, would suffer greatly for it. Death would be the only outcome.

~

Sitting in the window of her flat, watching the world go by, Cora sipped a much-needed cup of tea. She mulled over the museum trip. She was so confused about the origins of these items. Her parents had rarely travelled beyond the UK. Most of Dad's time had been spent managing the estate at Craigloch and Mum had worked part time as a secretary; hardly the world's most exciting jobs, but they enjoyed them. She was desperate to discover more but had very little to go on, and it seemed the only person who could help was spending the next six months in Egypt. She had come up against a dead end. She caught sight of Erica walking up the path and went to let her in.

"Shouldn't you be at work?" Cora asked.

"No. I finally managed to get a day off, if you can believe it. I've been calling you all morning. I was worried. Where have you been?"

Cora poured her friend a cup of tea and they sat.

"I went to the British Museum." Cora sipped her tea before continuing. "I can't believe I forgot to tell you." She went to her bedroom to retrieve the bag of items.

"When I was at Mum and Dad's going through their stuff I went up into the attic. You won't believe what I found. There was a trunk and inside were maps, and photos and an old book written in some kind of Arabic," she explained as she carefully took each item out of the box. "I've never seen them before. So I went to the museum to see if they could tell me a bit more about them."

Bemused, Erica raised an eyebrow.

"Wow! These are fantastic! And could they help?"

"Sort of. It looks as though they're linked to Egypt, of all places, but the professor I spoke to couldn't be more specific as it's not his field. The one person who could have possibly helped is unavailable, so I've hit a bit of a dead end."

"So what are you going to do?"

"I've absolutely no idea."

"I meant, what are you going to do with your life?" Erica said with exasperation.

Cora understood Erica's disquiet, but it was hard enough just getting up in the morning, let alone worrying about what other people were thinking. And she certainly didn't have the strength to make life changing decisions.

"I don't know. I'm just taking it one day at a time. Just like you said."

"But what're you going to do for money? You gave up your job."

"I have plenty of savings, and I guess my parents' estate eventually so money's not a worry."

"It's not healthy shutting yourself away like this. You need to get on with your life."

"And I will, Erica. Just as soon as I've worked out what that life is."

Erica persisted. Taking her friend's hand in hers, she forced Cora to look at her.

"I'm saying this because I care. I know the rest of your family aren't alive any more, but *you* are. They wouldn't want to see you sitting around and moping like this. They'd want to you to seize the moment. They'd want you to get out there and live your life. Please Cora, if you won't do it for me, do it for them."

A lengthy silence followed. The soundtrack of London continued on around them, puncturing the awkward uneasy stillness. Cora stared out at the world beyond her flat. On the other side of the glass everything continued as normal. People were going to work, children to school, and families were taking holidays, but she was stationary. She'd had her entire life snatched from under her, her family ripped from her arms, with no chance to say a proper goodbye to them. No chance of hearing their voices again. She would miss her brother and the way he would always joke with her and make her laugh. She would miss visiting her parents and seeing her mum roll her eyes as her dad disappeared into his office on the pretext of doing some work when they all knew he was secretly watching the cricket. But most of all she would miss her mum, her best friend and confidante. The woman who had taught her about life, taught her to cook and sew; the person Cora knew she could run to whenever she had a problem or needed advice. It felt as though the world continued to spin below her feet, yet she was fixed in place. There was no future. No present. Just a painful past.

The hurt, grief and loss had swamped her and continued to smother her. She was trapped by it, unable to move forward. She was unable to free herself from it, and it was pulling her deeper and deeper each day. Her life was no longer her own and, in that moment, she knew Erica was right. Her small flat had become her whole world. It was her refuge, a place to hide away from all of the pain and horror of everything that had happened. She was trapped and needed to change the way she was living but she had no idea how.

Another plane bound for Gatwick Airport passed overhead, engines humming as it banked. Cora stared up at it through the window, imagining escape. If she wanted, she could go anywhere in the world. All it would take was one flight and she'd be in another country, all of the pain and misery behind her, giving her a change of scenery, allowing her body and mind to heal, allowing the stress and grief to slowly evaporate. So what was stopping her? She sighed. *She* was. Subconsciously, her hand reached out to touch the leather-bound book and it drew her back from her thoughts. Picking it up, she clung to it tightly. When she held it, the feelings of loss faded and were replaced by strength and calm. It made her

WIND ACROSS THE NILE

feel close to her family. Stupid how an inanimate object could make her feel that way when nothing else could. She snapped back to the present, the seed of an idea growing in her mind. Was she brave enough? It was akin to a life-changing decision and she had told Erica she wasn't ready for anything like that. She took a deep breath before speaking.

"I think you're right, Erica. I've got to get out there and see the world."

"See? I knew you were in there somewhere!"

Holding the book in her hand she felt strength surge through her. Strength to carry on. Strength to sort her life out. Strength to start living again.

"I'll go to Egypt," she whispered.

"What?" Erica asked puzzled.

"I'll go to Egypt," Cora repeated with determination.

"Okay...Why Egypt?"

"I need to find Professor Foster."

"Who's Professor Foster?"

"He is the Egyptologist from the British Museum that I mentioned earlier. He may be able to help me with the book."

Erica stared at her friend in disbelief.

"It's a bit extreme. You go from not wanting to leave the house or talk to anyone to jumping onto a plane in search of someone you've never met!"

The look on Erica's face told Cora everything she needed to know. She thought she was mad and she could understand why.

"I'm absolutely fine. I need to do this. I need to find out why my parents had this book and what it contains. I've lost my entire family, Erica, and I know nothing about where I came from. My mum never talked about her side of the family, and Aunt Mary was so cagey when I asked her. Maybe this book is something to do with it? Maybe not. But if I don't try, I'll never know. The only way to find out is to go to Egypt and see if I can get it translated."

"I understand that you need answers, some kind of closure, but surely there are easier ways of doing it than disappearing to another country?"

"But don't you see? I have to! The maps, the photos, the statues, the book. They're all linked to Egypt. It's like a signpost. I'm supposed to go there."

Cora poured her heart out and suddenly realised how important it was to her. She had lost everything and was in the pit of despair. She needed a focus — a glimmer of hope — and as stupid as it may sound to some, the book was it. Her lifeline. Erica reached forward and gave Cora a reassuring hug.

"If this is what you want, then I support you. After all, I did say that you should see the world," Erica said. "When will you go?"

"Well there's no time like the present. I'll leave this weekend."

"That *is* quick."

"There's no point waiting. The quicker I go, the quicker I can get on with my life."

Cora grinned at Erica. It was the first time in weeks that she'd felt a small flicker of optimism amidst the grief and madness. Now she had a purpose, and a new chapter of her life was beginning. She had no idea what she'd get out of the trip. Perhaps nothing at all, but she had to do it so that she could move forward. Erica was right. It was what they would've wanted and it was time to try to step out from the dark shadows of grief.

CHAPTER FIVE

London, England, 2002

The seat on the plane was cramped and uncomfortable. Cora hated flying and it had been a lengthy wait at the airport with nothing to do except worry about the flight and the trip in general, and now, she had an uneasy flight of around five hours to endure. The farthest she'd ever been on holiday was to southern France, skiing in the Pyrenees with her parents. A trip to North Africa was something she'd never considered; now, here she was, staring out of the window of a plane that would shortly depart for Cairo.

Despite her nervousness, excitement had begun to stir in her again. At school, she had learnt a little about Egyptian history, but her knowledge was limited to topics of the pyramids, Tutankhamun and the River Nile. Not much for a country with more than five thousand years of history; fact she'd learned from reading the opening paragraph of a guidebook. She was looking forward to exploring the country and all it had to offer.

The plane started its journey to the runway to get ready for take-off. Cora stared at the tarmac as it steadily moved beneath them. This was the bit she hated: take-off, followed by being stuck inside a metal tube for hours with no means of escape. Upon reaching the main runway, the plane thrust forward and swiftly gathered speed. Gripping the seat arms so tightly her knuckles went white, Cora closed her eyes and breathed deeply to calm herself. Finally the aircraft lifted into the air, adjusting course. As soon as the lurch in her stomach had subsided and her ears had popped, Cora opened her eyes to gaze down upon the sprawling suburbs of greater London, which were becoming smaller as the plane steadily climbed. It banked over the city, once more adjusting course, to reveal a spectacular view of the River Thames as it weaved its way past such tourist sites as the London Eye and the Houses of Parliament. As they banked again, old tourist London was replaced by the office blocks and financial hub of the city. Somewhere in one of those ugly glass buildings sat her ex-fiancé and the life she had left behind.

Ex-fiancé. The words sounded alien to her. She had thought they were meant to be. Cora and

Damon. A couple that, in a year's time, would have been happily married, perhaps living in a picturesque house in the country, with a beautiful garden filled with flowers, and wisteria weaving its way around the front door. Settled and happy, the pair sharing a lifetime journey together as a family, with maybe a baby or two a few years later. But her dream had shattered, broken into a million pieces, a dream that could never be fixed.

Her fiancé was gone.

Her parents were dead. Her brother, too, and here she was, throwing caution to the wind, flying off to a strange country on a whim. A wild goose chase, some would say. She wondered in that moment, as the city disappeared, replaced with a blue horizon dotted by a blanket of white fluffy clouds, if she was doing the right thing.

"Oh well. It's too late now," she muttered to herself. "You're thirty thousand feet above France. There's no turning back."

The only sensible thing to do was sit back, try to enjoy the flight as best she could and see where the journey would take her.

~

As she disembarked and walked down the steps onto the tarmac outside of the arrival terminal at Cairo International Airport, Cora was hit by an intense dry dusty heat. It was a stark difference to the miserable cold, damp wintry weather she'd left behind in London. Once inside the terminal, she waited patiently in line to obtain her visa. Airport officials worked swiftly and once her passport had been checked and stamped, she blindly followed other passengers through the chaotic airport corridors.

Waiting patiently at baggage claim, Cora watched other weary travellers, wondering why they were here and if any of them had been through anything close to what she had been through recently. It was odd to think she was somewhere completely different and new, far away from all the trauma and stress in her life, and yet she still felt exactly the same. The grief and hurt of losing her family had travelled with her and still remained part of her. But what had she expected? You didn't just lose them in a few hours or overnight. Time would definitely be needed in order to heal. Her thoughts were interrupted as her case appeared on the carousel. She jostled with the crowd as she reached for it and dragged it from the moving belt. She got through Customs more quickly than expected and finally exited the terminal in search of a taxi.

The line of Egyptian taxis was easily identifiable, with choices ranging from old run down black and white Skodas, to white metered vehicles. Each driver was as desperate as the other for a fare. Unsure of the system, Cora chose the nearest vehicle, a battered old Skoda. After giving the hotel details to the driver, she watched in bemusement as he awkwardly stuffed her case into the smallest car boot she'd ever seen, before settling herself into the rear seat. Moments later, the driver was in the front seat and erratically pulling the car into the road, setting off on a journey that scared the life out of her and made her never want to get in a taxi again. It seemed there were no rules to driving on the roads in Egypt. Most drivers used their arms as indicators, pulling into any available gap in the road, even if it was barely large enough for a bicycle. The noise was unbearable, too. Every driver beeped their horn, whether it was necessary or not, and her own driver was no exception. The car didn't help either. The seat was ripped and uncomfortable and there were no seat belts. She gripped the handle on the door, praying all the way to the hotel that she would arrive safely and in one piece.

Forty-five minutes later, feeling a bit battered, but otherwise physically okay, her prayers were answered as they finally pulled up to the hotel. It was almost two a.m. and Cora was exhausted. Checking in was a blur and after entering her room, she pulled off her shoes and fell into bed, still wearing her travelling clothes. She was fast asleep the moment her head hit the pillow, sleeping better than she'd done for weeks.

~

Stumbling through the dream-filled blur that was the edge of waking, Cora eventually came to and found herself in an extremely comfortable bed. In the distance, she could hear the continuous sound of car horns. Slowly opening her eyes, she was momentarily confused by her surroundings. Where was she? Bright sunlight streamed through a gap in the unfamiliar curtains and it caught her attention, pulling her to full consciousness.

Cairo!

Rubbing the sleep from her eyes and still feeling a little disoriented, Cora hauled herself out of bed, and pulled back the curtains. She opened the patio door, and walked onto the hot, sunlit balcony. The exotic streets of Cairo sprawled before her in all their glory, good and bad. It was unlike any cityscape she'd ever seen and it took her aback. Directly below, the Nile sliced its way through the city. Sunlight sparkled on the coursing waters like a thousand glittering diamonds, as gentle waves, created by myriad boats going about their daily business, lapped at the shoreline. The river was lined with tall hotels, palm trees and other interesting buildings. Roads were cluttered with buses, taxis and cars, all with the same erratic driving she'd witnessed the previous night, the honking of horns ever present.

She stood for a while, content to just gaze out at the city skyline and its exciting chaos, before going back into the air-conditioned coolness of her room to shower, unpack and don fresh clothes.

~

The Egyptian Museum wasn't far, maybe half an hour on foot. Leaving the confines of the hotel,

Cora was greeted by the intense Egyptian heat and a throng of locals offering their services as taxi drivers and tour guides. Weaving her way through them, she politely declined, leaving them to lie in wait for other unsuspecting tourists. Walking over the Nile on the Qasr al-Nil bridge, she stopped for a moment to watch the boats as they sliced through the busy waters. It was cooler near the river and it briefly refreshed her before she continued her walk to the museum.

The iconic red brick building of the Egyptian Museum loomed before her and Cora marvelled at its size. It was quite imposing. After having her bag checked by security and paying the entrance fee, she made her way across the concourse. It was filled with palm trees, raised grass beds and large Egyptian statues hewn from granite, that gave visitors a small glimpse of the splendour to be revealed inside. She pushed through another set of turnstiles, walked up the steps and under the large white stone arch into the main building.

Inside the museum, Cora was struck by how different it was from the British Museum. This museum was dark, airless, gloomy and dusty. Many of the artefacts looked as though they had been haphazardly thrown about the space rather than logically arranged and presented. Cora smiled to herself. She loved it. It was more like a museum of old, one that had a multitude of stories to tell. It had none of the clinical feel of modern museums and it made her feel really close to, and part of, the artefacts. She wanted to walk amongst the displays and drink it all in; to learn about the history of this nation, and what better place to do it than in a building housing artefacts that told the country's story over thousands of years? It captivated her and she couldn't move. She could barely breathe at the wonder of it all.

A member of museum staff passed by, and she caught his attention.

"Excuse me."

"Can I help?" he asked in broken English.

"I hope so. I'm looking for Professor Foster from the British Museum."

"Who are you?"

She had always been good at thinking on her feet and the small lie that followed tripped neatly off her tongue.

"I'm one of Professor Foster's assistants. I was delayed leaving London."

"One moment."

The man rapidly spoke into a battered handheld radio. Moments later, a distant, tinny voice responded.

"Professor Foster left Cairo to go to Valley of Kings, Luxor."

Cora thanked the man and stepped out of the museum into bright sunshine and sticky heat. Her heart thudded as a wave of mild panic rose within her. She ran down the steps and sat on a stone wall outside the museum in the shade of an overhanging palm tree. She'd expected him to be here. Hadn't Professor James said he was going to Cairo? What on earth was she going to do now?

She was in a country she'd never been to before, trying to track down a man she'd never met, who wasn't where he was supposed to be, and was now on his way to another part of Egypt. She was such an idiot, running off to another country on a whim. Why hadn't she checked more details before leaving England?

Feeling despondent, Cora left the museum grounds and meandered her way back through the busy streets towards the river. As she stood on the bridge enjoying another respite from the heat, she stared out across the Nile and pondered her next move. She had absolutely no idea what to do next. Since the death of her family, life had been a complete whirlwind, she was emotionally battered and bruised and had little energy left for another fight.

Cora watched the sunlight as it sparkled on the water below. Egypt seemed to be an interesting place, full of life, history and excitement. So what was stopping her from exploring the country? This was meant to be an adventure; a voyage of discovery. Or at least that's what she'd told Erica. If so, what was stopping her from going to Luxor? She had both the time and the money. There was nothing to go home for, and it was a long time since she'd had the holiday her body and mind desperately needed. Cora had two choices: return home, or persevere and travel 400 miles to Luxor to see if she could track down this professor. It could end up being a complete waste of time but she just didn't want to leave Egypt yet. Her curiosity was pulling at her, making her want to stay, and she felt comfortable here, even in such a short amount of time. Her decision was made. She would go south to Luxor and enjoy the journey, wherever it ended up taking her.

CHAPTER SIX

Luxor, Egypt, 2002

He sat overlooking the tranquillity of the Nile, savouring a cup of strong thick coffee. He had watched the sun as it streaked its way through varying shades of pink, purple and orange on its final ascent to bright white, hot daytime. Luxor was still and quiet at this time of day and he was enjoying the peace whilst he had the chance. It wouldn't be long before the streets were filled with tourists.

Tourists. He detested each and every one of them. Each one seemed desperate to grab themselves a personal slice of history. They all wanted to have their picture taken next to an ancient monument or buy an "artefact" from a gift shop so that they could brag about it to their friends when they got home to their dull, insular little lives. Not that he particularly liked the hot, dusty, fly-ridden country himself, but at least he had more right to be here than most. Whereas they all paid through the nose for their two weeks in the sun as a means of escape, he was here through tradition and work.

Egypt was his, not theirs.

The vibration in his pocket pulled him back to the present. He really couldn't face talking to anyone. Whoever it was could leave a message. He was fed up with being told what to do. This was his situation and he would deal with it his way. As he took another sip of his coffee, the handset vibrated again. The caller was certainly insistent. Begrudgingly, he lowered his cup and answered.

"Yes!"

Listening to the voice at the other end, he absorbed the information. He was lucky to have so many people willing to do his bidding, but then, in his world, money could buy you a lot, especially when it came to information. The call ended as abruptly as it began and he placed the device back in his pocket, before lifting the cup to his lips again. The strong smell of coffee enveloped his senses.

His contact had given him good news confirming that she'd left her dull little life in London and found her way to Egypt, after making enquiries at the British Museum. It was interesting news. She was a lot braver than he thought, if a little stupid. Egypt was his playground and the

WIND ACROSS THE NILE

game would be played on his terms. On his turf. His way. Ultimately, he would win and she would lose, and she would learn the hard way. Draining the remainder of his coffee, he pulled on his sunglasses to shield his eyes from the ever-present glare. It was time to get back to work.

He was going to enjoy the coming weeks immensely.

~

Cora studied an Egyptian train timetable. Instead of flying to Luxor, she was taking the train to see more of the country. The next available departure from Cairo was at eleven that morning, arriving in Luxor around eleven in the evening. It would be a long day but that was what adventures were all about. She stuffed the timetable into her bag and downed the rest of her coffee. All that remained was to check out and find a taxi.

The short journey to the train station was just as eventful as the previous night when she'd arrived in the city, and she was relieved to get there in one piece. With barely forty-five minutes to spare before departure, she set about trying to locate the correct platform. To her frustration, everything was written in Arabic, and she had no idea where to go. She dragged her case over to a uniformed man to ask for help.

"Excuse me..."

The Egyptian waved at her as if to move her on, before turning and walking away. Frantically looking around, she spied a tourist policeman. His response was almost as short: *'No idea. I do not work for railway.'*

Cora was dejected and a little annoyed. She watched the hustle and bustle of the station, having no idea what to do next. She had no concept of the local language and no one seemed to want to help. She felt like giving up, ordering a taxi and going straight back to the airport to get the first flight home.

"Can I help you at all, Miss?"

Cora had never been so happy to hear another English voice in her life. Before her stood a tall, smartly dressed man. He wore a cream hat that perfectly matched his expensive three-piece suit. He had a gentlemanly air and reminded her of an aristocratic landowner who had become trapped in the wrong era. His manners were as impeccable as his suit.

"I need to get the eleven a.m. train to Luxor, but I've absolutely no idea which platform it's leaving from. I haven't even got a ticket yet."

"Let me help. I've lived here for years." The man smiled and guided her to a ticket booth. He spoke in Arabic to the man inside and Cora watched with pure admiration. When asked, she produced a wad of Egyptian Pound notes so he could pay for her ticket.

"You need platform nine for Luxor. It's that way. I'll take you to make sure you get on the right train."

"Thank you. I really appreciate your help, but you needn't see me all the way. I'm sure I can find it."

Despite her protests the man insisted, so she kept quiet and followed him through the busy station. As they reached the waiting train, he opened the carriage door allowing her to embark.

"Thank you for your help. I'm sorry but I don't even know your name. I'm Cora." She extended her hand to shake his, and he grasped it firmly, shaking in response.

"You're very welcome, Cora."

With that, he closed the carriage door, tipped the edge of his hat and walked away, losing himself in the bustling crowds. Bemused by the experience, Cora dragged her case along the train carriage and settled herself for the long journey southwards. Only then did she realise that she never got his name.

The trip to Luxor was absolutely draining and by the halfway point, Cora had begun to wish she had flown after all. Being adventurous was all well and good, but she was hot, tired and extremely uncomfortable. She had split her time between gazing at the endless passing scenery or trying to sleep but however hard she tried, she just couldn't get comfortable. It wasn't the adventure she'd hoped it would be and was thankful when the train finally arrived at its destination long after sunset, wearily, Cora disembarked and followed other passengers out of Luxor station into the darkness in search of a taxi.

"Hilton Hotel Karnak, please." The waiting driver nodded, muttering the price, and she nodded in agreement, far too tired to haggle over the cost.

The drive to Karnak was serene, and it wasn't long before they finally entered the gates of the hotel complex. In a haze of fatigue, she checked in, and was grateful to finally be able to close the hotel room door behind her.

~

Cora had no idea what the time was, but she could tell it was daytime, from the light that flooded through a gap in the curtains, bathing the room in pale yellow light. She dragged her tired and aching limbs from bed, then shuffled to the window and pulled back the curtains. Everything brightened in an instant and she stopped short. A truly wondrous sight greeted her, and she stared in fascination. The swirling waters of the Nile flowed right past the hotel grounds, which were vast and beautiful. The opposite bank of the river was empty, save for a few palm trees, a cluster of bulrushes and a smattering of other vegetation that clung to the water's edge. There were no buildings, just an expanse of land that stretched for miles, subtly changing from lush green vegetation to a sandy, jagged mountain range that finally merged with the most vibrant cornflower blue sky she'd ever seen. There was not a cloud on the horizon and bright sunshine beat down upon the world with a luminous radiance. She had arrived in Luxor. Transfixed, she couldn't think of anywhere more beautiful and serene. She was glad she had suffered the long and arduous journey to get here. The view alone made it all worthwhile.

~

Sitting in back of a hot, airless taxi, Cora grappled with a damaged window winder in an effort to get the glass to move. After much perseverance, she was finally successful and the window dropped a few inches allowing warm air to gently waft in. The vehicle weaved through the streets of Karnak towards the centre of Luxor. Compared to the western luxury of her hotel, the houses lining the streets were incredibly run down. Windows were little more than holes in the walls, and entrance doors were wooden slats or draped cloth, leaving the dwellings wide open to both people and the elements. Children ran barefoot along the street, their clothes dusty, their hands outstretched begging for money from passing tourists. Others swam in the Nile, their eyes wide and smiling, tinkling laughter coming from their lips. Cora had never been subjected to third world living before and it shocked her. In stark contrast, a line of sleek, modern coaches was parked up nearby.

A large ancient stone structure loomed into view. It was set back from the road and the entrance was lined with stone, ram-headed sphinxes.

"Karnak Temple," the taxi driver said.

It wasn't his last comment and, moments later, he spoke again as they passed an old hotel. Curved stone steps led up to the main entrance. A covered balcony sat just above the large front door, imposingly set between two large columns. Smart white balustrades ran the length of the building and a neatly clipped green lawn was flanked by palm trees. It was exceptionally grand, an old-fashioned hotel from a bygone era.

"Winter Palace Hotel. Howard Carter stay there."

Cora leaned forward to respond to the driver.

"Didn't he discover Tutankhamun's tomb?"

"Yes." The taxi driver grinned widely in the rear-view mirror. "Howard Carter very good man. My grandfather very good friend of his."

"Really?" The hotel looked nice and comfortable, the sort of place Cora could visit for a cup of afternoon tea.

"Luxor Temple," the driver uttered. Sure enough, another large stone temple similar to Karnak Temple appeared to their left. She took in the enormous statues and obelisk that flanked the entrance.

Cora smiled. She had no idea Egypt would be like this. Ancient alongside modern. Poverty next to wealth. Endless discoveries to be made. Maybe she had made the right decision after all.

The driver fell silent and Cora settled back to watch the passing scenery. Upon leaving Luxor, the road became edged with grass and dotted with palm trees. Open ground was tinged with an occasional residential building similar to those they had passed in Karnak, where small groups of cattle roamed. All too soon they were on Luxor Bridge passing the large modern Obelisk and Horus statues that welcomed drivers onto the structure. She stared out over the flowing waters of the Nile. It was so different to Cairo; quiet and calm with not a boat in sight. Exiting the bridge, they travelled a long, narrow vegetation-lined road. The breeze from the open window continued to cool her somewhat. As they turned towards the hills, the taxi driver spoke again.

"Memnon."

Cora thought he was uttering a curse in Arabic and ignored him.

"Memnon," he said again. This time he pointed his finger out of the window.

She looked, catching sight of two colossal stone statues depicted in a seated position. They stood proudly at the edge of the road, as if they'd been placed there to guard a lost ancient kingdom. She could only hazard a guess as to their height. How on earth had the Egyptians built all of this? Some construction companies could barely build houses or offices that lasted a century, let alone something that had lasted thousands of years.

Staring in wonder at the statues, Cora decided she would make time to visit these amazing sights. She may never get the chance again. She wanted to know more about them. She wanted to know why they were here and who built them. They intrigued her and she craved to learn more.

Fifteen minutes later, they arrived at the Valley of the Kings. Cora leaned over the seat to pay the driver, giving him a little extra for the guided tour, then stepped from the vehicle, putting on her sunglasses to protect her eyes from the glare. She paid her entrance fee and made her way along the dusty path through the world-famous Valley of the Kings. It seemed hotter on this side of the Nile. Everywhere she looked, she could see sand, dust and rock; a fairly inhospitable environment. She couldn't imagine working out in this heat all day. A man decked out in the recognisable uniform of tourist police sat astride a hissing camel and she approached.

"Excuse me. I'm looking for an English archaeology team. Do you know where they are?"

With an air of boredom, he motioned along the pathway, absently flicking buzzing flies away from his face. She thanked him before continuing along the path.

Finally she saw it: an area sectioned off with ropes, with a large mass of rubble and earth piled up against the mountainside. The people within the rope boundaries were steadily working, sifting earth through sieves as though they were panners searching for their first golden nugget. They all had hats, boots and long cargo-style trousers on. Shirtsleeves were rolled up and already grimy from the day's toil. In addition to the roped off area, there was a small tent awning that covered chairs,

WIND ACROSS THE NILE

a table, crates and plastic trays filled with odd pieces of pottery.

"Excuse me!" Cora shouted to a woman who was sitting on the ground, meticulously cleaning a tiny fragment of broken pottery with what looked like an old toothbrush.

The woman carried on cleaning and spoke without looking up. "If you're looking for Tut's tomb, it's back along the path, not here."

"I'm not looking for a tomb. I'm actually looking for Professor Foster?"

The woman stopped work. Shielding her eyes from the sun, she looked Cora up and down, making Cora feel self-conscious.

"Nick! Visitor!"

"Just a minute!" came the gruff response.

Cora patiently waited, whilst staring out across the arid landscape. Wherever she looked, the sandy-coloured ground merged with bright blue sky. It was unlike anything she'd ever seen, and it mesmerised her. She never thought she would have described Egypt as beautiful, but it truly was.

"Yes?" said an impatient voice behind her. "Who are you and what do you want?"

Professor Nick Foster wasn't what she expected. His piercing blue eyes the colour of the sky overhead, and handsome face brought her out of her reverie. Days-old stubble, a sandy colour that matched his tousled hair, graced his already tanned face. He was wearing khaki-coloured combat trousers, a creased white linen shirt and scuffed desert boots. Despite his good looks, his general demeanour was one of extreme boredom and irritability. With arms crossed, he impatiently tapped his fingers on his arm, waiting for her to speak. As though she were a child about to receive a telling off, Cora felt very uncomfortable and nervous.

"You must be Professor Foster. I'm Cora Thomas. I spoke to one of your colleagues at the British Museum. He said you spoke Egyptian Arabic?"

"What of it?" Professor Foster asked impatiently.

Cora stared at him. Professor James had been so pleasant and helpful. This man was arrogant and rude. She started to speak but the words fell over themselves. She was anxious and began to ramble. She had never been good at speaking up, and the professor's attitude flustered her.

"I've this book. I discovered it in my parents' home. The thing is, I can't actually read any of it. It's in Arabic."

"So what do you expect me to do about it?"

Cora's mouth had gone dry. She saw that the professor's colleagues had stopped working and were listening intently with great mirth.

"Um, well...I *was* wondering if you'd help me. Could you translate it for me?"

"That's what you came here to ask?" Professor Foster laughed derisively. "I've met some crazy people in my time, but I think you just made it to the top of my list. I hate to be rude, but you're completely wasting your time." The Professor took hold of her arm and guided her back to the pathway. "I'm not a translator. I'm a Professor of Egyptology. There are days when I don't even have time to eat lunch, let alone sit and read the ramblings of an old book. I need to get back to work so I suggest you leave me alone and go be a tourist!"

With that, he turned abruptly, returning to his team and his work, leaving Cora standing alone on the dusty path feeling like a complete fool.

CHAPTER SEVEN

Luxor, Egypt, 2002

He watched her as she left the excavation site, smirking at her naiveté. Was she really that much of an idiot, turning up unannounced, expecting an academic like *him* to help *her*? He watched as the dust she kicked up on her swift retreat swirled, dancing in the bright sunlight, before slowly settling to the ground. Everyone around him had gone back to work, and he should really do the same, but he just couldn't settle. In one brief sentence, she'd provided proof that the book truly existed. He needed to work out what to do next. He needed that book. Everything had led to this point. The book was rightfully his, but stealing it out from under her wasn't an option. He had to be smarter than that. In his mind, he replayed what had happened. He had watched her closely. She was so beautiful close up. She had her mother's eyes. They were beautiful and dark brown, like sweet, dark coffee meant to be savoured. Eyes that were permanently etched in his mind. They had come to life once more. Her mother's had become lifeless and cloudy as she had slowly slipped into death via his hands. He remembered it clearly. All three of the Thomas's had been given the opportunity to provide him with what he wanted, but they had resisted, and so he'd been given little choice. One by one, he had extinguished them, before staging their untimely traffic accident, the official cause of death.

He had been so pleased when the police believed his story. He had been out driving and came across the accident; a horrible mangled mass wedged between two trees. After calling for help, he had tried to help them — honest to God he had — but it was over in a few seconds. There was nothing he could have done for the poor family. The police had believed him, his statement had rung true. The authorities had put it down to an unfortunate piece of driving during bad weather that had sent a family careering to their death.

Now there was only Cora left and she had what he needed: a book that his family had spent generations searching for. So far, the book's existence had been rumour and conjecture, but now there was proof that it existed. All he had to do now was work out how to get it for himself.

Completely humiliated, Cora quickly walked away from the laughing academics. Once out of sight, she slowed and sat on a rock, catching her breath. That was it. It was over. The trip had been a mistake. What on earth had she been thinking? She had completely wasted her time and should have just stayed at home. It had been a ridiculous idea, flying thousands of miles in search of who knew what.

Sitting in the baking sun, swigging from a water bottle, she tried her best to pull herself together. She needed to calm down and start thinking rationally about the situation. As she stared out across the vista, the view imprinted itself upon her memory and she felt a sense of calm wash over her. She needed to remember why she was here. Yes, Professor Foster had turned her away and yes, she felt foolish. But was that reason enough to give up? Why did she always feel the need to run away when the situation was tough?

She surveyed the valley surrounding her. The Valley of the Kings was exactly that: a huge expanse of ground surrounded on three sides by mountains and hills. Sandy-coloured earth of the valley floor merged with the mountains, making it difficult to tell where valley ended and rugged ascent began. A bright cornflower sky, with not a cloud in sight, completed the view.

Walking through the valley, she became aware of lots of square cut openings that clung to the edges of the path. Tomb entrances. Each was a different size and shape, with a large metal gate that could be locked at night to protect it from vandals. She studied a large information board to get her bearings, before deciding to make her first stop: tomb KV62. The tomb of the young Pharaoh Tutankhamun.

Slowly descending into a rough-cut shaft, Cora plunged into semi-darkness, the area illuminated only by dull electric light. Upon reaching the bottom, she found herself in a medium-sized room hewn directly from rock. It had plain walls and was disappointingly unremarkable. Turning right to further explore, she gasped in surprise. Before her lay another rock-cut room but, unlike the first, its walls were painted mustard yellow and covered with reliefs. Ancient Egyptians were depicted in all their glory in the typical sideward stance. Rows of illustrated baboons sat worshipping the Pharaoh, and a multitude of other images and hieroglyphs were interspersed amongst them.

A large sarcophagus, covered with a protective see-through lid, sat at the centre of the space. Contained within was the mummy of the young Pharaoh. His frail body wrapped in linen, a pale comparison to the great ruler everyone knew him to be. She was completely captivated and all she could do was stand in the silence and stare in awe, losing herself in the rare moment of solitude, taking in every relief, carving and inch of the mummy.

Eventually the peace was shattered by a noisy group of tourists as they descended into the small cramped space. Cora decided it would be a good time to leave the Pharaoh to his eternal sleep.

The sun was hot and bright as Cora exited the tomb. Momentarily blinded by the sudden change, she quickly pulled down her sunglasses to protect her eyes.

Cora got a good view of the valley as she walked. It was set out specifically for tourists, with proper pathways, signposts and the odd amenity. Taking a moment, she stopped and looked around, trying to imagine the area devoid of human habitation, just bare jagged mountains and sparse valley floor, abandoned to the elements and seasons. She understood why the royalty of Egypt had chosen to bury their dead there. It was perfect royal graveyard that had been concealed for generations.

As she reached a signpost to the tomb of Ramses, she stepped aside to allow a large tour group to pass by. Cora turned and walked towards the tomb, then passed through the metal gate, making her way down the sloped wooden walkway into the depths. The walls were carved and painted with hieroglyphs, cartouches and other depictions of Egyptian life, all in bright hues of yellow, blue, red and brown. They were astonishingly well preserved. The ceiling was a beautiful shade of midnight blue, interspersed with small Egyptian figures, and framed with a small multi-coloured border. The tomb was truly stunning and much more interesting and vibrant than Tutankhamun's.

Cora spent over an hour studying each and every surface of the ancient burial chamber. At one point, eager to know more, she tagged onto the end of a guided tour, where she learned that the tomb had been decorated with a number of texts and pictures relating to the Egyptian *Book of the Earth* and the *Book of Aker*. The tour guide had explained that the ceiling was a depiction of the journey of the sun god Re travelling to the underworld and passing into the light.

Talk of dead books, underworlds and passing to the light sounded bizarre, but Cora's fascination was piqued, making her eager to know more. Ancient Egyptians, it seemed, had been an intelligent and creative people who believed in the divine and an afterlife; an essential part of their very existence. She liked the sound of that. Maybe she could learn something from these ancient peoples.

~

The hotel grounds were relatively empty when she returned, and Cora had the place to herself. She threw her towel and book onto a poolside lounger and ordered food from a passing waiter before walking across the deck to test the temperature of the water. Climbing down the ladder, she submerged herself into the welcome coolness, feeling the water wash over her as she sank to the bottom of the pool. Her hair fanned out around her and she stayed suspended in the calm solitude of the water for a few seconds, holding her breath, feeling the relaxation envelop her before ascending from the quiet depths. The hot sun struck her skin as she surfaced, and she kicked out, slicing her way through the pool.

After her swim, Cora sat in the shade and ate her food whilst reading a book about ancient Egypt, which she had purchased in the hotel gift shop. Her visit to the Valley of the Kings made her eager to learn more about Egypt's history. But the farther into the book she got, the more she realised the country's history was incredibly complex. Roughly divided into a number of different eras, each stage of their history was brought about by a specific event. It surprised her to learn that the history of ancient Egypt, as most people knew it, spanned thousands of years. Cora read about pharaohs and queens who lived during two specific periods, the Old Kingdom and the New Kingdom, including Tutankhamun, and the discovery of his tomb in 1922 by Howard Carter. The book noted that his funerary items were on display in the Egyptian Museum in Cairo. She wished she'd known before travelling to Luxor so that she could have seen them.

She glanced up from the book and saw that the hotel lights along the edge of the Nile were coming on and couples were slowly wandering down to the restaurants for dinner. A pink glow was cast across the sky as the sun descended behind the mountains on the opposite side of the Nile, ending another day.

The relaxing afternoon had made her feel much better, but the conversation with Professor Foster still bothered her. Nevertheless, she pushed it to one side and decided to stay in Egypt for a while before going home. It was time to forget about the book and have a holiday. Erica was right. It was time to think about herself for a change and have a break from everything that had happened. As of tomorrow she'd put the book to one side and go out and explore. It would be more interesting than reading about it.

~

Cora studied herself in the bathroom mirror. She noticed she had caught the sun and the bags under her eyes were much reduced. Even though she hadn't been in Egypt long, the country seemed to be good for her. She had phoned Erica the night before to let her know that she was okay and that she was staying for a few weeks. Erica had told Cora she was surprised at how upbeat she sounded, and that she hoped that it was a good thing.

Cora walked out of the hotel complex, feeling the heat of the day on her face and the warm breeze tracing its wispy fingers through her hair. She loved the climate here. It was a dry healing heat, and it seeped into her bones making her feel energised. It was good to feel the sun on her skin as it warmed her. Egypt, it seemed, was healing her, albeit very slowly.

Turning onto the main road leading to Karnak and Luxor, she pulled a shawl tightly around her bare shoulders so as not to offend the locals, and took in the many sights and sounds. She passed the same basic houses she had seen from the taxi. Egyptian children milled around outside. Some ran up to her, their grubby hands outstretched, shouting *'Baksheesh! Baksheesh!'* as they stared up at her through beautiful, innocent dark brown eyes that just melted her heart. She handed them a wad of dollar bills and they ran away exclaiming gratefully, *"Shukran English lady! Shukran!"* Cora knew she shouldn't give them money, but they made her heart wrench. The poverty and big doleful eyes were just too much. As she reached the imposing temple at Karnak, tourist coaches were already parked up and unloading sightseers. She took a moment to take in the large imposing walls of the site, with the line of ram head sphinxes in the foreground. It was spectacular and she tried to imagine pharaohs as they walked through the complex, going about their daily business as the sun shone down and the Nile gently flowed by. Turning away from Karnak Temple, she carried on and walked towards Luxor.

As she walked alongside the River Nile, she stopped for a moment. Small boats with triangular sails bobbed on the water, some with passengers, whilst others waited, tied to docks, for their next fare. Her waiter had explained that these vessels were called feluccas: the traditional sailboat of the river. They were boats from a forgotten era, floating serenely along the famous waters. In addition, Nile cruise ships boarded passengers and luggage in preparation for sailing from Luxor to Aswan. Across the water, the mountains continued to shield the Valley of the Kings from the rest of the world. Many who stood there on the Corniche would never have known it existed; an ancient secret that had remained hidden from the world for thousands of years. It was true what people said: Egypt really was a magical country, and Cora realised that her own journey in the country was only just beginning.

~

Luxor Museum was refreshingly cool inside. Sauntering through the space, she took in the artefacts, all of which had been discovered in the local area and related to what they called the Golden Age of the Pharaohs. It reminded her of when she was a young child and she had gone on a school trip to the British Museum. As they'd entered the Egyptian displays, Cora had been so scared when she'd seen the tall imposing mummies with eyes that never moved, but seemingly followed her around the room. Mummified animals had surrounded them and it had frightened her. She had burst into tears, giving her teacher no choice but to remove her from the exhibit. She smiled at the memory of her own childish behaviour. She had been mortified at what happened and her classmates had teased her for months afterwards. Now the artefacts completely fascinated her and she was eager to learn as much as she could.

A few hours later, she left the museum, and made her way back out into bright sunshine. It was extraordinarily hot, and she had been grateful for the museum's air-conditioning. She walked a little further into town until she reached the Winter Palace Hotel, where she climbed the grand sweeping staircase, and entered. She was entranced at the clean white interior decorated in a style that really wouldn't have looked out of place a hundred years ago. After speaking to a member of the staff, she was shown to the bar where she sat in a comfortable cushioned wicker seat overlooking the Nile, with a very English cup of tea, complete with teapot, bone china cup and saucer. Sitting in the breeze, away from the heat of the sun, she sighed with contentment. She was truly enjoying Egypt. She still missed her family terribly, but felt as though her grief was becoming slightly more manageable. There had been a few moments where tears pricked her eyes but she had fought them, replacing them with happier thoughts and memories. She knew it would take a long time before she completely healed, but it was a start.

The view from the hotel balcony was beautiful. Tourists passed by in horse drawn calèches, taking in the sights. Others got into feluccas for a short trip along the river. On the opposite bank, children ran and played, as cattle grazed at the water's edge. She couldn't explain how she felt, but she was very much at peace here. In an odd way, Egypt felt very much like home. She couldn't completely understand or truly describe the feelings, but they were growing stronger with every passing day.

CHAPTER EIGHT

Luxor, Egypt, 2002

Cora was so relaxed sitting on the balcony of the hotel that she had almost fallen asleep in her chair. Leaving the comfort of her surroundings, she crossed the road to stroll along the riverbank.

"Excuse me, Miss."

A voice broke through her thoughts and she turned to see a young English man walking next to her. He was average height, with brown hair and equally brown eyes. He was decked out in jeans and tee shirt, and had a battered leather satchel hung over his shoulder.

"Yes?"

"Aren't you the girl who visited Professor Foster yesterday?" He held out his hand for her to shake, before quickly continuing. "My name's Sam. Sam Anderson. I work for Professor Foster."

Bemused, she took his hand and shook it.

"Hi, Sam. Yes, I am."

"Cora, isn't it?"

"Yes, you have a good memory."

"I know. I'm one of those annoying people who remember everything, even the most irritatingly unnecessary things. I wasn't stalking you, I promise. I needed to come back to my digs to get some things and I saw you crossing the road."

"It's okay, it could have been worse. I could have bumped into your boss. Is he always that bloody rude?"

"Ah yes. The eminent, yet grumpy, Professor Foster. He has his off days. I'm intrigued to know what you were asking him about. We only caught bits and pieces. Whatever it was really annoyed him."

Cora looked at Sam thoughtfully. What harm would it do to tell him why she was here? She couldn't make any more of a fool of herself than she had already.

"Promise you won't laugh?"

"I promise." Sam held his hand up, palm out, and then motioned them to a nearby bench where they sat.

Cora turned to face him, taking a deep breath.

"My parents recently died. I found a book when I was clearing out their house. I can't understand any of it as it's written in Egyptian

Arabic. I took it to the British Museum, and one of the staff there told me that Professor Foster could decipher it for me."

"I see. And you came all the way to Egypt to find him and ask for his help?"

Cora groaned, realising how irrational it all sounded.

"I guess so," she muttered, blushing with embarrassment.

Sam laughed loudly, trying his best not to offend her.

"No wonder he was annoyed!"

"I didn't mean to upset him. Things have been rough for me lately. I guess the grief of losing my family has affected me more than I thought."

"I see. It's just that there are ways of handling Professor Foster, and dropping in on him unannounced with your particular request really wasn't the right way of going about it. May I ask what's so important about getting the book translated?"

"To be honest Sam, I'm not sure, but it was locked away with a number of other items relating to Egypt. I don't know anything about my mum's side of the family. I never met them or even knew who they were. I lost my family recently, so there's no one. I'm alone. I feel the book must be important or significant, and that it contains something that I *need* to know about. It feels too important not to try."

They sat in silence for a moment, Cora's words echoing on the passing breeze. A moment later, Sam smiled and spoke.

"If it's that important to you, Professor Foster isn't the only person who could help."

"No? Do you know someone else who could?"

"Well, I could translate it for you, if it would help?"

Cora suddenly felt hopeful. Was it really possible that Sam could help? Before she knew what she doing she leaned forward and hugged him excitedly.

"Oh Sam, that's brilliant! Could you really?"

He laughed at her excitement before gently releasing himself from the hug.

"Yes, I'd be happy to. Let me know where you're staying and I'll join you for dinner this evening and you can show me the book."

"I'm at the Karnak Hilton." She couldn't believe she had bumped into him and that he was going to help her. If she had left the Winter Palace two minutes earlier or later they may never have met. It was like a sign.

"You don't know how much this means to me, Sam."

"From the hug, I guess a lot. I'll see you at your hotel around eight tonight," he pledged. "I'd better run, otherwise I'll end up suffering the wrath of Professor Foster, too!"

Sam flagged down a passing taxi. He smiled and waved goodbye as the vehicle sped off in the direction of the West Bank.

Cora was so happy, she finally had someone to help her with the book! The trip hadn't been a mistake after all.

~

The sun had begun to set, casting a bright orange glow onto the mountains on the West Bank. Cora was enjoying the view. Egypt's sunsets were unlike any she'd ever seen. The colours were so vibrant, as though a painter had emptied every tube of orange, pink and purple into the heavens before haphazardly streaking it through with his favourite brush. She stood at the water's edge transfixed, feeling totally relaxed and at peace. A voice behind her pulled her back to the present and she turned to greet Sam.

"Cora. How are you?" Sam smiled as he held out his hand. Cora shook it out of politeness, amused by his formality.

"I'm good thanks. Shall we take a seat on the terrace?"

Sam followed her to the terrace. The grounds stretched all the way to the bank of the river, which was lined with small boats. An infinity pool hugged the river bank, and another swimming pool sat in the centre. There was also a bar and countless places to sit and relax. They sat at a quiet table under a canopy, once food had been ordered, Sam opened his bag and removed a notebook. With shaking hands, Cora produced the leather-bound book from her bag. As much as she wanted to know what was written within, she was slightly reluctant to hand it over to someone else.

"I guess you will need this."

Sam took it from her, carefully opening it to the first page. He was silent for a few minutes as he studied the beautiful swirling script but, to Cora, it felt like an eternity.

"It's definitely Egyptian Arabic. It's been written by an Egyptian woman called Randa. Wow." He paused and looked up at Cora.

"What is it?"

"You won't believe it. She actually lived here in Luxor, although in those days it was called Thebes. The date at the top is 1900. I think it may be some kind of diary."

The waiter appeared with their drinks, and Sam carefully placed the book on the table whilst they were served. Cora stared out across the river at the lush green banks beyond. Her brain was buzzing. The book's owner had a name. Randa. Maybe she was the woman in the photographs? If so, who was she and how was she connected to her family? Still gazing out across the water, a multitude of feluccas floated past, bathed in the final breaths of sunset. It painted a heavenly scene, one she knew she'd never forget. To think she would have missed all of this if she had stayed home.

"It's beautiful, isn't it?" Sam remarked, breaking her train of thought.

"Yes. Completely beautiful," she replied with barely a whisper.

WIND ACROSS THE NILE

"This is my second time working in Luxor and I still have moments where I stop and can't quite believe what I'm seeing."

"So what made you take up archaeology as a career?" she asked.

"I'm actually an Egyptologist. The career choice was down to my family. My mother is a historian, my sister as well. My father and grandfather were both Egyptologists. It's a family tradition."

"You must have very interesting dinner parties!" Cora laughed.

"You could say that, although they do become a bit competitive. Who's doing the latest research? Who's about to go and work on the most ground-breaking dig? That sort of thing."

"Sounds like fun!" Cora replied with some envy.

"Not really, but that's family for you. What about you? What do you do when you're not escaping life and running half way across the world with unusual books?"

"Not much. Life had been been normal and boring for me, until my family died. Just a steady job in an office in London, and a fiancé who I recently spilt up with. That about sums it up."

"It doesn't sound boring at all. We all have to do what is right for us, not everyone can do the same thing in life. It would be very tedious if we did. Do you have any brothers or sisters?"

Cora stared into her drink, it was the first time she had encountered this kind of conversation since her family's demise. A lump rose in her throat and she felt her eyes prickle. It was hard to keep the conversation going without her emotions taking control. The last thing she wanted was to break down in front of Sam.

"I had a brother but he died.'"

"I'm sorry. Was it recent?"

"Yes. He and my parents were all killed in the same car crash. I only buried them recently. My life's a bit topsy-turvy at the moment. I ended things with my fiancé because he missed the funeral, and then I found out that he was cheating on me with some woman in his office, it was so meaningless. But, because of them I also resigned from my job. My life has literally been turned upside down and I don't know who I am or where I'm heading anymore."

She paused to drink some water. Her throat was dry. She was finding it hard to talk about it all. The book on the table caught her attention, and she reached for it. The merest touch gave her the strength to speak again. "I found the book completely by accident. It was locked away in the attic with some of my parents' belongings. It pulled at me. It seemed important to learn more about it, so I decided to come here and find Professor Foster to see if he could help me."

"I'm sorry, Cora. It sounds like you've had a really rough time. I promise I'll do what I can to help you."

"Thank you, Sam."

The waiter appeared holding two plates laden with aromatic grilled fish served with salad and bread, and they ceased conversation to tuck in. By the time they cleared their plates, the sun had completed its descent behind the hills, and the stars and moon shone brightly overhead. Lamps along the edge of the river twinkled brightly; small moments of brightness against the starkness of darkening night.

"How do you want me do this, Cora? Should I take the book away with me, translate it and then bring it back once I've finished and then go through it with you?" Sam asked.

Cora mulled it over. The evening had passed so swiftly and she had hoped they would have gone through it and learnt more, but she had to admit, she'd been happy just to sit and talk, enjoying her meal with good company. She'd already waited weeks, a few more days would hardly matter. When it came to the book, however, she couldn't let it out of her hands. It was too important to her. She had lost so much already, and even though it was just a book, she couldn't let it out of her sight.

"Would you be okay with meeting up when you can, in order to go through it? It's not that I don't trust you, Sam, but I've only just met you and I can't risk the book getting lost or damaged."

"I understand. I'll come and see you in a few days if that suits?"

"That's great. I hope you understand, Sam. I know it's only a book, but I've lost so much already."

"Of course, that's fine."

Sam smiled and they continued talking late into the evening, until finally they bade each other goodnight with the promise to meet again in few days, when Sam's job permitted.

~

It was three days before Cora and Sam were able to meet up again. He was too busy with the excavation and hadn't been able to get away. Cora had been restless and frustrated, desperate to know more about Randa. She wondered what kind of life she had led, and what was so important about her that her own parents had kept her diary hidden away all these years, but Cora had to be patient. So she filled the time by settling herself pool side, reading books and wandering around Luxor. The infinity pool had become her favourite place to unwind. It hugged the river's edge and she loved leaning on the side, kicking her legs in the water, feeling the sun on her back as she stared out across the Nile.

England and its myriad troubles now seemed far behind her, and she was sleeping better than she ever had in London. The grief had barely waned and often still caught her unawares. When it did, she dealt with it as swiftly as she could and tried to move on. Perhaps she was avoiding her feelings, but that was the best she could do at the moment. She was tanned and looking healthy and she felt reasonably happy and relaxed.

Cora finally received a message from Sam, asking her to meet him at the Winter Palace Hotel at eight that evening. She was so excited she could barely contain herself. Every time she looked at the clock, she swore the hands were going backwards. Eventually, however, eight o'clock arrived. Cora was at the meeting place and Sam arrived on time. Instead of going into the opulence that was the Winter Palace Hotel, he steered her into the vibrant back streets of Luxor to a small local restaurant. Once they had found a table and ordered, Sam took the book from her and began to translate. Cora sat in silence hanging on his every word, taking it all in.

Thebes, Egypt, 1900

My name is Randa. I am an Egyptian woman, and I was born in Thebes in Egypt in the year 1883. I live with my parents and my two brothers Ishaq and Hakim, and we are good children. My brothers help my father. He works with the archaeologists and other foreign treasure seekers who are invading our small town in the hope of making their fortune. I spend my days with my mother. We clean the house, cook and tend to the chickens. We also help my father and brothers when they ask. I am lucky as my father has taught me to write the language we speak, a skill he learned working with the treasure hunters. As a woman I am lucky to have learned this. We are Copt's, that is to say we are Christians and we pray regularly, this keeps us healthy, happy and safe.

The year is now 1900, and I have met an Englishman that I am in love with, but I cannot tell anyone. I fear that someone may discover my feelings and I must be careful not to let anyone find out. Many girls of my kind have suffered at the hands of others for spending time with the English men. The punishment is harsh and they are treated cruelly. I am writing it down and hiding this book, this wonderful book that he gave to me as a token of his affection, so that I can, in a way, share my news, and remember everything that happens. My Englishman is very handsome, he is tall and has beautiful eyes. He is one of the treasure hunters that I have grown to hate so much. His name is Albert and despite my hatred for the treasure hunters, I cannot help but love him. He is so very different from the rest of them. He is working with my father in the Kings Valley on an excavation. If not for Albert's generosity my father would not be working, so he provides the food on our table and the roof over our head. For that I am grateful.

The first time I met Albert I had gone to see father. I do not normally go to the excavation site, as father does not like it, but grandfather had fallen and was being treated by the doctor for a leg that had broken. Father was urgently needed to pay our debts. I saw Albert and he caught my eye as I arrived and he smiled at me. I knew at that very moment the stars had aligned and we were meant to be. I knew I would see him again, and that it would be the start of a long course of discovery and love.

My future had begun and I was unable to stop it.

Sam stopped reading to take a drink, and Cora's mind began to wander. She was surprised, and couldn't believe the book was so old. She was learning about a woman's life, a life that had been lived over a century ago, when times were very different for men, women and children. Cora knew very little about her family. Her parents had never discussed her ancestral history and each time she had tried to bring up the subject, she had very firmly been told that the past was the past. She was gripped by what she was hearing: Randa was laying her life bare, page after page. She had a story to tell and felt the only way to tell it was by writing it down. Cora felt an empathy with her. Randa, it seemed, was a strong character but she felt she had to hide that strength away in the pages of a book. It seemed she was playing a dangerous game, one that could see her outcast by her family and her friends for how she felt. Cora herself had spent her entire life trying to avoid confrontation. She didn't like it. She hated ending up in situations where she did the wrong thing and upset people, and she felt an affinity to Randa and yearned to learn more about her.

Cora brought her attention back to Sam and listened intently as he continued to read.

Thebes, Egypt, 1900

Mother sent me to fetch the bread today and I saw him again. He was standing on the Corniche looking out across the Nile. His hat was tipped forward to protect his face from the blazing sun, he was wearing a smart white suit and held in his hand a tobacco pipe, which he raised to his lips and puffed upon. Grey wafts of smoke disappeared into the clear air, as he slowly exhaled. Suddenly he turned, looking straight at me. It was almost as if he had known I was there. His eyes bore deeply into me, as though he was searching for my very soul. His smile lit up his eyes and my heart melted. I knew that stopping to speak with him was wrong, but I did not care, I was drawn to him, like a moth to a flame, I had no choice, he pulled me in. I cannot explain why. I wished him a good morning, and surprisingly he responded in excellent Egyptian. He was kind and made me laugh. We talked and he told me all about his purpose for being in Thebes and his relationship with my father.

I had been unaware that they had known each other for years, and that they were great friends as well as work colleagues. I walked a while with him, listening to him talk, he had such passion about everything and told me all about his life and where he was from. He said he was born in a place called Oxfordshire in England. He was the son of rich landowners, who owned a great estate in the heart of the English countryside. I felt as if I was in the presence of English Royalty, although Albert assured me he was just a normal man. As I bid him good day and turned to leave he asked me to have dinner with him. I desperately wanted to say yes, but it was forbidden, my parents would not like it. Sadly I said no and hurriedly parted ways and went to buy the bread, but my talk with him remained with me all day leaving a warmth in my heart and a secretive smile upon my face.

"That's the first two entries," Sam said as he lowered the book allowing a waiter to place their food on the table. "There seems to be a lot here," he observed as he flicked through the pages. "I think it's going to take some time to go through it all, but we'll get there."

"It's okay. I know you have a job to do. I'm just grateful someone is helping me."

"You're welcome." Sam smiled as he returned the book to Cora. He continued, "I meant to ask. We, as in 'the team', are finishing early and having a night out tomorrow to celebrate one of the girls' birthdays. We're taking a felucca down to one of the small islands to have some local food and entertainment. Would you like to come along?"

"I'd love to, but are you sure I would be welcome? I don't think Professor Foster likes me very much."

"Don't worry about him. Professor Foster just gets grumpy when people distract him from his work. He'll be fine. Anyway you'll be *my* guest, and I would like it if you came along."

"Alright, I'll come, just as long as I won't be intruding."

"That's great and, no, you won't be intruding. Meet us at the dock by the Mummification Museum, at seven in the evening."

"There's a Mummification Museum?" Cora asked in horror.

"Oh yes, it's really interesting. You should go."

"I think I'll give it a miss, but thanks all the same."

"Chicken! I always say when in Egypt…"

She laughed at his barefaced cheek. "I'll think about it."

Cora suddenly realised it was Sunday. A week ago she'd been on a plane, on her way here. Since arriving she'd travelled halfway across the country, visited some tombs and a museum, made friends with an Egyptologist and begun to understand a little about the book. The more she learned, the more confused she became. Only time would tell if this whole episode turned out to be a mistake or not.

CHAPTER NINE

Luxor, Egypt, 2002

Cora took Sam's advice and visited the Mummification Museum the following morning. She wasn't sure what to expect. She hated anything remotely gruesome, and what little she did know about mummification was that it was likely to be just that. Filled with trepidation, she wavered on the Corniche outside the museum, not sure if she could do this. With renewed determination, she banished her fears, stepped into the museum, and paid her entrance fee. She wandered through the semi-darkened rooms viewing the displays. The museum wasn't gruesome, just weird, with the practise of mummification thoroughly explained. The removal of organs from a corpse, using natural minerals to dry out the body, preserving it for the afterlife, and then saving essential bodily organs in jars for use in that afterlife was an odd concept. She wondered how the Egyptians had come up with it.

What surprised her most was the variety of mummified examples. There were cats, fish, ducks, and even crocodiles. As well as mummified remains, there was a full array of equipment that would have been used during the process. Cora found it interesting and completely overcame any fears she had.

After leaving the confines of the museum, she took a pleasant stroll back along the Corniche. She hadn't failed to notice that wherever she went in this country, she was continually harassed by the locals. Horse drawn calèche owners often drew alongside asking if she'd like a ride to her final destination. Shop and market stall owners begged her to view *their* wares. Felucca owners promised the best sail of the Nile in *their* boat. Children ran along beside her, begging for baksheesh. Cora was grateful to have learned two basic words in Arabic, *'La'* and *'Shukran'*, meaning *'no'* and *'thanks'*. When combined, and said firmly with a polite smile, it seemed to do the trick, and they left her in peace. Even though it was a little tedious, it wasn't unpleasant; it was just a way of life in Egypt.

Cora spent the rest of the day lazing in the infinity pool at her hotel. This beautiful country was seeping into her bones, making her feel relaxed and very much at home. Nothing about the country fazed her. Cora had overheard some fellow tourists complain about the heat, the begging and, occasionally, the less than clean conditions, but all it made her do was smile. She felt that Egypt wouldn't be Egypt without these trials and tribulations. Leaning her arms on the edge of the pool, she stared out at the picture postcard view. If things in her life hadn't changed so suddenly, so dramatically, she would have been sitting at her desk in her old job right now. Emails would be backing up in her account; the phone would be ringing off the hook as her boss shouted at her for some missing papers that he himself had misplaced. She had definitely made the right decision. Leaving her job was the best thing she had done. Why was it that people were content to stay in a job they were so unhappy doing? Why had *she* put up with it for so long? It was a question she just couldn't answer. All she knew was that her life had changed, and it was time to work out how to create a new one.

~

Cora arrived at the dock on the Corniche to find Sam already there, leaning on the rail with his back to her. She watched him thoughtfully. She had come to like him, even though she had only met him twice. He had a good sense of humour and he was helping her when most people wouldn't have bothered.

"Hi, Sam."

He quickly turned. "Cora. I had a feeling you'd be early."

"You did?"

"Yep, that's why I got here a bit earlier. I didn't want you getting hassled by the locals. The others should be here soon, but why don't we get on the boat now?"

Cora followed him down a rickety gangplank that led onto a pale blue and red felucca which gently rocked from their weight. The owner greeted them, grinning from ear to ear, and passed each of them a glass of hot red liquid. Not wanting to offend him, Cora took it before whispering to Sam. "What is this? It looks like hot Ribena."

"Hibiscus tea. They serve it in all the cafés. Try it, you may like it."

"Sammy!"

A young woman ran at full pelt down the precariously wobbling gangplank and leaped into the felucca, making it sway violently as she landed. Cora held the tea at arm's length to prevent it from staining her trousers.

"Sorry!" the girl exclaimed grinning wildly, as she threw her arms around Sam and hugged him.

"Cora, this bundle of excess energy is Alexandra Chambers. She's an Egyptologist and generally causes chaos wherever she goes. It's her birthday we're celebrating today, hence the fact that she's even more excitable than normal," Sam explained.

Alexandra grinned, plonking herself on the seat and pulling Cora down next to her. "Hi Cora. You can call me Alex."

"Hi Alex."

"So, what brings you to Egypt?"

Cora laughed. Sam wasn't wrong about her being excitable. It was like a whirlwind had descended upon the boat. Cora liked her though. Alex was full of life and a complete breath of fresh air. Cora immediately felt at ease with her, which was unusual as it often took some time for Cora to warm to new people.

"It's a long story, Alex, but the short version is that it involves an old book."

"Oh my god! *You're* the book girl. He talks about you all the time."

Cora turned to Sam, raising an eyebrow just in time to catch a faint blush creeping up his face. Quickly he turned away to talk to the owner of the boat.

"Does he now? You must tell me more."

Before Alex could say another word, a small group of people was making their way down the gangplank. One by one, they clambered into the boat and Sam introduced them.

"Everyone. This is Cora. Cora you've just met Alex, next to her is Lucy Griffiths, then we have David Johnson and finally our boss, Nick Foster."

Cora greeted them all with a smile and a wave.

"Have we met?" Nick asked gruffly, a look of confusion passing across his face.

"Cora's the book girl," Alex pronounced loudly.

"Ah, yes. The woman who expected me to give up my valuable time to help out with some hare-brained quest to decipher a book. How's that going by the way?" His comments dripped with sarcasm and his eyes flashed fiercely.

Shocked at his rudeness, Cora was lost for words. How dare he talk to her like that! He didn't even know her. She wanted to yell at him for being so impolite, but decided it wouldn't be a good idea when he was surrounded by all his staff. Reluctantly she let it go. This time.

Taking a deep breath, she spoke. "It's going well, thanks. Someone else kindly agreed to help."

"I heard. A member of my staff, I understand. Make sure that you don't distract him from his *actual* job. We barely have enough hours in the day as it is." With that, Nick turned his back to her, and struck up a conversation with David.

Cora blinked back tears that were threatening to rise to the surface. She was so embarrassed and couldn't believe how rude he was being.

"Listen, Sam, I think I'll give tonight a miss. I don't want to spoil Alex's birthday."

Overhearing, Alex leaned in to speak before Sam had a chance.

"Don't you dare! Just ignore Nick. He's been a miserable sod ever since his divorce came through. It's my birthday and I want you here. Tell her, Sam."

"You heard the girl, Cora. She doesn't like taking no for an answer."

"Oh. Okay. If you insist." She smiled weakly, still feeling uncomfortable, but she didn't want to upset Alex on her birthday. "I'll stay, but keep your boss away from me."

Sam smiled and put a comforting arm around her shoulder. "Don't worry. I'll protect you."

The owner untied the ropes and pushed the felucca out into the gentle flowing waters of the Nile. The sails unfurled, turning the boat into the familiar picture postcard view of feluccas that Cora had seen so many times from the banks of the river. She felt the soft warm breeze upon her face; light willowy fingers calming her as they traced her skin. The group settled back, chatting, relaxing and sipping hibiscus tea as the swell of wind against sail serenely carried them along. Sam pointed out the expanse of Luxor Temple. It looked so long from this angle on the river, a dominant sight on the horizon, a reminder of Egypt's plentiful history.

The boat found its way into the river's main currents, and navigated its steady journey upstream, carried along by nothing but sail and wind. Despite the early hour, the sky had begun to turn a gentle orange, increasingly flecked through with pinks and purples, heralding an end to another day. As they rode the currents, Cora gazed in wonder at the passing shoreline. Dark green vegetation hugged the bank of the Nile and crept back onto the land, occasionally touching small dwellings that looked like mere hovels compared to Western standards. It was hard to believe that people lived in these homes. Fields were filled with crops, and barefoot children ran along the shore, kicking old footballs between them. Others hailed the passengers by waving madly and Cora smiled, waving back. Buffalo grazed near the waterline — great hulking beasts that waded through dense vegetation in search of sustenance. One shook its large frame to rid itself of a bird that had settled upon its back. Farther along, camels sat next to Bedouin tents, lazily chewing and grunting. Their owners sat around open fires, talking and eating, lost in their own world, not even noticing the vessel of foreigners as it sailed on by.

"Amazing, isn't it?" Sam's voice broke through her thoughts.

"It is. Each time I look up I see something new. I keep expecting to see a pharaoh and his entourage appear on the shoreline. It's like I've been transported back to another world, like time has frozen and I'm an interloper."

"I felt the same the first time I took a trip on a felucca."

"Thank you for inviting me, Sam. I wouldn't have missed this for the world."

"My pleasure."

They fell silent, their voices replaced by the gentle sound of water lapping against the bow, only occasionally disturbed by the chatter of the others in the group.

"Come on you two," Alex pulled at Cora's arm. "Don't be so unsociable."

"Sorry, I was admiring the scenery," Cora said, reluctant to turn her back on it.

"Oh sod that. It's my birthday and we're celebrating!" Alex laughed, looking at the shocked expression on Cora's face. "You're new to all this, aren't you?"

"Yes."

"Don't apologise. I was the same when I first came to Egypt. It's an amazing place. Go on, you have about twenty minutes to enjoy it before we get to Banana island."

With that dismissal, Cora went back to enjoying the view, one she would never tire of. She wondered how many others had felt like this upon visiting Luxor. She had completely fallen in love with Egypt and all of its mysteries. She had never felt like this before about any place, but knew that when she left Egypt, it would remain in her heart forever, and she in turn would leave a little of hers here.

As Alex predicted, they arrived at the island around twenty minutes later. There was no jetty, just a long creaking plank of wood that deposited them straight onto the riverbank. It was precarious, to say the least, but they all made it without injury. As she finally scrambled onto the bank, Cora turned to Sam.

"Why do they call it Banana Island?"

"Well...because of the bananas," Sam laughed as he grabbed her hand, pulling her up the slope to follow the others. Minutes later, after walking a wide footpath under large tree boughs filled with ripening bunches of bananas, they arrived at a clearing. A large canvas tent stood to one side above rows of tables and chairs. An open fire, with an earthen wall covered in dishes, sat at the edge of the clearing. Cora looked around, noting they were not the only people here.

"Wow! What on earth is all this?"

"Do you always ask this many questions?" Sam asked.

"I'm interested, that's all."

"It's a clearing with tents, a fire pit, bread ovens and tables, where we're spending the evening. The other people are tourists. It's entertainment the locals put on. Come on, let's grab a seat."

Cora followed him and they all sat at a table just inside the tent.

"Why are they wearing those coloured tunics?"

"Each tourist is given a *Djubbeh* or tunic as you called it, to wear. It's to make the evening more authentically Egyptian."

"Do we have to wear one too?" she whispered.

Sam laughed loudly. "No, don't worry. You're safe."

An Egyptian man stepped into the clearing holding a basket filled with cobras. The rest of the team hurriedly found seats and settled back to watch the show. Cora shivered at the sight of the reptiles. She had a strong aversion to snakes.

Unlike her, the rest of the audience seemed transfixed as the cobras danced and weaved at the man's every command, as if captivated by his voice and music that swirled about them. He was rewarded with a huge round of applause once he had finished. With the cobras safely back in their baskets, a group of young men in traditional dress then stepped forward. Holding various instruments, they proceeded to entertain the crowd, with a blend of intoxicating Egyptian music. Dancers swirled and moved hypnotically in time to the music, an amazing spectacle of colour and pure talent.

After an hour of entertainment, a man stepped forward to announce that food was served. They left the confines of the tent to join the queue. As she ducked her head under the edge of the canvas, Cora felt a hand grip her arm. She was swung around and found herself face to face with Nick. His cool blue eyes were stern and unforgiving. It made her uneasy. She wanted to escape his grip, but couldn't as he was just too strong.

"Watch yourself with Sam," he growled in a low, whispering tone.

"I'm sorry?" His vice-like grip hurt her arm and his words unsettled her.

"You heard, what I said. He's not to be trusted."

"What is your problem? You have been so rude and, frankly, quite horrible since we met. You know nothing about me, and yet when you *do* choose to talk to me you have nothing nice to say! Is this how you talk about all of the people who work for you? You must be so popular, Professor Foster. Now let go. You're hurting me!"

"I'm only saying it for your own good." He continued to hold her, but his touch was lighter. She stared into his eyes, trying to read him. She had expected hatred but instead she saw a glimmer of concern and it both surprised and confused her.

"I can make up my own mind, thank you." Somehow she managed to shake herself free. She was furious, and wanted to storm off, but a chair blocked her way and she had to struggle to get by.

"I know him, Cora. You don't. I've known him and his family for a long time."

She stopped and turned to face him, anger coursing through her veins.

"I'll choose my own friends, thank you. Mind your own business and leave me alone!"

With tears pricking her eyes, she walked as quickly as her legs would carry her so she could join the queue for food. Her heart was thudding in her chest and her palms were sweaty. She hated confrontation and was upset at being spoken to as if she were an idiot. For some reason, Nick Foster seemed to dislike her and she had no idea why. The argument with him had spoiled what had been a lovely evening. She had to push it to the back of her mind and try to forget about it. It was Alex's birthday and she needed to keep the peace for her sake.

WIND ACROSS THE NILE

Turning her attention back to the food on display, she heaped her plate full, then returned to the table to join the others, sitting as far away from Nick as possible.

"So, Cora. What have you been up to since you arrived?" David asked whilst shovelling a mountain of couscous into his mouth.

"The usual. Reading by the pool, seeing the local culture. Today I went to the Mummification Museum."

Alex laughed loudly. "Really? I've never been. Is it worth the trip?"

"Yes. I thought I should learn more about Egypt's history. It was very interesting." She turned to Sam and winked, who in turn smiled knowingly.

"I suppose you have to do something whilst waiting for Sam to do your bidding," Nick muttered under his breath.

"For goodness sake, Nick. Stop being so bloody miserable. You're ruining Alex's birthday," David snapped. Turning to Cora, David said, "Tell us about this book, Cora. All we know is that Sam's translating it."

Cora looked at Sam and he smiled encouragingly. Ignoring Nick, she recounted the whole sorry sordid mess. Her family's demise. The break up. Her resignation. And finally her decision to come to Egypt. When she'd finished, five sets of eyes, filled with sympathy and support, stared at her. Even Nick's, albeit fleetingly.

"Oh, Cora. That's so sad." Lucy took her hand supportively. "Look, don't just feel that you only have Sammy to talk to whilst you're here, you can always talk to us."

The others nodded in agreement, except for Nick, who bowed his head and stared at his plate, avoiding eye contact. What a bloody miserable man he was, Cora thought to herself. She was glad he wasn't translating the book. She couldn't think of anything worse than being stuck in a room with him. Sam on the other hand was a polar opposite; friendly, funny, and a pleasure to be around.

"So what archaeological work are you doing here in Egypt?" Cora asked, interested to learn more about her new friends.

"We're supporting a number of digs out here. It involves a few months at the Valley of the Kings and the surrounding area, and then we fly up to Cairo to work on some excavations around the Giza Plateau," David explained.

"So there are still things to find?" Cora asked in amazement.

"Oh yes, but no one knows how much. There could be hundreds of buried tombs, artefacts and temple remains, but it's unlikely we'll ever find it all. Some have been looted, some vandalised and others destroyed by earthquakes, landslides or flooding. There are still so many mysteries out there, though, and we hope to find something of interest soon."

"I guess you all love it?" she asked in fascination.

"Absolutely. I think we would all agree that we have the best job in the world." David smiled and the others nodded in agreement.

Despite her confrontation with Nick, Cora had a good evening. It was almost pitch black as they scrambled down the grassy bank to board the felucca that would take them back along the river to Luxor. The group was silent as the boat travelled towards the small town. The moon was full and high in the sky, bathing them and their surroundings in an ethereal silver light.

All too soon, the twinkling lights of the town appeared, and the boat was being secured to the jetty for them to disembark. Once on dry land, they said their goodbyes and went their separate ways. Sam hailed a taxi for Cora and offered to escort her, but she declined. It was only a short distance to her hotel and, sure enough, ten exhausted minutes later she was riding the lift to the second floor. She closed the door firmly behind her, and fell into bed, feeling happier than she'd felt in a long time.

CHAPTER TEN

Luxor, Egypt, 2002

He awoke in a cold sweat. The bed was drenched from his body's reaction to the frantic nightmares that had plagued his brain. Lying in the darkness, he tried to piece together the violent visions and why they had begun to torment him. He had finally discovered there was truth in the rumours about the diary, and was on his way to ensuring a brighter future for himself; a way out of the career he hated so much. It would be a surprise to some. His eminent name had ensured a rightful place as an Egyptologist, but it wasn't for him. He wanted none of it. His dreams and ambitions lay elsewhere. So why the nightmares? Was his own conscience trying to deceive him? He had hated seeing her tonight. Laughing and joking with the team. It had made him angry, an anger that had simmered beneath the surface, wanting to escape, but one that he had managed to keep buried. He had enjoyed listening to her talk about the death of her family. Seeing the sympathy on the face of his colleagues had only made him feel better. *He* had done that, *he* had caused that pain and they would never know.

Pushing away the damp sheets, he rose from bed, and crept silently across the room. Opening the top drawer of the cabinet, he rummaged through the contents, finally locating the photograph. By the light of the moon he could make out the figures in the aged sepia image. Two men, both of whom had been good friends as well as work colleagues, but one had betrayed the other, and a life had been violently lost. Even now, generations later, that death and betrayal still hurt. So much so that it had become a curse around the neck of their descendants. This was why he was doing all of this. Revenge. Pure and simple. Whether he liked it or not, it was his family duty.

Climbing back onto the saturated sheets, he lay on the dampness with his head on the pillow. He closed his eyes, silently begging the nightmares not to return. He clutched the photograph, the vision of both men imprinted itself on his memory until finally he fell into a fitful sleep.

Another glorious day welcomed Cora as her eyes fluttered open after a contented night's sleep. Turning onto her side, she lay on the bed staring out of the window watching the activities of the hotel and the Nile beyond. She hadn't bothered closing her curtains the night before, preferring instead to lie in bed, gazing at the moon and stars as she drifted off. It was a completely different world out here, away from the stresses, strains and dullness of London. Never had she imagined a world so far removed from where she lived. Even though Egypt was mostly desert, Cora loved the rugged beauty of it. The country was vibrant, colourful and interesting, and she was making the most of it.

The walk to Karnak Temple took twenty minutes. As Cora navigated her way towards the main entrance, through parked coaches and milling tourists, she marvelled at the size of the structure. Walking a long stone ramp, she passed along a paved area lined on both sides with large ram headed stone sphinxes. As she reached the huge entrance wall, she got a clear view through the gap — her first glimpse of the temple's inner sanctum. She rummaged in her bag, then pulled out a guidebook and read as she walked. The huge wall was called a pylon. Many temples across Egypt had them, including the ones at Luxor, Philae and Medinet Habu. Walking through the towering stone structure into the open courtyard, she was greeted by an enormous granite statue that dominated the space. Pharaoh Ramses II stood straight and tall, his arms crossed over his chest holding what the guidebook described as a crook and flail. He was missing his nose and the upper part of his face was also damaged. At his feet stood a small female figure, which was completely dwarfed by the pharaoh that towered above. It was just a small glimpse of the power and glory of the Golden Age of Pharaohs.

Strolling through the temple, she continued to read, her brain becoming a sponge, soaking up historical facts. The temple was reported to be the largest surviving one of its kind, and was a UNESCO World Heritage Site, but its history was a chequered one. Rather than being one temple, it was actually an enormous complex, made up of a number of different temples, each one dedicated to a different Egyptian god. Cora read that Karnak Temple was originally built by early Egyptian rulers when the ancient city of Thebes had first been founded. The temple had been changed and augmented many times by different rulers who had all wanted to add their own signature to it. As she entered a vast area called the hypostyle hall, she stood at its heart, gazing in awe at the mass of gigantic stone columns. Each one was decorated with figures of ancient Egyptians, mysterious looking hieroglyphs and other inscriptions. Looking skywards, she saw that a few of the roof lintels were still in place, intricately carved and still with the original paint on them — brilliant hues of green, blue, yellow and red — vibrant against the stark sandy colour of the rest of the temple. She barely dared to breathe; the hall was spectacular. The sun peeked its way through the gaps in the roof lintels and the space seemed almost heavenly. In her mind's eye, she was instantly transported back thousands of years to pharaonic days, when priests would have walked the halls following their adored king. Shutting her eyes, she allowed her mind to wander. Her imagination heard the muttered prayers, saw the worship of the ancient people and she swore that she caught the faintest smell of incense that wafted around her from a long-gone era.

Leaving the hypostyle hall, Cora continued exploring. Bright sunshine greeted her once more, and she found herself in the central court, where the monuments were fairly ruinous. Rising skywards were two large obelisks, reminiscent of Cleopatra's Needle in London. Who would have thought that the grey, smog-coated relic sitting at the edge of the Thames had started life somewhere as beautiful as this?

In the midst of the complex was an enormous sacred lake. Taking a seat on a low wall, she drank from a bottle of water. The lake was huge, and the temple's structure reflected on its still surface. Cora put the guidebook to one side and watched the comings and goings of the tour guides and their charges, wondering how many people had visited this place, and how many of them had been as gripped by this country as she. How she wished her family could have been here with her. Cora lifted a hand to her cheek and felt the tears. She had done a good job of keeping her feelings at bay since she had arrived in Egypt, but something about this particular view made her miss her parents and brother so much. Unable to move, she sat on the wall and allowed herself to cry. It was all she could do.

~

Stepping from a taxi at the Valley of the Nobles, Cora caught sight of Sam. She greeted him with a friendly wave.

"Hi, Cora. Glad you made it."

"It's good to see you again."

"You, too." Sam smiled.

"Why are we meeting here? I thought you were working in the Valley of the Kings?"

"We are. When you saw us the other day, we were doing some preliminary work there," he explained. "For the last few days we have been here helping a team with a local mapping project. It's something Nick was involved in last year and he offered them some of our time. We've almost finished, which is good, as we're desperate to continue work in the Valley of the Kings."

"So will Nick be here this morning then?"

"No. He's gone to the office to deal with some paperwork."

Cora was relieved. The news that she wouldn't have to see the professor improved her mood greatly. She had been nervous about seeing him again after their argument. She pushed it to the back of her mind as she followed Sam along the dusty path that wound its way to the site as Sam explained the area to her. It was completely different to the other temples that she'd visited. The remains were basic single storey, rough stone dwellings, which she learned had housed workmen used by pharaohs and nobles whilst building the tombs and temples in the surrounding area. The remains had a grey and, in some places, almost white colouring and opened out onto the main ancient thoroughfare or other narrow alleyways.

Sam explained that, despite the basic look of the Valley of the Nobles, it had actually proven to be a great discovery. Artefacts found in previous excavations had included papyrus and ostraca, which helped to document how people had lived and what their jobs were. Cora was looking forward to seeing what the team was working on. Sam obliged by showing her the site on the edge of the workmen's village. From what she could understand, locals had built their homes on the land on top of ancient remains and, after much conflict the authorities had recently moved them on, leaving the area free for the archaeologists to work.

Cora greeted the team whilst Sam explained how they were plotting the landscape and anything that lay beneath the surface. The information would eventually give them an accurate record of the ancient sites both above and below ground.

"That's very clever. Is it the first time it's been done?"

"No, there have been other mapping projects too, but they'll always need updating. New things are being discovered every year."

She watched the team, and it was so obvious that they were all very committed to their work. Despite the elements and tough environment, she thought they were lucky to have found something in life they were happy with. She wondered if she would ever find that kind of contentment.

It was hot, dusty work and, by late morning, the sun had risen high in the sky, throwing intense rays onto everything. Not even the shade could keep the heat at bay. Cora's skin was a hot, sticky mix of sweat and dust. She was glad she'd worn a hat. It protected her face and head from the excesses of the sun, preventing her face from burning. Her linen trousers and cotton top weren't faring so well. They were drenched from rivulets of sweat that were running down her back and arms, and her feet were boiling in socks and boots. Sam had advised her not to wear sandals, as there were plenty of snakes, scorpions and other nasties in the area. The last thing she wanted was to accidentally tread on one and get bitten.

It wasn't long before they broke for lunch, taking shelter in the welcome shade of an ancient stone wall. Cora pulled the book from her bag and passed it to Sam. He turned the delicate pages and began to read.

Thebes, Egypt, 1900

Father announced to the family that he was holding an important dinner at our humble home for all of the wonderful benefactors of the excavations. As I carried food to the table, set up on the veranda, I saw him. My Albert! My hands shook with excitement and I could barely contain myself. All evening I had to serve food with my mother and was not able to talk to him. I could only glance sideways at him when I thought no one else was looking, my eyes desperately trying to search out his. It was unbearable and I felt as though I was being punished for talking to him a week earlier.

Later as the men sat smoking outside Albert came in and caught me alone in the kitchen. I was fearful someone would catch us, but Albert was reassuring. He asked me to have dinner with him again, but I had to decline once more, even though I wanted to, so very much, but I was just too scared of my parents finding out. I could not bring shame upon them. I loved them too much to break their rules.

Albert was kind and did not push me, he just smiled and said he would see me again, whatever it took. I liked the sound of that, and secretly hoped that he would be true to his word.

I have not seen Albert for almost two weeks. It makes me sad. I have missed his presence. Maybe he had not liked me as much as I thought he had? I tried to push it from my mind by keeping busy. I helped my mother about the house, and Hakim, my brother, with the animals. Each day has been torture and I am beginning to think I was a fool. Why would Albert like me? He is a rich English Gentleman who could have any woman he chose. He would never love a woman like me, a lowly peasant. I was stupid to think he ever would.

Thebes, Egypt, 1901
Today Hakim and Ishaq, told me to accompany them to the excavation to see my father. I am not normally allowed to go there, but Ishaq was insistent and in father's absence he was to be obeyed. When we arrived I climbed from the cart, helping Hakim with baskets that were in the back of the cart. Once unloaded I hung back stroking the faithful donkey's neck. I watched my brothers from a distance, they seemed at home here, greeting everyone as though they were a long lost friend. I searched the landscape with my eyes for my father, but I couldn't see him anywhere. When Hakim returned he told me father was down in one of the trenches directing the workmen. Not wanting me to be in the way, Hakim told me to go wait in the storage tent, while they conducted business. I did not know what business they were talking about, but I had learned long ago never to question my parents or my brothers.

Quietly I obeyed, slipping inside the tent. It was cooler away from the heat of the sun and I spent the time looking at the old pieces of pottery and other finds that were spread across the table. The ancient pots and stone felt strange in my fingers, I took in their feel and texture. I ran my loose fingers over larger artefacts, pots and small ancient statues, all of them a key to our ancestors and our being able to survive here in this arid landscape we so lovingly called home.

I was startled by a noise behind me. As I turned I saw the silhouette of a man in the doorway. Even before I saw his face I knew it was him. As he moved forward to greet me he spoke my name with barely a whisper.

My Albert.

It had been so long since I had last seen him. I knew if my father found us together he would be furious, but I could not move. It was as though my feet were stuck to the floor. All I could do was look at Albert's handsome smiling face. He asked me to sit and I obeyed as he sat opposite me. He told me I was the most beautiful woman he had ever met and he had fallen in love with me. He told me he could not stop thinking about me, and he wanted, so much, to be with me. My head was telling me to leave, get out and do not look back. But my heart told me to stay. For the first time in my life I let my heart take control and it soared, making me feel alive. I told Albert I loved him too, but that it was impossible for us to be together, my father would not allow it. Albert said he would talk to my father, but that terrified me. I pleaded with him not to, he must not tell my father, he would be so angry and it would be the end for both of us.

Albert agreed to abide by my wishes, but told me he would never stop loving me and someday we would have to tell him.

It was too much for me and I fled leaving him sitting there in the tent, I pleaded with Hakim to take me home, telling him I felt too ill to stay. My brother obliged and I ran into my room at home and cried tears of sadness for the man I loved with all my heart, who would never become part of my life.

CHAPTER ELEVEN

Luxor, Egypt, 2002

Cora had been transported back to another time; feeling, living and breathing the burgeoning love affair of Albert and Randa. She could barely think straight. She had so many unanswered questions.

"Are you okay?" Sam asked, placing his hand lightly upon her arm.

"I'm stunned. Who were they?"

"I don't know. Has anyone ever mentioned an Albert or a Randa before?"

"No, never."

Over lunch they sat discussing the diary, trying to figure out who the couple were and what it could mean for Cora, but all they came up with was supposition.

After lunch, Sam suggested Cora visit the Ramesseum, which wasn't far from the Valley of the Nobles, and assured her it wouldn't take long to walk there. After saying her goodbyes, she set off down the dusty slope towards the main road. As she waited for an approaching taxi to pass before crossing the tarmac, out of the corner of her eye she saw the vehicle stop. Quickly she continued towards the temple to avoid having to speak to the driver, but she stopped when she heard an English voice shouting her name. Turning, she saw Nick Foster striding towards her, as the taxi disappeared into the distance in a hail of dust and small stones. His demeanour was one of anger and she groaned. It was the last thing she needed: Mr. Self Bloody Righteous. She ignored him and continued towards the temple.

"Cora! Stop!"

She heard running footsteps and gave up, turning to face him head on.

"What?" she shouted in exasperation. She didn't want another argument. She just wanted to be left in peace.

"Are you okay?" Despite the anger that was etched on his face, his voice was filled with concern.

She was taken aback and didn't know what to say. He finally caught up with her and was steering her away from the road onto the dusty desert edge. Despite his unusually warm demeanour, she was wary. Her protective walls went up and she stood her ground.

"I'm fine. But thank you for your concern," she responded tersely, before gently twisting her elbow out of his hand and turning to walk away once more.

"Will you keep still for one minute? I was worried when I saw you out here alone. Has something happened? You've not been attacked or anything, have you?"

Cora was completely taken aback. Who was this person and what had he done with the irritable Professor Foster? She was thrown by his helpful attention. He was nothing like the rude arrogant person she had met before. Maybe she had gotten him wrong and he'd just been having a few off days? The memories of how he treated her came flooding back and she reminded herself how rude he *had* been. She steeled herself, not willing to soften just yet.

"Not that it's any of your business but I was at the site this morning. Sam read me some more of the book, but I didn't want to keep him too long. He suggested I come and visit the Ramesseum. So that's what I'm doing."

"Just because we are used to wandering about on our own, doesn't mean to say you are. Sam should have known better!" Nick spat.

"I wondered how long it would take," Cora sneered as she shook her head. And there she was thinking he actually cared!

"What's *that* supposed to mean?"

"You, Nick. You've been bad tempered and, quite frankly, rude ever since we first met. All you've done is give me grief for talking to Sam since I arrived, when he actually seems like a perfectly nice guy who is only trying to help. Which I hasten to remind you is something that *you* wouldn't do. What is your problem?"

"My problem? I don't have a problem."

"Oh, I think you do."

"Well I don't!" he shot back defensively.

They stood in the heat of the blazing sun at the side of the dusty desert road glaring at each other. Anger bubbled in both of them and neither knew what to say or do next.

Eventually Nick sighed, "Look, Cora. I'm sorry. I think we may have got off on the wrong foot."

"No kidding," she said sarcastically. Despite his apology, she wasn't letting him off that easily. He had a long way to go before he made up for his poor behaviour towards her.

"Let me walk you to the Ramesseum."

She studied him for a moment. She could see his anger had subsided, which was a start, and from the look on his face she could see that the offer was genuine. Warily, she relented. She really didn't want to spend the afternoon standing at the side of the road at loggerheads with a man she barely knew.

"Okay. But I'm not sure I've forgiven you yet. You've been an absolute bastard to me. Just so you know my feelings."

They turned down the pathway towards the temple in silence, as dust kicked up from each step it swirled about their feet. The cries of a local bird could be heard in the distance, occasionally punctuated by the sound of a passing taxi or tourist coach. It was quite peaceful, but Cora couldn't bear the awkwardness of the silence any longer.

"Why do you hate people so much, Nick?"

He laughed loudly. "I don't hate *people*, as you so eloquently put it."

"Well you certainly gave the impression that you couldn't stand me when you first met me, and you haven't exactly been nice about Sam either. You keep warning me off him every time you see me. Why is that, Nick? Am I missing something?"

"Firstly, I don't know you well enough to dislike you. I think you're probably a very nice person, but you have to admit that turning up out of the blue, in a strange country, asking someone you've never met before to translate some old book you've found, makes you sound a bit crazy."

Cora thought about it for a moment. Maybe he was right, maybe it did sound a bit odd. Was that why Erica had tried so hard to dissuade her from coming out here?

"I didn't think of it that way. I guess I've been all over the place since the funeral. I'm sorry."

"There's no need to apologise. I know how tough things can be sometimes. It just wasn't the smartest thing to do. Despite being a great place, parts of Egypt can be unsafe for lone travellers, especially females."

"Oh." She knew he was right and that she had been foolhardy making such a trip at such a precarious time of life. Sighing, she stared out across the expanse of land that undulated its way from mountain to river. Yes, maybe she had been stupid but, on the other hand, if she hadn't come she would have missed all of this. She knew if she went back in time knowing what she did now, she would still make exactly the same decision.

"And Sam? What is it with you two, Nick?"

They had arrived at the Ramesseum, and stopped as Nick leaned upon the entrance gate and sighed. Cora tried to read what was going on behind those crystal blue eyes, but they were a closed book.

"Sam is difficult to explain. He can be a nice guy, but he never takes anything seriously; gets easily bored. Women, cars, even jobs. We come from similar backgrounds, both sons of Egyptologists, both destined for the same career, but if Sam had his way, he'd be sitting somewhere hot and sunny, relaxing by the pool with a girl of his choice by day, playing the roulette wheel at night. He's a lazy chancer and I just don't trust him."

"That's harsh."

"Unfortunately, the truth always is. I've known him a long time." He paused. "All I'm saying is, don't trust him too much, Cora. He may seem friendly and helpful now, but eventually he'll get bored. You seem like a nice person and I don't want to see you get hurt, especially after everything you've been through."

Cora was stunned. For the first time since they had met, Nick was being completely candid. She had no idea how much of what he said was true, but if it were, he was saying Sam couldn't be trusted. Was Sam really that flaky and unreliable? She had pinned all her hopes on him and she hated to think he might suddenly give up on her. She really liked him; he had been so nice and helpful. But he, too, had been scathing about Nick. It seemed they both loathed each other and she had somehow, unintentionally, got caught in the middle. It wasn't a position she liked being in and she disliked the confrontation. She no longer knew who to trust. Maybe they were both right? But then again...

"Come on, let's not talk about it anymore. You're a big girl. You'll make up your own mind when you're ready. In the meantime, let me show you around the Ramesseum,"

"Are you sure you don't need to get back to work?"

"No, it's fine. David's there. They can cope without me for a bit longer. It's not often an Egyptologist offers to give you a guided tour. People pay good money for this you know." he replied with a chuckle.

"Well as you're offering, it would be rude not to accept," Cora laughed, and followed him into the complex. Secretly she was excited at the thought of having her very own Indiana Jones showing her around.

~

The Ramesseum turned out to be much smaller and more ruinous than Karnak Temple. Cora still found it fascinating, though. As they walked through the site, Nick told her all about its history. As they meandered through the crumbling structure, she learned it had once been an important temple connected to Pharaoh Ramses II, with views that stretched out across the Nile. Nick was easy to listen to, and explained things well and she was enjoying having her own personal guide rather than reading about it in a book. A while later, they sat on a wall in the shade, overlooking the site.

"It's so beautiful here. Thanks for showing me around, Nick."

"My pleasure. I enjoy showing people the country's history. I don't get to do it very often anymore."

"Well I'm glad you stopped me. It's made the day special."

"Can I ask you a question, Cora?"

"Yes of course."

"Why is the book so important to you?"

"I have no idea. I know this will sound odd, but my family is all gone, and the book feels like the only link I have to my past. I have a feeling that my family hid something from me and the book is the key." She paused looking at Nick, who was smiling. "I sound mad, don't I?"

"No, not at all. I can understand that you've lost everything and you want to find some kind of connection to the past. But don't dwell on it too long, Cora. You also need to grieve properly, too. Don't get so caught up in this book that you forget to accept what happened and learn to live again."

She sighed; it was uncanny how much he sounded like Erica. "I won't. If it was just the book then I wouldn't be on such a mission, but I found photos, too, and some old maps of Egypt. There were also a couple of Egyptian statues. I think your colleague said they are called shabti or something? I just know that there's more to it." She was trying her best to explain but couldn't seem to find the right words. She persevered in the hope that he would understand.

"When I first landed in Egypt, I instantly fell in love with the country. The heat, the people, the culture, even the annoying things you're supposed to hate. I know this probably sounds weird to you, but I feel at home here, like I truly belong. More so than in London where I actually live, or in my family home in Scotland where I grew up. It's like Egypt is part of me and I'm a part of her. Does that make any sense at all?"

"Wow. I know people come to Egypt and love it, but I don't think I've ever met anyone who has completely fallen for it in the way you have."

"I must sound like an idiot."

"Not at all, you sound like a person who has found happiness in something. After everything that's happened, I'm pleased for you. But just remember what I said: give yourself time to grieve, too, and watch who you trust whilst you're here."

She rolled her eyes. It had come back to this again.

"You mean Sam, don't you?"

"Yes."

"And what about you, Nick? Can I trust *you*?"

"I certainly think so, but only you can decide that."

She turned away from him to gaze out over the beautiful landscape. She liked Sam, he had been so friendly and so amenable. If it hadn't been for him, she would be back home sitting in her flat, watching the rain fall, kicking herself for not seeing things through and wondering what to do next. Instead she was here, she was still living, still moving forward. Sam had given her hope, and he had been there when she had needed it most, and she was grateful. So, to that end, it was hard to heed Nick's warning, and his words left her in turmoil. And what about him? Nick hadn't exactly made her feel welcome when she had first met him. She knew he and Sam detested each other. But, and it was a big but, he'd spent the afternoon with her making amends for his poor behaviour, when he should've been working. She'd finally pushed the grumpy miserable man she'd first met to one side and stumbled upon someone she could, if given the chance, come to like as a friend. But could she trust him and could she trust Sam? Her head was spinning, and there was still no answer. For the time being, all she could do was take both men at face value and see what happened.

Glancing at the handsome Egyptologist next to her, she smiled.

"I think you're okay, Professor Foster. Just don't be so bloody grumpy all the time."

"Okay, I promise, but please don't call me professor, it makes me sound so old!'

"Nick it is then," she agreed as she stood and dusted down her trousers. "I guess I'd better let you get back to work."

"I guess so," he agreed, following suit.

They walked back to the road whilst Cora filled the silence by telling him all about the recent diary entry in the book. As they reached the road, Nick flagged down a passing taxi.

"Why don't you take the taxi back to the hotel and you can drop me at the site on the way?" Nick suggested.

"Okay, that sounds good."

Nick opened the door, barking instructions at the driver in Arabic, before motioning for Cora to get in. She slid across the seat and smiled at Nick as he closed the door and the taxi set off.

At the site, the taxi slowed and stopped at the side of the road and Nick passed Cora a handful of pound notes.

"Nice to spend time with you, Cora. Just remember what I said."

"I will." She smiled at him.

Nick climbed out of the taxi, and closed the door. Cora waved at him as the taxi drove off and headed towards the Nile. It wasn't long before they'd passed over the river and were making their way up the driveway of the hotel complex.

~

He stared out across the Nile, watching the sun slowly disappearing in the west. The gentle evening breeze caressed his skin, teasing the hairs as it went. Thoughts of her ran through his brain, taunting him. He was grateful he'd been able to spend time with her. She was finally beginning to trust him and he had learned from the book that Hakim existed. But progress was slow and wearing. He wished there was some way of speeding it up, but he knew he had to let things run their course. He had watched her beautiful eyes light up as she talked and it reminded him so much of her mother. So beautiful. But he had to stop thinking of her like that!

The slow gathering of information and working out facts wasn't his strong point. Ironic really, considering his job. It would be much easier if he could just wade in, beat the information out of people and then dispatch them. Sadly, a trail of death and destruction only brought unwanted attention, and left him having to carefully cover his tracks. So he was forced to play the waiting game.

His phone rang and he answered it with the boredom he felt. Listening intently, his attention shifted. Speaking to his father always required close attention. Despite feeling as though he was in charge, he knew that the mantle had only been handed to him out of family obligation and that his father would always be firmly in charge until the day *he* died. Briefly slipping into a world of his own, he wondered how easy it would be to kill his own father. How would he accomplish it? Was it something he would have the nerve for or would he chicken out at the last minute? Brought back to the conversation at hand, he reported everything he'd learned before taking further instructions and ending the call.

The consensus was that the girl would be useful for a while longer. But once she outgrew that usefulness, she would go the way of her family. She would be another sad unfortunate accident, which would be so much easier and more fun to accomplish here in this stinking cesspool of a country. He laughed quietly to himself, thinking of all the different ways he could kill her once her time was up.

Oh, he was enjoying this immensely.

CHAPTER TWELVE

Luxor, Egypt, 2002

Sam arrived at the hotel relaxed and eager to get on with the day. The team had a rare day off and he had chosen to spend it with Cora. He had settled himself in a chair at the edge of the river with a coffee, and was waiting for her to arrive.

"Good morning, Sam." Cora pulled out the chair opposite and sat, before ordering another coffee from a passing waiter.

"I hope it was okay to come and see you."

"Of course. I was glad you rang."

"I heard you saw Professor Foster yesterday."

"I did. He showed me around the Ramesseum. It was fascinating."

"He seemed in a better mood. You must have caught him on a good day," Sam said.

"Is he always in a bad mood?"

"Not really, but he has seemed more irritable recently. I don't know why, but I did hear rumours about his wife cheating on him. One of the team said he only signed the divorce papers a few days before coming here. So maybe that's why he's a bit miserable."

"How awful for him."

"I suppose. That's the trouble with this kind of career. We're away from home a lot of the time. I suppose it's only natural for some people to stray," Sam shrugged.

Cora wasn't sure she agreed with him. After what had happened with Damon, she could never condone anyone cheating. If you were unhappy in your relationship, surely it was better to be honest and just split amicably rather than hurting and betraying someone?

Sam placed his coffee cup back on the table.

"Anyway, enough about my boss. I'm here to learn more about the book, or should we now call it a diary?"

"I think diary sounds good."

"Diary it is. Shall we get started?"

She nodded, passing it to him. He opened it and carefully flicked through to where he'd last finished reading.

Thebes, Egypt, 1901

I spent an unhappy day trudging through the house doing my chores. It was only yesterday that I had seen Albert, but I knew that I had to forget about him. However much I love him, he is an English Gentleman and I am just a peasant. He is from a different country and culture and I can never be with him. I have to forget he ever existed, or I will lose my family forever, and I just could not bear that. Worse than that I could lose my life.

I was out in the yard feeding the chickens, watching them peck and cluck noisily about my feet, when a young boy arrived with a note for me. I was surprised, why would anyone send me a note? I told him it was a mistake and to leave. But the boy was insistent. The note was for me. Warily I took it from him, and thanked him, giving him some eggs - my parents would never miss them, the chickens were always good to us. Walking away from the house, I sat in the shade of a palm tree and opened the note with shaking hands.

Somehow I knew it would be from Albert. He had written to me in my own language, and I traced the swirling script with my fingers. I had been lucky to learn how to read and write when I was young, very few women did, but it was one thing my father insisted upon.

Albert wanted to meet me. The time and directions were in the note. He knew it would be a hard decision for me and told me he would wait for me all night in the hope I would come. I went to bed filled with a mix of dread and excitement. I desperately wanted to meet him, but I had doubts. What if my parents caught me sneaking out? How would I explain where I was going?

Finally I heard my parents and brothers go to bed. The moon had risen high in the sky, and the stars were shining alongside it. I made my decision in that moment with nothing but the heavens for company. I would go. Quietly I slid from my bed and dressed, before tiptoeing from the house. My bare feet barely made a sound on the rough dusty floor. Opening the door I squeezed though a small gap, leaving it ajar so I could return making as little noise as possible.

The moon bathed the world outside in such a beautiful silver blue light. The silence was deafening and once I was far enough away from the house I ran as fast as my legs would carry me, down the road to where Albert had said he would meet me. All the way I worried about my parents catching me, or worse, that it was a cruel trick and Albert would not be waiting for me at all.

I saw the light from his lamp as I turned into the lane, and I breathed a sigh of relief. Albert. He was wearing his best suit and smoking his pipe. He greeted me with a polite bow and led me farther down the lane into a field hidden from the road by a few sparse trees. On the ground lay a blanket and a wicker basket, silently Albert motioned for me to sit and I obeyed. Nervously I watched as he opened the basket, passing me bread, cheese, cured meats and fruit. He was treating me to the dinner I had tried so hard to refuse, and it was the most wonderful meal I had ever shared with anyone. He placed his hand on my face telling me I was the most beautiful woman he had ever set eyes upon, and if it was possible, at that moment, I fell in love with him even more.

Once we had eaten Albert and I sat and talked. He told me of his life in England. He had grown up in a big house with servants to wait upon him and his family. The house had lush green gardens filled with flowers, trees and ponds. He rode horses and attended hunts and celebrated birthdays and other occasions in the large ballroom of the house. They had money to buy whatever they wanted and he often went to London for parties, to lunch with friends or on business with his father. It all sounded wonderful to me, a world away from my meagre existence with my parents, Hakim and Ishaq and I could not even begin to imagine a life beyond the dust and heat of my beloved Egypt.

In turn I told him about my life in Thebes. I explained about my parents and my two brothers, Ishaq the oldest child, Hakim younger than myself. How we farmed what little land we had, and had hardly any money other than what my father brought in from working with the treasure hunters. He learned how close my family are and how I was a good girl who obeyed their every wish and command and how I rarely left the house and how my time was spent with my mother helping her and looking after the house and family. That was my purpose in life.

It reminded me that I was disobeying them, and I felt torn between two very different worlds.

Just before the sun began to rise I bade Albert goodnight. I was sad to leave him, but I did not want my parents to catch me away from home on my own. If they did I would be severely punished. Quietly I crept back into the house fearful of being confronted by angry parents, but everyone was still asleep. Climbing into my bed I fell fast asleep in an instant dreaming of the beautiful evening and the goodbye kiss I had shared with Albert.

Sam paused to drink some coffee. Cora had hung on his every word, enthralled by what she was hearing. She had great admiration for Randa. She was a woman from a different time, someone who was brave and fighting to be more than she was, for something she loved; a man she had fallen for. Cora knew that Randa was a very special woman, and wanted to know more about her. Swigging back the last of the strong liquid, Sam smiled at her and turned to the next entry and continued.

Thebes, Egypt, 1901
I am so scared. My brothers went to the site with my father again today, but they all came home early. There was an argument. I do not know what about, but my father and my brothers are all upset and they have continued to argue all evening. My mother wails, begging them to stop, but they ignore her. They keep looking at the door as if they expect someone to turn up, but no one comes.
I went to bed, I could not bear to hear them yell at each other. I lay there unable to sleep, the sounds of raised voices continued into the night. Finally I

slept until I was awoken by a sound and saw Hakim pass my door. He looked like a ghost and I whispered to him. He came and sat next to my bed and cried. The bruises on his face are horrible. Father must have been very angry with him. I have never seen Hakim cry before, he is a strong man. I knew something very bad has happened, but he would not tell me what it was.

Something is very wrong. My family is breaking into pieces and cannot stop it. I tried to hold back my tears but could not.

Thebes, Egypt, 1901

It has been weeks since the arguments and nothing has been said. I have continued to meet Albert in secret and our love has grown stronger with each meeting. I know that what I am doing is dangerous. But I cannot stop. Two days ago my father, Hakim and Ishaq were called to Cairo, so my mother and I were left to keep each other company. It is rare that my father leaves us alone, and I know that if he had ever known about Albert and I it would have completely broken his heart.

Last night I crept out to meet Albert again. I always look forward to our late night picnics. When I arrived he had a donkey and cart with him. Silently he helped me into the cart and we made our way down the track towards the banks of the Nile. The moon was once more bright in the sky and stars twinkled in the heavens, there was no sound other than the noise of the donkeys hooves on the track. Finally we stopped and Albert jumped from the cart tying the donkey to a nearby tree, before reaching up and helping me down. Before us a waiting felucca bobbed on the rivers gentle currents. Reaching for my hand Albert helped me in to the battered boat before paying a local boy who was silently waiting in the shadows. The boy nodded and then climbed into the cart and moved off along the road. Albert pushed the boat out into the river and jumped in allowing it to be gently carried along on the slow river currents. As the boat gently floated along, Albert lay back on a blanket and without hesitation I joined him.

We lay in each others arms silently staring up at the beautifully lit heavens. The light breeze continued to bob the felucca along in the currents guiding us gently downstream. When Albert kissed me I kissed him back without hesitation. He untied my hair letting it fall over my shoulders, telling me I was beautiful and he loved me with all his heart, and whatever happened he would never leave me. I knew he wanted more and despite everything, despite the risks, I let it happen.

Tenderly he removed my garments and I helped him with his, and we lay naked in the bottom of the boat, feeling the warm Nile breeze caress our bare skin. We kissed and touched each other until we were so intertwined I did not know which limb was mine and which his. I knew it was wrong. I knew my family would forbid it, but I could not stop and I finally gave in feeling the ripples of unending love and contentment course through my body.

Afterwards we just lay there until the sun began to rise, blotting out the lights in the heavens as an orange glow of a new day began. Albert returned the boat to shore. Tying the boat up, we climbed into the waiting horse and cart and made our way back to the house. I managed to make it to my bed a few minutes before my mother rose to start another day. I lay on my bed unable to sleep, the evening had been beautiful but I was filled with shame, and silently cried tears of heartbreak into my pillow.

Sam placed the book on the table. It felt like he had been reading for hours, and the story seemed to have gripped him as much as it had Cora.

"I can't believe the lengths they went to in order to see each other," Cora said. She couldn't even begin to comprehend the sacrifice Randa had made. She must have truly loved Albert to risk losing her family.

"It certainly was brave of them," Sam agreed.

"Would her parents have been that angry?"

"Oh yes. It was a different time back then. It was one thing to come to a country like this, but for an Egyptian woman to fraternise so freely with an English man was unheard of. She would have brought great shame on herself and those she loved. Her parents would have disowned her at the very least. Some may have even been so ashamed that they would have killed her."

Cora was silent. She hadn't realised how much Randa was risking for her love affair with Albert. Cora wasn't sure she could ever be that brave.

"So what are your plans, Cora? How long are you staying?"

"I'm not sure. I feel like I need a complete break from everything at the moment. I know I can't stay here forever. It costs money. But I'll probably stay for a few more weeks."

"Well there's plenty more to see." Sam ran through a list of ancient sites she could visit, and she assigned them to her memory, noting to follow his advice and see as much as she could before returning home.

"By the way," Sam continued," I asked my parents if they could help with this diary. I know that Albert and Oxford wasn't much to go on but there was an Albert MacKenzie alive at that time who used to work here in Egypt. There were a few news articles in the local rags of the time about his trips to Egypt. Other than that, he seems to have completely disappeared off the radar. They're going to dig a bit deeper and see if they can find out more. I hope you don't mind me getting them involved."

"Of course not, Sam. Thank you so much."

"No problem. I should get going. I'm meeting friends for lunch, but I'll see you again soon." With that, he downed the remainder of his coffee, stood, slung his leather bag over his shoulder and left Cora in the shade of an umbrella, mulling over everything she'd just learned.

CHAPTER THIRTEEN

Luxor, Egypt, 2002

The heat and glare of the Egyptian sunshine was never-ending. Nevertheless, the walk was a pleasant one. A gentle warm breeze emanated from the Nile and Cora was grateful. It could get so hot sometimes and, without the movement of air from the river, it would have bordered on unbearable.

Luxor Temple was a smaller version of the temple at Karnak. A similar line of stone sphinxes led up to a large entrance pylon which was flanked by two seated black granite statues. One was accompanied by a towering obelisk covered with hieroglyphs. Walking through the gap in the pylon, Cora tagged onto a guided tour, listening carefully to what the guide was saying as they made their way through the ancient site.

The guide described Luxor Temple's history, how it had been built specifically for celebrating ancient Egyptian festivals and that the sphinxes at the entrance ran all the way from Luxor to Karnak Temple marking a ceremonial route. He pointed out other statues that looked as if they were standing proudly at regular intervals, similar to the ones flanking the entrance. Some were so life-like, Cora half expected them to step off their plinth and join them on the tour. Cora preferred Luxor Temple to Karnak; it was much smaller but wasn't in as much disrepair.

Abandoning the group in the peristyle court, she sat on a wall and watched tourists as they milled about, taking photographs and studying the ruins. She thought back to her last meeting with Sam, and pondered Randa and Albert's relationship. Their story was so beautiful and Cora was pleased to finally be learning more about them. She was still at a loss as to why her family had this diary locked away in the attic, though. She was becoming impatient for an answer and just wished she and Sam could sit down for a few days to go through it rather than doing it in fits and starts.

Gazing across the hall's open courtyard to the tall columns beyond, she thought back over her time in Egypt. The country had definitely made its mark on her. Its culture and history had seeped into her bones making her yearn for more. It made her resistant to go home, and left her with a longing to immerse herself in everything Egypt for as long as she could. Her mind returned to Sam again. So far, he had been true to his word in helping her. Though, since her talk with Nick, she wondered *why* he was being so kind to her and what he was getting from it, but she had pushed it away. For now she was just grateful that someone was willing to help.

Nick also crept into her thoughts. He had surprised her at the Ramesseum. She hadn't expected him to be so friendly, he was a completely different person to the one she'd first met. She hoped it would last. Underneath it all, he seemed like a nice enough man. The last thing she wanted was to fall out with him again.

The courtyard suddenly filled with the arrival of two coach groups. Her peace and quiet shattered, she walked back through the columned walkway and out of the temple, making a beeline for the Winter Palace Hotel. She couldn't resist a refreshing cup of tea.

~

After polishing off delicious tea and sandwiches whilst overlooking the Nile, Cora left the Winter Palace, turned her back on the river and entered the heart of Luxor. It wasn't long before she stumbled into the tourist bazaar, an area made up of shops and stalls where owners proudly showed off a multitude of goods. On one there were statues of ancient Egyptian deities, clothes and scarves made from Egyptian cotton. Another had bags, purses and shoes hand sewn in camel skin. A third, Jewellery in gold, silver and precious stones, all designed to lure the tourist in. One stall caught her attention, so she strolled over and watched with interest as the owner explained the ancient art of making papyrus. It was fascinating. He took a piece of river reed and cut it, before squeezing it and releasing the excess liquid. He laid it out in criss-cross strips, finally producing a square of parchment. Once done, he placed it to one side to dry before painting exquisite Egyptian reliefs on it. She marvelled that this ancient practise had been handed down for thousands of years and was still being done in the modern age, even if it was only for tourism.

An intoxicating smell of perfume and spices infused the air and mingled with a lingering smell of coffee. Beads and other trinkets were also readily available and the occasional merchant tried to entice her by giving her a small turquoise bead in the shape of a scarab beetle. She had accepted them so as not to offend. Others beckoned her to join them to browse their wares by offering her a cup of the thick black coffee or glass of hibiscus tea. Politely she declined, content just to let the sounds, sights and smells envelop her as she meandered through the market.

Eventually she found herself on the main shopping street. She walked along, taking in cafés alongside chemists, and other miscellaneous shops selling groceries, clothes, household items and spices. Spices, it seemed, were everywhere, and the smell was enticing. It enveloped her and she knew it was a sensation that she would always remember, one that would be forever Egypt.

Cora enjoyed these quiet times when she could drop herself into the colour and culture of the country and enjoy being part of the everyday life here. She still missed her family terribly, but distance was helping: distance from cold and gloomy England and the accompanying stresses and strains of everything that had happened. She missed her regular chats and dinners with Erica, but she wouldn't be here forever. Her head had already become so full of the past, brimming with ancient history, but she had a feeling she had only just scratched the surface.

Back on the Corniche, she watched the boats drifting by on fast flowing waters, soaking in the warmth of the sun. She felt relaxed and, for the first time, she didn't feel a huge wave of grief wash over her when thoughts of her parents passed through her mind. They would have loved it here. Her mum would have hated the dust, dirt and begging, but she would have put it aside for the beauty of the scenery and the wondrous sites. As the sun moved farther over the hills, Cora knew it wouldn't be long before the sky glowed pink and orange, ending another day. She had nowhere to be and nothing to do but relax and enjoy her surroundings, which she did with a big contented sigh. If someone asked her right now, this very moment, if she would ever return to England, the truth of her answer would be a very definite no. She could never return.

CHAPTER FOURTEEN

Luxor, Egypt, 2002

Still half asleep, she searched the bedside table for the hotel phone which was ringing loudly. Lifting the receiver, she was greeted by an excited Erica; a sound that dragged her to full consciousness.

"Morning, Cora!"

"Erica, hi. Do you have to be so chirpy this time in the morning?" she groaned. "Some of us are on holiday!"

Oops sorry, but it's eight-thirty here. Wakey, wakey!"

Cora rubbed the sleep from her eyes and sipped some water as she looked at the clock. She had slept later than usual.

"This better be good, Erica."

"It is. Firstly the flat is fine and the plants are still alive, which is good as you know how crap I am at looking after plants." Cora heard Erica pause for dramatic effect and she allowed her to carry on, knowing Erica would always do her own thing in her own way in her own time. "The good news is that your brother's place has sold! It's subject to contract and all that, but the agent thinks it should go through quickly."

Cora sat bolt upright. She hadn't expected it to happen so quickly and, despite a wave of sadness, it was positive news, and it brought her another step toward closure.

"That's good news. Thanks for letting me know."

"So how's the trip going?"

"Good. This place is amazing, Erica. I finally tracked down the professor and his team, and I've been to some of the sites and watched the team work, too. Sam has been so kind, translating the book for me. It turns out it's actually a diary."

"Who's Sam? Tell me more!" Erica teased.

Cora rolled her eyes at the insinuation. "Nothing to tell. He's one of Professor Foster's team and he offered to translate the diary when the professor refused."

"Boyfriend potential?"

"Bloody hell woman, don't you ever think of anything else?" Cora laughed.

"No. You know what they say. The best way to get over a man is to get under one."

"Right," she agreed, humouring Erica. "If that's all, I'm heading for the shower."

"Okay, okay. I know when I've said too much."

They said their goodbyes, promising to speak again soon and Cora hung up. Still smiling from the conversation, Cora climbed out of bed and pulled back the curtains, allowing the sunlight to spill into the room. She was looking forward to relaxing by the pool with a book.

~

Later that day, seated under an awning in the hotel grounds, Cora and Sam shared a large pitcher of iced lemonade. Sam sipped from the glass before placing it back on the table, the condensation ran down the outside of the glass forming a small puddle on the tabletop. Picking up Randa's diary, he flicked through the now familiar aging leather bound pages, found the right page and began to read.

<u>Thebes, Egypt, 1902</u>

I have been secretly meeting Albert for months now and there have been many more nights like the first beautiful night on the felucca. I have been unable to write everything down as I have been so busy with my family. The guilt of what I have done still follows me and haunts me at night, but I love Albert more than my own life and I am in too deep to stop now. It is the middle of the night and I am unable to sleep, I crept out of the house to sit on the step to write by the light of the full moon.

Every time I see Albert he is more gentle and caring than the time before. But I am beginning to worry. With each day I wake feeling tired and so terribly sick, my symptoms are becoming more and more like my mother's when she had Hakim. I fear that I too am expecting a child. It is making me ill with worry. I cannot concentrate, I am nervous and I am completely fearful of what is to come. Is this my punishment for defying my family? I know that I have sinned greatly and I am now paying the price for that sin.

Yesterday I finally confided in Hakim. I knew telling him was a risk, he is a man and by rights he should have told father straightway but he did not. I have always been able to trust Hakim, and this time was no different. He understands me and is not at all like my parents, he was very happy for me, and he told me he knew Albert and I were in love, he can see it in our eyes. This scared me as I feared my parents may have seen it too, but Hakim assured me they were too blind to see real love. Hakim said he would help me and Albert in any way he could. He told me I have to tell Albert, but I am too frightened. What if Albert stops loving me? I do not want to be alone. I could not bear it.

<u>Thebes, Egypt, 1902</u>

It has been a week since I spoke to Hakim and tonight I finally found the courage to tell Albert. My heart was filled with dread as I gave the news to him. I waited for him to call me names and disown me but he did not. He was joyful at the news, and it made my heart fly, he was excited to be a Father and told me he was the happiest man on earth. He showed me just how happy he was by taking me out on a felucca. Under the silver light of a full moon he took my hand and gently kissed it. He knelt before me, telling me he would always love me and our child, we were precious to him, more precious than his own life. Tears of joy slid down my face as he placed a beautiful ring onto my finger, asking me to be his wife and spend the rest of my life with him. Without hesitation I told him I would.

The weight of the metal band was my whole world, but also a reminder of the obstacles that we would have to overcome and a future that would continue to be an uphill struggle. Despite these worries, I have no reservations. I am going to marry my Albert, and I am blissfully happy.

When I returned home I hid the ring. As I fed the chickens with Hakim I could not hide my excitement, I told him, but begged him to keep it secret. He was so happy for me, he told me he wanted what was best for me and he told me he liked Albert and knew he would look after me. Hakim did not want to see me grow old and tired like our mother, working too hard for others and having no life. I knew from that moment that Hakim was right, this life was not for me. I was made for better things. I knew my parents would be furious as this was not what they had planned for me, but Albert and my child meant too much. All of my life I have lived in everyone's shadow, I want to break free and live my live for me. I deserve it and so does my child.

Thebes, Egypt, 1902

Albert came to the house the following evening, and he asked to speak with my family. I sat at the table next to my mother and there was a deathly silence in the room that seemed to go on forever. My hands sat in my lap and they nervously twisted. Butterflies swirled in my stomach making me feel sick and nervous. I wanted it to be over but for ages the air was dense and heavy, like an electric storm patiently waiting to choose its moment to strike.

Eventually Albert spoke. He told my family that he was in love with me and he was going to marry me and we were expecting a child. My father's anger was all too visible. He knocked over his chair as he stood and it clattered to the floor, the start of the horrifying crescendo that was to follow. He shouted at Albert in our own language cursing him for betraying him and for defiling his one and only precious daughter. He yelled so loudly unable to contain the anger. He smashed pots and threw anything he could get his hands on. I had never seen my father like this and it scared me. My father continued to shout as my mother cried tears of sadness. Her sadness only made him more angry. Did Albert not know he had betrayed his trust? Did Albert not know he had brought shame on me? On our entire family? My father tried to grab me by the hair, but Albert stopped him, pushing me behind him to protect me. I sobbed knowing that my father would never love me again.

It went on for what felt like hours, before father finally stopped yelling. I had remained behind Albert and felt the shakes of fear coursing through my body, as the occasional tear escaped to skim the surface of my skin, before rolling down my face and neck, then disappearing into the folds of my clothes. Father turned his attention to me again. His face was a twisted seething mass of hatred. He told me I was shameful. I was a fallen woman, no better than a slut and a whore, who had no right to be under his roof. I had brought disrespect on the family. I fought so hard to hide the tears, to be brave, but they refused and fell fast. I turned to my mother and felt my heart break as she cried and buried her head in her hands, wailing uncontrollably. It was then I felt the shame. Ishaq would not look at me and from that moment on, my father refused to even acknowledge my existence. Only Hakim looked at me, and it was with pure love and sympathy. I knew he would always be there if I needed him.

Finally my father instructed my mother to take me to my room to collect my belongings, she stood in the doorway and watched me in silence as I gathered what few possessions I had. As I left the room I tried to kiss her cheek but she turned from me, wailing and collapsing to the floor, the loss of her only daughter too much to bear. Before I had the chance to comfort her, Ishaq was at my side pulling me roughly from the house. Albert was already standing on the veranda waiting for me.

Ishaq released his tight grip on my arms, pushing me harshly and I fell face first into the dirt, he turned his back upon me, disappearing into the house. Gently and without words, my beloved Albert lifted me from the ground. I saw my father, his angry eyes now with a hint of sadness about them. His hands shook as he told me I was no longer welcome and was never to return home. In one final blow to us, he instructed Albert to collect his belongings from the excavation site. My father no longer wanted his money and Albert no longer had a job, my father was having us moved to Cairo. With heavy hearts, Albert and I turned leaving my home behind me, forever.

As I climbed into the waiting cart, I turned one last time to look at my beloved home, the place I grew up, the place I learned to cook with my mother, the place I played as a child with my brothers. The placed I called home. Used to call home. Tears fell from my eyes and I sobbed as I left, crying myself hoarse as we travelled the lonely nighttime roads of Thebes. As I fell to sleep that night, in Albert's bed at his lodgings, I placed my hand over the swell of my stomach, the child who had not yet been born, but who had already lost so much. I had no idea what my future with Albert would hold now that we were outcasts, but I had to try and stay positive for my unborn child, I had to believe it would be okay. I had no other choice.

Cora wiped away a stray tear. Randa and Albert's story was devastating. A sad, yet beautiful tale. She couldn't even begin to understand what they had gone through. Yes, Cora had lost her parents and brother to an accident, but they had loved her, loved her unconditionally for who she was, whatever she did in her life. How would she have coped if she had lost them as Randa had hers? She doubted she would ever be able to live with it. She had so much respect for Randa and had no idea where her courage had come from. She was so much stronger than Cora would ever have been.

Sam's voice broke through her thoughts and she turned her attention back to him.

"Sorry, Sam. I was miles away."

"I was asking if you have any other plans for today."

"No, why do you ask?"

"I wondered if you might like to visit the mortuary temple at Deir el Bahri?"

"Yes, I think I need a change of scenery after hearing all of that. It was quite gut-wrenching."

"I'll go and order a taxi from the front desk while you get what you need from your room. See you in a few minutes,"

Forgoing the elevator, Cora ran upstairs and grabbed her bag and a shawl for her shoulders, a few minutes later she met Sam back in reception and together they walked out to the waiting taxi. The vehicle sped along the Corniche, stopping at the passenger and vehicle ferry by Luxor Temple. After paying the driver, Sam and Cora, boarded the waiting ferry.

"I didn't know this was here, Sam. I've always taken a taxi across to the other side via the big bridge."

"I normally do too, but this is much more fun. The ferry goes to El-Gezira and you can walk up to Deir el Bahri. It doesn't take long."

The ferry completed its short journey across the river and they disembarked at El-Gezira, avoiding offers of help from the locals. Soon, they passed the El-Gezira Hotel, and turned onto a track that ran along the edge of the El Fadliya canal. Large palm trees lined the road, their shade all too brief. Stooped, wizened bodies of locals were working in the lush green vegetation. Sam explained how the irrigation system worked and how the farmers managed to maintain the sectioned land so well. Soil along the Nile was extremely fertile, enabling farmers to grow cotton, clover, sugar cane and rice. It was a practise that had continued since Pharaonic days and little had changed.

Continuing to talk as they walked, she learned more about Sam's childhood. It seemed his parents were often away on excavations or researching in museums and he was brought up differently to most other children he knew. Whilst his friends were watching cartoons, playing football or out on their bikes, he was traipsing around historical sites and museums. It was hardly surprising he had ended up where he was. Cora laughed as Sam told her about the time he hid in a sarcophagus and jumped out on his sister and her friends, scaring them half to death. His parents hadn't been as pleased, as he had damaged a part of the ancient relic in the process and his father had had a lot of explaining to do.

In turn, Cora told Sam more about her life growing up in Scotland and how she had left home in her early twenties to live in London where, a number of years later, she'd met Damon. She poured her heart out about how she thought she and Damon had been happily engaged but that, in reality, it had all been an illusion that had ended very badly.

Although the conversation had some serious topics, it was an enjoyable walk and Cora felt like she had found a friend. Although she still didn't know Sam that well, she really enjoyed his company. He was easy to get along with, funny, and very knowledgeable. She still didn't understand why Nick hated him so much. She hadn't seen a bad side to him, but then that was the thing about people: everyone was different, and you never really knew what went on behind the scenes.

They turned off the track onto another road that led them past the Abdul Kassem Hotel and the remains of the Temple of Seti I and Ramses II. Sam highlighted the ancient temples, explaining their history as they went. Sadly, they were now barely recognisable, but she was still fascinated. Pharaohs, it seemed, had had a passion for building big; making their mark on society and history. She wondered what it would be like to go back in time and walk the same path. Would the whole area be covered with temples, tombs and perhaps open areas waiting for the next temple to be built?

Reaching a road junction, Sam pointed out the large site of Deir el Bahri which loomed before them. It was an enormous temple complex built on several levels, with a large upward slope leading onto a long wide terrace. At intervals, life-size statues of kings were depicted in the standing position, with arms crossed, holding the crook and flail. Their heads sported the pharaonic crown and beard.

"It's huge, Sam!"

"It is, but just wait until we get closer. I love this temple. It has one of the most interesting stories. It was built for the Pharaoh Hatshepsut."

"I've not heard of him, was he a great ruler?" she asked with interest.

"She," Sam corrected.

"Did you say 'she'? I don't understand."

"An Egyptian called Thutmose III inherited the throne, but he was considered too young to rule. His Aunt Hatshepsut, who incidentally was also his stepmother, stepped in and became his successor. The story goes that she actually took the job so seriously that she decided to rule as a man, and used to dress as one even choosing to wear a false beard. She was known as the Pharaoh Hatshepsut."

Cora laughed, shaking her head in surprise; a female pharaoh. She'd heard it all now! "A feminist for ancient times!" she declared.

"I guess so. The whole story surrounding her is really interesting. People nowadays think that she was almost erased from history because Egyptians at the time didn't believe in what she was doing, but I think there is more to it. She did rule for around fifteen to twenty years, which for that time is a lengthy reign. It is more likely that she incensed her people by having an illicit affair with one of her courtiers, a man called Senenmut."

"It's never a dull day with the ancient Egyptians, is it?"

"No, it's not. If you dig deeply enough, you'll find all sorts of interesting stories — interfamily marriage, war, murder, deceit — but they were also a people who were extremely talented and advanced for their time. Their architectural and engineering feats were second to none. They worked precious metals including gold, and reigned for thousands of years, keeping the country relatively stable, bar a few minor blips."

"The more I hear about them, the more I understand why you and the rest of the team do the job you do. The other day, I bought some books to read up on the history and I've become obsessed by it all but there is so much to learn."

"There is. I've been doing this for years and I'm learning new things all the time."

"It sounds like you really love it. Now come on, show me round Hatshepsut's temple and tell me more about this affair between her and her courtier."

Cora grabbed Sam's arm and dragged him up the ramp as he began to recant the history of the site.

CHAPTER FIFTEEN

Luxor, Egypt, 2002

Cora and Sam spent almost three hours at the site and he had been right, there was plenty to see. The wall carvings alone were stunning. Some were in colour which, Sam explained, was unusual for temples. In most temples, over time the colour had been damaged or had simply faded, due to the elements, ultimately returning the stone back to its natural hue.

Cora's favourite was the large depiction of Anubis. Most people thought Anubis was a figure to be feared but, to her, he was astute and proud. Anubis was a revered Egyptian god of the underworld who was also protector of the dead and his job was taking those who had died to the *weighing of the heart ceremony*. He was just doing a job, heart and feather weighing aside.

As they reached the bottom of the ramp, leaving the temple behind them, Sam steered her to one side where mounds of ruinous blocks lay scattered about as though a child had tipped over a box of play bricks. They were remnants of two other temples belonging to Mentuhotep II and Thutmose III. Cora imagined them nestled into the hillside, standing proudly next to Hatshepsut's temple. It would have made an incredible sight on the horizon; a show of power and strength to all those who had a shadow of doubt about their great leaders.

"I've one last thing to show you," Sam said, directing her past the temples to jagged rocky outcrops at the base of the mountains, away from the parked coaches and milling tourists.

"This is the royal cache tomb."

Cora looked at the big ragged hole in the ground. It wasn't very spectacular and she wondered why Sam was showing it to her. Seeing the confusion on her face, he explained.

"This unremarkable hole in the ground is very significant. When it was discovered, archaeologists found it contained the mummified remains of more than fifty missing kings, queens and other nobility. They also found funerary equipment used for the burial of Hatshepsut."

Cora looked into the hole again. "All of that was in there?"

"Yes."

"Do they know why? I thought Egyptian royals had their own tombs?"

"They did, but at some point — no one knows when — the bodies were secretly moved to protect them from looting."

"Who was doing the looting?"

"We don't exactly know, but we suspect ancient workers went back after the royals had been buried and the tombs sealed. They would have been the only people who would know where the tombs were and what was in them."

"I wonder why they did it?"

"Sometimes they re-used them for their own burials. But more often it was because many of the tombs contained precious metals and jewels, which were taken and melted down or sold to traders."

"Did any of them ever get caught?"

"Sometimes. There are accounts of robbers being punished. Some were whipped, others had hands or ears cut off."

"That's horrible!"

"It is, but to the ancient Egyptians the afterlife was everything and having their tombs raided was sacrilege."

"The Egyptians were a very complex people, weren't they?"

"They definitely were."

Sam and Cora had turned full circle and were walking back towards the road. Sam directed her to a small refreshments tent at the side of the temple, where he bought them each a glass of hibiscus tea. They sat looking up at the imposing temple, watching as tourists swarmed among the ruins.

"Doesn't this ever get to you, Sam?"

"What?"

"All these people trampling over the sites."

"Not really. We tend to work during some of the quieter parts of the year. It can get a lot busier than this."

"Really?"

"Yes. There are certain tombs and pyramids that only open for short periods of time to protect them and others don't open at all now. But tourism is also good. Egypt needs it to bring money in for locals. It's a difficult balance to get right. Egypt's very proud of its history and they do all they can to look after it."

"That's good to hear."

"Shall I read some more of the diary whilst we drink our tea?"

"Yes, why not."

Sitting in the shade out of the midday heat, sipping the fragrant floral tea, Cora listened intently as Sam read to her.

<u>Cairo, Egypt, 1902</u>

It is a week since I last wrote and so much has happened. At my father's request Albert and I made the slow and difficult journey northwards to the Delta eventually finding ourselves in Cairo. I was sad to leave Thebes, it was my home and I loved it dearly. It is all I have ever known. I had never been to the City before and it was hot, dusty and dirty and it overwhelmed me, but it was also full of new experiences, sights, sounds and smells. Once I got over my initial fear it began to feel familiar. Albert found us a small lodging on the outskirts of the City, it is basic and cramped but we have a roof over our heads and we can gratefully call it home. I miss my family and beautiful Thebes, my father kept his word and found Albert another job, working at Giza, but my family still refuse to have anything to do with us. Albert is so happy to be doing what he loves. I hope this excavation will be more fruitful than the last, his father has told him that he wants a return on his investment.

I am less happy though. Whilst he is working I am left to the solitude of our new home, I still feel terribly sick each morning and the baby is restless. I have no friends and no one to speak to, and I am lonely without Albert here to keep me company. Occasionally I am able to walk to the market for food, but it is a struggle and I am unsure how much longer I will be able to do it.

<u>Cairo, Egypt, 1903</u>

It has been months since I have written, I have been so tired and unwell with carrying this child. I have been unable to leave the house at all and feel like a caged animal. Most of the time I sleep. I still have no friends here and I miss my family so much, if not for Albert and the new life I am bringing to the world I would just throw myself into the Nile and end it all, surrendering myself to the swirling depths would be bliss compared to the daily hell I feel.

<u>*Cairo, Egypt, 1903*</u>

A happier day arrived. Albert surprised me. He gave me a dress so beautiful that I was unsure if it was actually for me. Once I was wearing it he took me to the local church where we married. I did not know that this would be possible and I am reluctant to ask how he managed it, although I suspect he paid the priest. It was a small affair, just me, him and the priest. He was so happy and for the first time in months, so was I. Albert knew an archaeology friend who could make a photograph. It was bizarre to see us captured forever on a sheet of thick paper. But I am happy. Now I can look at it forever and remember the happiest day of my life. I am now Mrs. Albert MacKenzie!

My happiness was not to last. A few weeks later Albert returned with bad news, he is worried, the excavation is not as good as he had hoped. The finds are poor, and they may have to close the site down. Worse still his father keeps threatening to take money from him and the excavation team have become dismissive of him.

I hope for all our sake things get better soon. They have to.

~

It is only a month now until I am due to give birth.

Things for Albert and I have become so much worse. They still have not found anything at Giza and Albert's father has now stopped sending us money. Albert begged and pleaded with him but his father just refused. Albert eventually told his father that he was married and I was due to give birth and at first his father was happy, he wanted to know all about me and where we had met. So Albert told him. When he learned the truth Albert's father lost his temper, he told Albert he had ruined the family name by marrying me. In the letter he sent, Albert's father called me horrible names, he said I was nothing more than a whore of a peasant. It hurt so much, but I tried not to let it show, Albert felt bad enough already. Albert has now lost everything, his father has disowned him. The big house in the country with the beautiful gardens where he grew up and learned to be a man, his inheritance, and his pride, they are all gone. We only have what money he brought with him to Egypt and that is fast disappearing. Albert is despondent and I do not know what to do to help him. All is lost to him, gone forever, taken by a family who no longer love or care about him, and it is all my fault.

<u>Cairo, Egypt, 1903</u>

My beautiful baby, a girl, has been delivered to us safely and is in good health. Albert was so very happy and he adores his new daughter. It is the first time I have seen him smile in so very long. His eyes lit up when he saw her and I saw a spark of the old Albert in there. We have decided to call her

Florence, as this was Albert's grandmothers name, even if his family want nothing to do with us, we still want them to be a part of our lives in some way. My beautiful girl has my hair and eyes and her fathers nose and when I sit with her Albert smiles at her with such love. Florence being here makes it all better, we are a family. We have a purpose now.

<u>Cairo, Egypt, 1903</u>
Our joy did not last. It has barely been a week, since I last wrote and Albert has now lost his job and no one else will employ him. He says our money is running out and the only sensible thing to do is go back to England, Albert says he can use his name to our advantage and get work there. I am reluctant to leave my beloved Egypt, despite our troubles I love it so much and I have heard that England is cold and damp, but Albert is my husband now and I must abide by his wishes. If he thinks that England is better for us then I must try and put aside my own feelings. Albert told me he has already visited the shipping office and they had a good price on tickets so we leave in two months from the Port of Alexandria. Reluctantly I have agreed to go with him, I love him and have no other choice.

I feel a dread in my soul that once I leave the shores of Egypt I will never see my family or my beautiful country again, and the thought of that is heartbreaking.

WIND ACROSS THE NILE

Southampton, England, 1904

It has been months since I last wrote. I could not bear to write what I feel, because if I did, it would make my life real, and to me it still seems like a horrible dream. I am sitting in my new home, feeling the cold and damp seep into my tired aching bones. The rain is pouring outside, drenching everything in sight, running in small rivers. I do not think it has stopped since we arrived.

Before I left Egypt, I sent a note to Hakim to tell him all of our news. I will miss my brother so much, and I know he will miss me too. I was dreading the journey to England and did not want to go but I had no choice. I stood on the deck of the boat as it left the Port of Alexandria and I cried tears of sadness watching as my homeland slowly disappeared from sight. If Albert had not been there to steer me downstairs to our cabin, I would have thrown myself overboard, into the swirling cold waters of the ocean, to put an end to all of this hurt and pain that I constantly carry with me. As I numbly walked down the boat steps I had shivered with the cold. In our berth Albert sat me down and cleaned my tear stained face before pulling a blanket over Florence. He is such a patient man.

I was glad to finally arrive in England, the movement of the boat made Florence and I so ill, I barely ate and when I tried to take on food it just came back up again. Florence liking it even less than I, cried and cried until she finally howled herself into fitful sleep. We disembarked in a place called Southampton. In a weary daze I obediently carried

Florence following Albert who was looking after two small cases. I waited patiently, sitting on an old wooden chair, tiredness overwhelming me, whilst Albert sought lodgings. Mercifully he found some later that day we were shown our new home by our landlord, a man who was in great need of a wash and smelled strongly of alcohol. I did not trust the way he looked at me and I averted my gaze, hiding behind Albert.

We have settled now, there is a bedroom and another room housing a stove and space for a few chairs and table. There is also a small courtyard behind the house, the toilet is in a small wooden hut out the back and we share it with the neighbours. The house is dirty, cramped, and smells of damp, and is very dark inside. It is not an ideal place to bring up a child, and I hate the rats and other vermin that come out at night rustling around in search of food scraps.

I feel so far from my home and family, and I fear I will never go back and I worry that this pitiful existence is all that is left for me. Albert has tried his best to get work, but he has been finding it hard, I know it is hurting his pride not being able to provide properly for his family. I wish there was something I could do to help him, I feel like such a burden and a failure and often wonder why he fell in love with me and married me.

He would be better off if I had died. Everyone would.

~

Cora blinked, wiping away the tears. She felt like hours had passed. She had finished her tea and was now sipping water.

"She sounds so unhappy. She gave up everything for the love of a man and ended up living in a complete hovel in an unfamiliar country."

Sam placed a sympathetic hand on her arm. "It is a sad story. Life was much harder in those days." Then, steering the conversation elsewhere, he said, "I'm starving, Cora. Shall we go and get something to eat?"

Cora quietly nodded, she was hungry too. Standing, she grabbed her bag, stuffed the diary inside and followed him.

~

The delicious aroma of food hit them before they entered the café and Cora hadn't realised how late the hour was. Their order was quick to arrive and they sat in silence enjoying a mix of bread, couscous and chicken.

"So this is how you spend your days," a familiar voice spoke and Cora saw Nick standing next to her.

"Hi there!" she grinned through a mouth full of bread. Quickly she chewed it down so that she could talk properly.

"I've had a great day. Sam's shown me around some of the sites. He's also read some more of the diary, too. Sit down and join us. I'd love to tell you some more about it."

Cora saw the look pass across both men's faces. It was obvious that neither of them relished the thought of being in each other's company. Despite that, Nick pulled out the chair next to Cora. He sat and ordered coffee from a passing waiter. Sam sat in silence as Cora replayed what they had learned.

"That's some story. You still have no idea how it relates to you?" Nick asked.

"None at all."

"Well I hope you find out soon. It's good you're helping her out, Sam."

Sam nodded in agreement as Nick drained back the last of his coffee, pushed back his chair and stood.

"Well, it's been nice to see you again, Cora. Sam."

He turned and exited the café as swiftly as he had arrived. It wasn't long before Cora and Sam had also finished their meal and left the café. The sun was still shining brightly, but the tourists were starting to dissipate, heading back to their hotels at the end of a long tiring day of sightseeing. Sam walked Cora to the edge of the road and flagged down a taxi to take them back to the East Bank. The taxi stopped briefly on the Corniche to let Sam out before speeding on to drop Cora at her hotel. It had been a fun day and she was looking forward to a swim in the pool.

As she entered the lobby, her happiness disintegrated when the receptionist informed her that Damon was waiting for her on the terrace. Sinking to a chair, she closed her eyes and tried to squash down the feeling of utter panic. Her hands were shaking and she felt sick. Damon was here? What the hell did he want? Opening her eyes, she realized she needed to get to her room, so she stood up and glanced around, but all was quiet. Sneaking across the reception, she managed to make it into the lift and up to her room without seeing him. Anger coursed through her as she looked out across the flowing Nile. Who had told him that she was here, and why had he even come?

Hadn't they said everything that was left to say back in Scotland?

CHAPTER SIXTEEN

Luxor, Egypt, 2002

He drank the whiskey he had managed to procure. With every sip it took him back to her. Her body, face, hair, eyes. Those beautiful eyes. It had been good to see her again, despite his hatred for her. Yes, he hated Cora and everything she represented, knowingly or not. She was a part of a history that was unresolved and it grated on him and his family. But he had also begun to realise that he was a man with needs. She was very attractive. No, he was lying. She was beautiful, incredibly beautiful, almost exotically so: long shiny raven locks, almost flawless skin, dotted with a few pale freckles, and intense dark brown eyes. Eyes like deep pools that caught hold of him and dragged him under until he felt as though he was about to drown. He wanted her, and that was a new feeling for him. This was a game changer. This was not meant to happen.

It had begun to distract him. Seeing her smiling face today had only begun to reinforce the feelings that were bubbling below the surface, threatening to release themselves like a dormant volcano roaring to life before blowing its top, changing life forever. He needed to rid himself of those feelings and keep sight of why he was here. She was a stain on his family's existence that was only good for one thing. Information. Once he had that information, she would go the way of her parents. A horrible accident, one he was still planning, and he would make it a good one. She deserved something special; a death like no other. There was more at stake here than lust and his own selfish needs.

There was revenge and truth, and that was far more important.

~

Cora heard an insistent knock at the door. Reluctantly, she looked through the spy hole, expecting to see an angry Damon but instead she saw Nick Foster. It had only been a few hours since she'd last seen him and she smiled at the sight of the good looking man the other side of the door. He really was very attractive. Taken aback by her thoughts, she mentally chided herself. He was someone she barely knew and she was definitely not on the market after everything that had happened. She opened the door.

"Nick. Hi. What are you doing here?" she asked curiously.

"I thought this may interest you." He held an envelope in his hand and looked slightly uncomfortable.

Cora took the envelope from him and opened it. Pulling out the thick card, she read the embossed script.

"You're inviting me to a talk?" she asked with surprise.

"Yes, but only if you're interested. It's a lecture being held tomorrow at the Luxor Museum, about last season's dig. It probably isn't something that would interest everyone, but I thought you might be?"

She smiled, noticing how nervous he was. It surprised her.

"Thank you, Nick. It's very kind. I'd love to attend."

"Really?"

"Really. It would be great to hear more about the work you and the team do. I'm getting very hooked on all this Egyptology stuff."

Nick laughed, visibly relaxing.

"That's good to know. There are people who come out here and either sit by the pool all day never setting foot outside the hotel, or they do venture out and end up hating every minute of their holiday and can't wait to get home again."

"Well, not me. I'm throwing myself headlong into everything!"

"So I've heard. I have a bit of spare time now. Would you like to get a coffee downstairs? I could tell you a little more about the event?"

Cora paused for a moment. She really didn't want to see Damon, but then again it was *her* hotel. She had come here first. Why should she stay locked in her room just to avoid *him*?

"Do you know what? That would be lovely. Thanks, Nick."

Grabbing her keycard, she slid it into her pocket before closing the door behind her. On the way downstairs the lift was full of other tourists so they didn't talk much. Cora directed Nick as they walked out onto the sun scorched terrace, where they located a free table under the shade of an umbrella, overlooking the river. Scanning the grounds, Cora couldn't see Damon anywhere and hoped that he'd changed his mind and left.

After ordering drinks, Nick spoke.

"I've not been to this hotel before. It's a bit out of the way, but definitely worth it for the beautiful view."

"That's why I like it. I didn't know it was this far out when I booked it. I just chose it because it's a Hilton but, as you noticed, the surroundings are beautiful and the view is to die for. They have some great restaurants, too."

Nick studied her for a moment before speaking. "Are you feeling a bit better now? I mean after all of the trauma you've been through?"

"A little, but then there are moments when the reality of all that's happened, and all I've lost, hit's me and it hurts. I miss my family so much. There have been so many times when I've wanted to call them and tell them about the fantastic things I've seen, and then reality sets in and I remember they're no longer alive. The distance and change of scenery is helping to distract me but it's going to take time to come to terms with what's happened. Losing a loved one is bad enough, but I lost three members of my family in one go. Everything changed and it's been incredibly hard to deal with."

"I can understand. I have friends who've been through similar situations, but I think you're really brave coming out here the way you have."

Cora was surprised. "You think I'm brave?"

He laughed. "Yes I do! Don't look so shocked. And I think it's doing you a world of good. You look much better than you did when I first saw you. The climate's working for you."

"Thanks." Cora felt herself blush a little, as she didn't always feel deserving of compliments. Swiftly she changed the subject to help ease her embarrassment. "So tell me about this invitation."

Nick recounted a little of the previous year's dig to her. As head of the excavation, he had been asked by the Egyptian authorities to give a talk at the Luxor Museum to a group of sponsors, officials and eminent archaeologists and Egyptologists. Cora learned that she was one of the few non-academic attendees and felt privileged to be asked.

"It sounds very interesting. I look forward to it."

"Don't expect it to be too exciting. We academics have a tendency to drone on a bit and we can get quite boring!"

"I'm sure it will be very interesting," Cora reassured with a chuckle.

A natural silence fell. It was now early evening and the sun would soon begin its descent for yet another day. She still had a nagging feeling that Damon was around somewhere and it unsettled her.

"Are you okay, Cora? You seem distracted."

"I'm sorry." She explained to Nick about Damon.

"I know hate is a strong word, but I really do hate him," she continued. "He managed to single-handedly turn the worst time of my life into a nightmare. I was finally able to distance myself from him then he has the nerve to turn up here and I don't even know why. I wish he would just leave me alone."

"He sounds like a right piece of work."

"He is. I never thought I would say it, but he truly is. I really do wonder what I ever saw him in the first place." She shook her head, embarrassed at her own lack of judgment.

"That's life, Cora. It isn't always straightforward and it does have a habit of throwing awkward and unwanted situations at you sometimes."

WIND ACROSS THE NILE

"I guess you're right. Thanks for understanding, Nick. It's been good to talk about it."

He smiled at her, placing a friendly hand over hers. "You're welcome. I know we haven't known each other long, and we started off on the wrong foot, but I'm always here if you need someone to talk to."

"Who the bloody hell is this, Cora? I've been worried sick about you! I thought you'd gone missing. And yet here you are, happy and healthy, cozying up to another man, who quite frankly looks like he could do with a shower and some new clothes!"

Cora knew she would bump into Damon at some point. He was like the proverbial bad penny. He leaned over the table pointing viciously at Nick. Nick swiftly released her hand before pushing back his chair and standing in one swift movement, and then holding out his hand out to Damon in a gentlemanly act of friendliness.

"Hi there. I'm Professor Nick Foster. I don't think we've met?"

Cora couldn't believe how calm Nick was. Damon on the other hand was drunk and looked like he was about to explode. She tried her best to keep a straight face, stifling a laugh that threatened to escape as Damon swiped Nick's hand away in disgust.

"No, *Professor Nick Foster,* I don't think we have. What the hell are you doing with *my* fiancée?"

"Fiancée? I'm sorry, I got the impression the two of you were no longer together."

Cora knew Nick was only trying to help, but it was the wrong thing to say to Damon, especially when he was in this drunken state. It would only make him more angry and combative. She wished Nick would keep quiet and let her deal with it.

"That, my friend, is where you're wrong." Damon prodded Nick in the chest swaying unsteadily. "Cora and I are very much in love. We're getting married. In fact she's coming home with me tomorrow, the wedding is next week."

Nick raised an eyebrow at Cora. She couldn't believe what an idiot Damon was being and, more to the point, what the hell she ever seen in him to begin with. She was so embarrassed. Damon was being extremely disrespectful to both her and Nick. To top it all, he was drunk in public, an insensitive and disrespectful thing to do in Egypt. Damon grabbed hold of Cora's arm, roughly pulling her out of her chair.

"Come on. We're going."

Cora tried her best to wriggle free from Damon's crushing grip as he dragged her along behind him. He didn't get far, as she tripped over the leg of the table, and fell to the ground. Damon landed heavily on top of her. The stench of alcohol wafted over her, making her feel sick. The touch of his skin repulsed her and she somehow managed to find the brute strength to push him away and stand up. Embarrassed, she stepped towards the

WIND ACROSS THE NILE

safety of Nick. Anger overwhelmed her and she rounded on him.

"I am *not* your fiancée any more, Damon! It's over. It's been over for a long time. I hate you and I never want to see you again. For the last time, leave me alone!"

Damon pulled himself to his feet and stood, swaying dangerously, he pointed a finger at her, venomously spitting words.

"You'd be nothing without me! Nothing! You're an ungrateful, selfish bitch! I spent a lot of money to come here. Now do as I say. You are coming home with me!"

Nick stepped forward, pushing Cora behind him.

"She's not going anywhere. I think you should leave before I call hotel security."

"This is none of your business, *mate*. This is between me and her."

"Tough. You got me involved."

Damon glared at her.

"Cora. We're leaving. Now!"

It was a stalemate.

Suddenly without warning, Damon lunged at Nick, fist clenched, but Nick was too quick and side-stepped him. Damon fell headlong into the table, sending it and the contents crashing to the floor. Crockery shattered and bounced along the paved area. Two waiters came running, unsure of what was happening. Seeing the drama that was unfolding, they stood perplexed, unsure of what to do next. Horrified, Cora looked on, praying it was all just a horrible dream. She actually pinched herself, hoping she'd wake up in a cold sweat, thankful that it was just some horrific nightmare. But she remained where she was, unfortunately awake the whole time, watching as Damon struggled to his feet to take another swing at Nick. He succeeded, catching Nick off guard, hitting him squarely on the jaw. Cora winced when she heard the crack as fist hit jaw bone.

"Enough!" was all she could yell.

Hotel security guards arrived at a run and they jumped in to grab Damon, and before he knew what was happening, he was being firmly held down until the police arrived. From then on, everything became a blur. They were taken to the Security Office of the hotel where all three were heavily questioned and statements taken by the tourist police. They also had to produce their identification and give their reasons for being in Egypt. Seeing that all was lost, Damon confessed to what had happened, including punching Nick. He was swiftly bundled into a police car that departed the hotel soon after. Cora stood, in the main Reception, Nick alongside her, and watched him go.

"What will happen to him, Nick?"

"They'll probably charge him with misconduct, before deporting him."

Cora turned to look at him and passed him an ice pack that she had borrowed from the bar staff. Nick smiled and winced a little as he held it to his face, where a dark purple bruise was spreading.

"Does it hurt?"

"A little, but I've had worse. Come on I think we both need a drink."

Cora followed him back outside. In their absence, the waiters had cleaned up the mess and re-set the table. It was as though the argument had never occurred.

"I'm so sorry you got involved in that, Nick."

"Don't worry about it. Things happen."

"I guess, but I still feel bad. Could I buy you dinner to say thank you?"

Nick smiled, flinching as the pain in his jaw set in.

"You don't have to do that."

"I'd like to, though."

"Well, if you insist. Dinner would be nice. Thank you."

CHAPTER SEVENTEEN

Luxor, Egypt, 2002

Cora bounced out of bed eager to begin a new day. Now that she knew Damon had left, the heavy burden and stress of the previous day had lifted. Better still, she was going to an event at Luxor Museum tonight. She was looking forward to it but realised she had nothing appropriate to wear, so made plans to go into the city to find something suitable. As she walked through the backstreets of Luxor, passing shops and stalls containing an eclectic mix of tourist-related garb, she spotted a small shop filled to the brim with scarves, dresses and other accessories. Gingerly stepping inside, Cora was taken aback. There were so many nice things that she couldn't even begin to decide what to buy. With a little help from the shop owner, she eventually chose a traditional Egyptian cotton top in sea green. Embellished with embroidery and tiny beads, it was beautiful. She also chose a matching cotton shawl, and some bangles that gently tinkled and glittered in the passing light. She would match the new clothes and jewellery with a pair of brown linen trousers that were still bunched up in her suitcase.

On her way back to the hotel, she lingered at a café for a coffee and something to eat. She was excited about the lecture but was also nervous about seeing Nick again, especially if Sam was there. It was obvious that they didn't like each other much, and their meeting in the café at Deir el Bahri had been more than a little uncomfortable. She hoped becoming friends with both of them wouldn't cause problems. She'd had enough aggravation to last a lifetime.

~

Later that evening, filled with nerves, Cora stepped from the taxi. Walking across the pedestrian area in front of the museum, she joined the small queue outside, and waited patiently to enter the building. Once inside, she walked along the plain but bright corridor towards the main exhibit space. She searched for the Egyptologists and spotted them huddled in a far corner. Weaving her way through the throng of smartly dressed attendees, she caught sight of Nick at the front of the room, and did a double take. He was wearing a black dinner suit and bow tie. He was clean shaven and had even had his hair cut. He looked incredibly handsome, and it surprisingly took her breath away. He gave Cora a discreet smile and wave mid-sentence, before turning his attention back to the men standing next to him. She smiled and continued making her way towards the rest of the team.

"Hey guys."

Sam and the others turned, greeting her with surprise.

"Cora! I didn't know you were coming." The shock of seeing her was all too visible on Sam's face. He looked annoyed that she had been invited, and Cora could only guess that his annoyance was because she was building a friendship with his boss.

"I didn't either until yesterday. Nick gave me the invitation."

Alex hugged her, grinning widely. "It's so great to see you! We've been asking Sam where you were as we all wanted to see you again. We thought he was trying to keep you all to himself."

Sam blushed and left the group momentarily, returning with a drink for her.

"Thanks."

An announcement advised the visitors to take their seats and she joined the others in a row halfway back. It wasn't long before the lights dimmed and Nick was introduced to the crowd by the museum curator.

Cora watched the lecture with pure admiration. Nick was an amazing speaker. She thought it might have been a bit dry and boring, but it wasn't. Nick was animated and at times very funny. He spoke in such a way that the subject came alive and was easy to understand. She was completely captivated and the world around her melted away.

Thirty minutes later, the room broke into rapturous applause and, after a short session of questions, Nick stepped from the podium. As the room filled with light, attendees stood and moved forward to congratulate him or mingled to discuss what they had just heard. Cora and the others huddled in the corner again waiting for Nick to make his way through the throng of congratulations. When he finally reached them, the male members of his team slapped him on the back and the female ones hugged him, words of congratulations all around. Cora wasn't quite sure what to do, so she just smiled.

"It's good of you to come, Cora, and you look lovely."

She blushed upon hearing the compliment.

"That was a great speech and the photos were fantastic."

"Thank you. I hope you understood it all."

"I did. Well, most of it anyway," she laughed.

"I have to circulate a bit more, but I'll come back soon. Don't go anywhere."

As he disappeared into the crowd again, lost in a sea of congratulatory handshakes and praise.

Cora chatted with the team, catching up on what they'd been doing since she last saw them. David explained that the excavation at the Valley of Kings was going well and they had documented some interesting finds. He also noted that the local mapping project at the Valley of the Nobles was on schedule, and wouldn't require much more of their time. Once they finished it, they would move back over to the Valley of the Kings to continue there. Cora listened and then told them the latest news about the diary, and the relationship between Albert and Randa.

A few hours later, the last of the guests finally said goodbye, and Nick wandered over to the team, grinning widely, as he undid his bow tie and unbuttoned his collar.

"Are we bored yet?" he asked. His team was all now slumped in chairs at the back of the room, looking tired.

"No!" they chorused in unison, trying their best to show happy faces.

"Well, you're all free to go, or if you want, we could make a night of it and all go for dinner?"

"Dinner!" was the resounding answer.

"Right. Let me just finish up here meet you at the usual place as soon as I can."

The group swiftly gathered their belongings and made for the exit, but Nick gently took hold of Cora's arm, holding her back.

"I need to speak to you," he whispered.

Sam turned and caught sight of Cora lagging behind with Nick.

"Come on, Cora."

"I'll bring her with me. You go with the others, Sam. We won't be long."

Cora saw the look of reluctance, perhaps even annoyance, cross Sam's face. The situation between with the two men was getting awkward now. She felt a bit like a pinball in a machine, tossed about from one to the other. She wished she knew why they disliked each other so much.

"It's fine Sam, I won't be long. I'll see you and the others in the restaurant in a few minutes. Save me a seat!" She smiled warmly and watched as he went to join the others.

Cora took a seat and watched as Nick shut down his laptop and packed his papers into his briefcase. He looked very different in his suit tonight, his hair was less messy and, for once, he was dust free. She was pleasantly surprised at how well he scrubbed up.

Yes, quite attractive. She shook the stray thoughts from her head, still surprised that she was even having them.

"You okay? You looked miles away." Nick's voice broke through her thoughts and she smiled.

"Yes. I'm fine."

"Good. Listen, before we go and eat, I wanted to show you something. It's not very exciting but I thought you may like it."

Intrigued, she followed him through the small museum until they reached a dark recess. He stopped and pointed at one of the exhibits.

"I wanted to show you this."

Cora stared at a carved stone head hanging resplendently on the wall. It certainly caught her attention. Intrigued, she looked more closely. It was different to other statues, and she hadn't paid any attention to it when she'd visited the museum before. The features were extremely feminine and the face was elongated, not at all like other ancient Egyptian faces. It was as though it had been stretched. The lips were fuller and eyes were like large almonds. Despite its outlandish look, it was strikingly beautiful.

"It's exquisite."

"I thought you'd like it. It's the Pharaoh Akhenaten. He was known as the heretic king and he completely turned the Egyptian way of life and thinking upon its head. He abandoned the traditional Egyptian religion of the time, which was based on the god of Amun and introduced a religion based on the Aten, the name of the sun-disk. It wasn't a popular decision and didn't last long." He paused. "I think all Egyptian art and architecture is beautiful, but this is truly striking. It has to be one of my favourites."

Cora agreed. There was something magical about it. The simplicity of the carving said so much about the man who had once ruled these lands.

"Cora, could I ask you something?"

"Of course."

"How are things going with Sam?"

"Fine. Why do you ask?"

"I'm not sure, and I don't want you thinking that I'm getting at him, but he's been acting strangely. The other day, two men I've never seen before turned up to see him. Their behaviour was furtive. I didn't trust them at all."

"Have you asked him?" Cora said.

"No. I thought I'd ask you first, since you've been spending a lot of time with him."

She sighed again, interrupting him before he could continue.

"I haven't noticed anything, Nick. I do remember him mentioning meeting up with some friends on his day off. Maybe that's who you saw?"

"Maybe that was it. Thanks Cora, you've helped put my mind at rest a bit. I was worried about asking you. I didn't want you to get cross."

"Why would I do that?"

"Well you've been protective of him in the past, and jumped down my throat on more than one occasion."

"Ah that. Well I know you better now, and if you're worried about him then it means you care, regardless of your personal feelings towards him. It makes you a great person and good boss."

"Thanks, Cora. I'm not the grumpy bastard everyone thinks I am. Things have been tough over the last few years and I don't like having lazy people working for me. It makes life harder for me and my team and, unfortunately, Sam is lazy. That's what makes me grumpy, and it doesn't help that the others tend to cover for him, especially the girls. It pisses me off."

This surprised Cora. She had no idea Sam was like this at work, and she felt a little guilty for taking him away from Nick and the team to read the diary.

"I understand, and I'm sorry if I've taken him away from work. He's been lovely to me, but there *is* something about him I can't put my finger on. I still don't quite understand his motives for helping me. I don't know what he's getting out of it, to be honest, but then I think maybe he's just being kind?"

"I know what you mean. Listen, I really am sorry that I was so rude to you the day you arrived. I was having a particularly bad day and you caught me at the wrong time. I haven't really gone into it with the others but I feel I owe you an explanation." He paused, staring back up at Akhenaten. Cora could only see his face in profile and knew whatever he was about to share was a big deal for him. She let him continue in his own time.

"I was married, and things between my wife and I became strained. One day I received photos of her in bed with someone else. To this day I still don't know who it was. His face was covered, but what I could see in the pictures was proof enough. When I confronted her over it, she blamed me." His laugh was hollow and Cora could tell how much he was still hurting. She wished she could do something to help, but knew it was something only he could resolve.

"After six years of marriage, she blamed me. Told me it was my fault, for working away, for never being there. She had always known what I did for a living and she'd been happy about it when we first got married. I don't know what changed. Things turned nasty. She screamed at me, threw things, spat venomous words and I just stood there and let her, watching with sadness as the woman I loved turn into a seething mass of hatred before my very eyes. She no longer loved me. In fact, in her own words, she despised me. So I filed for divorce. It only came through a few weeks ago. I'd spoken to my solicitor the morning you turned up, and, well, I guess I still had a lot of the bitterness coursing through me." He paused shaking his head. "You just happened to be in the wrong place at the wrong time, and I'm truly sorry if I took it out on you, Cora. I shouldn't have done that."

"It's okay, Nick. I understand and forgive you. I'm so sorry to hear about your wife. It must have been so awful for you. Does it still hurt that you don't know who the other party was?"

"If I'm honest, it does. But I'm not sure it would do any good to find out. I'd probably only smack the bastard on the jaw, and that would make me no better than Damon. I just have to get on with my life and learn, as best as I can, to live with it. It doesn't make it any easier, though."

Cora had no idea how his wife could have done that to him. It was so cruel. She didn't know him that well and he seemed decent enough despite how rude he'd been to her when she first arrived, but he had now apologised. She'd give him the benefit of the doubt and see what happened.

She did feel sorry for him. So what if he had worked away? The woman knew that when she married him. It was part and parcel of his job. As far as Cora was concerned, his ex-wife was the one who had been selfish, not Nick.

"Do you still love her?"

"No. I thought I did, but I realised I was still in love with the idea of us being married. I have no feelings for her at all now."

The silence enveloped them and they both looked up at the overtly feminine features of one of the world's greatest rulers, each of them lost within their own thoughts, neither knowing what to say or do next. Nick was the first to shake himself from the reverie.

"Come on. We'd better get going or the others will think we've got lost."

"Good idea. I'm starving."

They left Akhenaten to once more rule over the quiet solitude of the museum, and thanked the curator on the way out. Outside in the still warm night air, they walked along the Corniche towards the centre of town. Ten minutes later, Nick was leading Cora down some slightly questionable back streets and into a vibrant local restaurant. The others were seated, tucking into a feast of local fare. Cora and Nick planted themselves on the two remaining empty chairs before diving in and piling their plates high. Sam had saved a seat next to him and she was able to talk to both men equally, sharing her time between them.

The meal was great fun and Nick's team praised him on his lecture. Cora felt privileged to be part of the group, especially now that she and Nick were on better terms. The meal lasted a few hours but finally, just past midnight, they said their goodbyes and all made their way back to their temporary residences.

CHAPTER EIGHTEEN

Luxor, Egypt, 2002

He dreamed of her that night; persistent, clawing, vibrant dreams that had him waking in a cold sweat, terrified to go back to sleep. He just couldn't get her out of his head. She had looked so beautiful, the earthy tones of her clothes perfectly matching those eyes and that hair. Did she know, deep down, who she really was, or was she still so blissfully unaware? He had felt her eyes taunting him that night. He had watched her as she threw her head back with laughter, nervously winding her fingers around the ends of the soft hair that fell neatly about her shoulders. He was very jealous. He had hated seeing her with *him*. He hated that the two of them were getting so close. If the bastard wasn't careful, he would end up going the same way as the others who had got in his way. How many had he killed now? He'd lost count, but the thrill remained with him and he savoured the moment of each death. Staring out of the window at the clear night, he wished he could get past the feelings of intense jealousy. He wanted — no, needed —to treat her like the enemy she was. Getting her on his side and gaining her trust had been important and he had finally managed to do that. He had revealed so much of his life to her already but, in doing so he had awakened a longing for her that bordered on animal lust. Try as he might, he couldn't bury it and it was beginning to take over. He was torn by what his body wanted and what he had to do.

At night, his brain played tricks on him, forcing memories of what he had done to rise to the surface. It was the same tonight. Cora's beautiful living face had merged with her dead mother's once again. The eyes had held him, captivated him and he had been incapable of resisting. The only thing that had shocked him from the intense feelings was when her mother had cried out in pain and anguish. Cora's mother had known she was about to die and all he could see was himself, leaning over her body, taunting her. He knew these feelings would pass during the day and he would get on with his job, being the professional Egyptologist that he was. But as night arrived, he would again crave the darker side of his life, a mix of death and lust that confused his brain and made him wake in terror. It was a vicious circle. One that was dragging him deeper and deeper into the pit of hell and he knew there was no stopping it.

~

Cora waved to the team as she trod the uneven stony path to where they were working. She noticed that the large landslide had all but disappeared and they had now started preparing the ground. As she passed Nick, he grinned, winking at her before returning his attention to the new trench that had been opened.

Sam looked up as she approached and smiled.

"Hey, you're early."

"Yes. Don't worry I'll wait until you're done."

"I won't be long. You can sit and watch if you want."

She took him up on his offer and sat on the dusty ground listening as he explained how excavations worked, how they sectioned out the area, noting and sorting any finds they uncovered, before writing a report to go back to the Supreme Council of Antiquities in Cairo. The Supreme Council was meticulous about any work that took place in the country, and the archaeological teams worked under strict guidance, with support from the locals.

Cora hung on Sam's every word, taking everything in. A multitude of tools, ranging from scrapers to brushes, sat in a pile on the ground next to him, and he methodically worked, occasionally switching from one tool to another. She noticed how big his hands were but how delicate they were when dealing with the archaeology, only disturbing what was vital. It was fascinating and she admired how he and the other academics didn't get bored, as it was a job that definitely required boundless patience.

Twenty minutes after retrieving his find, which, to Cora, looked like nothing more than a broken piece of pottery, Sam stood, brushed off his trousers and stepped out of the trench. She followed him over to the flank of mountain and sat beside him in the limited shade, plucking up courage to speak before he read some more of the diary.

"Can I ask you something?" She kept her voice low so others couldn't hear.

"Of course."

"You seemed very quiet last night and someone on the team mentioned they were worried about you. They saw two strange men hanging around the other day. Are you in trouble?"

Sam sighed, running his fingers through his hair. "I'm fine Cora. The last thing I want to do is worry people. The men in question were just old college friends. Their demeanor's always been a bit unsavory, but they are completely harmless."

From the look on his face, she wasn't sure if he was telling the truth or not, but decided to let it go. At least she'd made him aware that she was thinking of him.

"Well that's good. I'm sorry to ask, Sam, but I was worried. I care about you and wanted to make sure you were alright.'"

"Thank you. It's nice to know I have someone looking out for me." He grinned, nudging her with his shoulder. "Shall we see what Albert and Randa have been up to?"

Southampton, England, 1904

I have tried to make things better by scrubbing and cleaning the house. Try as I may it still remains damp and dirty. Yesterday the woman who lives next door came to see me, she is very nice and keeps me company during the day. Her name is Nance Potter, she has a big round face with pink cheeks and a great big laugh, and is always smiling. She seems to find pleasure in the smallest of things. I found it hard to talk to her as I still do not speak a lot of English, and she knows no Egyptian, but we get by. It's just nice to have the company.

She adored Florence the day she met her, and often sits there bouncing her on her knee. Nance has three young children of her own that are always running around laughing and playing. Whenever she comes in to visit she always brings me scraps of food, and old bits of cloth. I am so grateful to her and it is helping me to make the house a bit more of a home. I think I would have been driven to utter madness had I not met Nance, she has become my saviour.

CHRISSIE PARKER

<u>Southampton, England, 1904</u>

It has been a few weeks since I last wrote but I have very good news, Albert has found a job, and he will be working at the shipyards labouring. He is not earning much money but we are able to buy food and keep the roof over our head. Nance and Albert have been teaching me to speak more English. I know this is something I have to do to get by now that I live in England, especially now that we have Florence. I am learning well, it is giving me something to do and I practice all the time. It is helping me fit in and I am so grateful to both of them. I can name everything in the house now and can have small conversations with people in the market too,

I have also met some of the other neighbours. They were wary at first, but Nance introduced me to them and they all love Florence and ask me all about Egypt, as if I am a princess and it is some kind of magical place that only exists in story books. I love talking about my country and where I grew up, but it also makes me sad, as I have not heard from my family and I miss them so much.

I do not feel like as much of an outsider now as I did. But deep down I always know that I am, and always will be different.

<u>Southampton, England, 1904</u>

I have finally heard from my brother Hakim! He has written to me and I was so happy to finally get a letter from him. It had been forwarded from Cairo by a friend of Albert's. For so long I have waited for contact from my family, I prayed every day that they would write to me and finally my prayer was answered.

I have been granted a miracle, but it wasn't the happiness I hoped for.

A man knocked at the door and handed me an envelope, it is so strange to think it has travelled all the way from my beloved homeland. All I could do was stare at it turning it over and over in my hands, barely daring to open it, but also anxious to know what it contained. Eventually I gathered courage and ripped at it with shaking hands. Disappointment fleetingly greeted me as there was only a single sheet of paper within, but I knew from the writing that it was from Hakim and not my parents. Slowly I read, taking in the contents. What I read upsets me and I feared for Hakim and what would become of him, it is such a shameful thing he has done and yet I know that he only did it for the greater good. I wish I had known before, so I could have helped him. I am so far from my brother and the rest of my family and there is nothing I can do, and I so wish that I could help. I am glad he wrote to me, but my happiness was swift, now all I feel is a dreadful burden. One I must bear alone. My parents have now lost two of their children to sin and I pray they will not lose a third. I wonder what they did in their life for them to suffer so much.

Cora placed a hand on Sam's arm. Her heart was pounding and she dared not breathe. The turmoil she felt was unlike anything she could describe.

"What does she mean? What does the letter say, Sam?"

"I don't know." He tipped the book and gently flicked through the leaves to release any stray papers, but nothing fell.

"There isn't one."

"There must be!"

"I'm sorry, Cora, but there isn't."

"It must've got lost." Disappointment filled her. "I wonder what it said."

"I wish we knew. Maybe there's something about it later on."

Calmly, Sam continued to read.

Southampton, England, 1905

It has been a whole year since I last wrote. I could not bring myself to write. It was all too much. The news I received about Hakim sent me into shock and I have not heard anything else from him or my family. I miss Hakim so much, I worry greatly about what happened with him and the authorities, and I hope and pray he is well. More than that, I hope he is still alive. He has to be.

I cried in Albert's arms the day the letter came and he comforted me, offering to take me home to see if I could help, but I knew I would not be welcome and it would have been too expensive, so I threw myself into my life here and Florence takes up much of my time. Not much has changed, we still live in the same small cramped dwelling. Florence grows daily and now walks. She is always running about and looking at things. She tires me out as I have to watch her constantly. She had started to try to stand too and I think she will walk very soon one of these days. Florence is what Albert and Nance call a handful. I call her a child with a mind of her own. Albert and Nance see her as unruly and naughty but I try to explain that she is exploring, interested in life and needs room to breathe and grow. I like her this way, it means she will be a strong, independent woman and be able to fight her own battles and not have to rely on anyone else.

Albert has gone from labouring job to labouring job. He hates what he is doing and misses his old life. He tells me he will one day earn enough for us to return to Egypt where he will be able to work on the excavations again, but I do not believe him. He can barely earn enough to keep the rent paid and buy us food. I like his dream very much, but it is just that. A dream.

Albert's family still refuses to talk to him and his friends have abandoned him completely. Sometimes I think it would be easier if I left him, he would then be able to go back to his life of plenty, with his money and status. He tells me Florence and I are the best things in his life and he would die if he lost us, so I stay. I clean the house, not an easy job with Florence being so active, I mend our clothes and I am always cooking, there is no time for anything else. Nance still lives next door with her growing family, she is due to have another child in a few months. I am so lucky to call her my friend, I would be lost without her.

My family have not been in touch and I now know that they never will. I do not hate them or blame them, but I wish for Florence's sake they could see it in their hearts to at least ask after her. She will lose so much growing up without knowing who her family truly are.

<u>*Southampton, England, 1906*</u>

Another year has passed and things are worse than ever. I almost gave up writing in my book, but I want my daughter to have something for the future. I want her to have something that shows her where she came from and how we lived. Even if I only write once a year.

Life hurts so much now. It is all just too unbearable.

Albert stills works as a labourer, but he has taken to going to the public house with the other working men on his way home. I cannot blame him, I know that everything he does, he does for us, but he is spending money that Florence and I need so desperately for food and clothing. He swills the foul smelling liquid down his throat, losing himself in it until he is barely able to stand or see straight. He has taken to the drink in a bad way and he falls through the door later and later each night. Florence barely sees him now. I do not trust him around her when he drinks. He is becoming less of a father as the days go by. Nance is sympathetic and has started slipping more bits of food and cloth to me, but she can barely afford to do it. I feel like I am losing the man I love and I do not know what to do to keep him. I fear he loves the drink more now than he loves me and Florence. I fear that my punishment has only just begun and I will eventually lose everyone I have ever loved and cared about. My heart is slowly breaking and I have no way of fixing it. I should have thrown myself into the Nile when I had the chance. At least I would have been at peace in my beautiful Egypt. Instead I live each day in hell.

<u>*Southampton, England, 1907*</u>

It has been another year and life is worse than ever, even when I read what I wrote last. Albert now brings the drink home with him. I am lucky that he is a kind drunk and not a violent one like the husband of Mrs. Nutter who lives opposite. When Albert drinks he kills me with kind words rather than beating me senseless like some women's husbands do. Mrs. Nutter's husband came home drunk one and hit her in the face, because she was too busy talking to the neighbour Mrs. Meegan and not cooking his tea. I am glad Albert is not like that, but I do fear for Florence. She is still so small and I worry that his behaviour will scare her, she is still as inquisitive as ever, and now understands some of what is happening around her. She lights up my life, and I smile each time I look at her. Florence is the only reason I am still alive.

Sadness has reached me from home too, Hakim finally sent me another letter, I was glad to learn he was alive, but it was not the good news I had expected. With every beat of my heart I wish I could do as Hakim asks but I am unable to feed and clothe my family let alone travel to my homeland to do his bidding. I can only pray that he finds peace. I do not want him to die.

Cora wiped the tears from her cheeks with the back of her hand. She felt foolish for crying again, but hearing about Randa's plight was really upsetting her.

"Oh Sam. I'm not sure I can listen to anymore. I dread hearing what comes next. I wish we knew more about the letters. I'm desperate to know what Hakim has done."

They sat against the wall overlooking the excavation site, allowing the silence to wash over them. Sam knew Cora could take no more today; she was emotionally exhausted. He passed the diary to her and, as she went to take it, it fell and landed open at the rear page. Reaching for it, Sam went to hand it back to her and then hesitated. Cora looked at his face, and saw excitement pass over it, as though he had just discovered something.

"What is it Sam?"

"Have you seen this?" he asked, showing Cora the page.

"No, why?" She took the book and stared at the aging paper.

"I'm not quite sure. There are words on this page that I haven't noticed before. They're in a list with random dates next to them and some of it is

WIND ACROSS THE NILE

in Arabic and some in English." He paused and looked up at Cora, "Do you know someone called Elizabeth Thomas"

"That's my mum!"

He leaned closer to her, pointing to the writing. "Her name's here at the bottom of the page. At the top is Randa's, between the two are Florence MacKenzie and Emma Sanders." He paused before looking at her and smiling.

"I think this is a family tree. If I'm right, then Randa is your great-great-grandmother."

"My what?!" Cora couldn't believe what she was hearing. It made her feel sick, nervous, excited and so sad all at the same time.

After everything she had just learned about Albert and Randa, it was too much. She needed space. She needed to think. Jumping to her feet, she paced back and forth, unable to contain the nervous energy that coursed through her veins. Her brain tried its best to disseminate the information, but she was at a loss. Was it true that the book was a family heirloom, and she was descended from an Egyptian woman and an English aristocratic landowner? Had her mum ever known? If she had, why had she kept it a secret? Cora's brain raced at lightning speed, questions continuing to tumble around her head, with no answers to follow. It was almost paralysing. She could no longer think straight.

"This is amazing, Cora!" Sam was standing next her grinning. Seeing her stricken face, he paused and placed a comforting hand on her arm.

"I know today has been a bit overwhelming for you, Cora, and such a huge shock. Maybe you should leave the diary with me for a bit. I can read it and see what happens next so you don't have to hear about any bad stuff. It might be easier on you?"

"I'm sorry, Sam. I can't do this. It's too much."

Quickly she stood, thrusting the diary into her bag. Without another word, she walked away from him and the site, her brain buzzing with unanswered questions. What did this all mean? Was her family cursed? Her parents and brother had died suddenly. She had never known her grandparents because they, too, had died young. No one ever talked about her mum's side of the family. When she had tried to ask questions, she had been told in one way or another that the past was the past. Why was that? Were they ashamed of something? Or was it something else? Stumbling over rocks on the dusty path, she picked up speed. As tears fell, it was all she could do not to collapse in a heap and sob. Avoiding surprised stares of passing tourists, she blindly ran as fast as she could, heading towards the road.

As she had passed Nick looked up. He rose and followed in her wake, running to catch up with her.

"Hey, Cora! Slow down. What's wrong?"

Cora stopped, unable to run any further in the heat.

"She's fine, Nick," Sam said, swiftly appearing at their side.

Cora just stood there, out of breath, unused to the heat, her body numb, unable to move. An Egyptologist stood on either side of her, blocking her way. She wished they would just get lost and leave her alone, but she no longer had the energy to argue. Gently Nick took hold of her shoulders and turned her to face him.

"Look at me. What's happened?"

"I'm fine, Nick. I just need to leave. Please, let me go," she pleaded.

"Will someone please tell me what's going on?" Nick demanded.

"She's fine, Nick. Come on Cora. I know you're in shock, but don't leave. I can help you. It's what you wanted wasn't it?"

Cora was unable to move or speak. In a way, Sam was right — it was the reason she came to Egypt — but the stakes had dramatically increased. So much had happened in her life recently and she was so confused. She just didn't know what to do next. Turning to Sam, she spoke through her tears.

"Sam, I know you're trying to help, and I do appreciate it, but I need time to think about this. Please."

Nick's temper got the better of him.

"For the second time, will someone please tell me what the bloody hell is going on?" Nick shouted.

"It looks like Cora's diary may have been written by her great-great-grandmother." Sam said.

"What?" Nick took a step back visibly shocked.

Sam continued, "There's a family tree in the back of it, with her mother's name on it. I'm fairly certain the diary was written by one of Cora's ancestors." Sam explained further, "It freaked Cora out and she said she wants to leave and take the diary with her. I was just trying to persuade her to let me keep it and find out more for her to save her any more despair, but she ran away."

Cora hated it when people talked about her as if she weren't there.

"It's too much for me to take in, Sam. I can't make any decisions about it at the moment. I just want some time on my own. I need time to think."

"But Cora...," was all Sam could say before he was swiftly interrupted by Nick.

"If that's what Cora wants, then leave it. It's her diary."

She smiled weakly at Nick, grateful for the support.

"Thank you. I know you're just trying to help Sam, but I need some time alone to work things out in my head."

Sam shrugged, not looking particularly happy. "If that's what you want, I understand. But remember I'm here if you need me."

"I know, and thank you Sam. I really appreciate everything you've done for me so far. Now, if you don't mind, I'm going back to the hotel."

Both men walked her down to the entrance to flag down a taxi. Once she'd left, they walked in silence back to the excavation site, both fuming for different reasons.

CHAPTER NINETEEN

Luxor, Egypt, 2002

Cora slammed her hotel room door so hard that the mirror on the wall shook. Throwing her bag to the side, she sank to the bed and cried, the floodgates fully opening. She hadn't felt like this since the death of her parents; utter loss and despair all over again, but this time it was much worse. She felt completely betrayed. Her mum had kept such a huge secret from her and it hurt that she hadn't trusted Cora enough to tell her. She had just started to come to terms with the fact that her family was gone, only to discover that she may be part Egyptian and have distant relatives who had no idea she even existed. Why had her family kept such a huge secret from her? Did they think she'd never find out?

Cora had no idea what to do next. She felt awful for running away from Sam and Nick. They had both been so nice to her, especially Sam, but she just couldn't handle it. She was a complete mess and she had to sort out how she felt and what she was going to do. Climbing from the bed, she wearily made a cup of tea before picking up the phone and dialling.

"Erica, it's me. Thank goodness you're home."

"Cora? You sound upset. What's happened?"

Tears sprang forth once again and she poured her heart out, recounting everything whilst Erica listened intently, allowing her friend to speak and get it all out of her system.

"So the diary belongs to your family? You're telling me the author is an Egyptian relative? Cora, that's huge!"

"I know, but I'm so confused, Erica. Why didn't Mum tell me? We were always so close; we talked about everything. She never kept secrets from me, ever."

"Until now."

"Until now," Cora agreed ruefully. "I trusted her, why couldn't she trust me? What do I do?"

"Well you have a choice. You either stay there and tough it out or forget about the whole thing, come home and just get on with your life."

"You make it sound so easy."

"Isn't it? You went there for a reason. To find out what was in the diary and just as it starts to get interesting you do what you always do. You run away."

"I'm not running away! It's just so much to take in. So much has happened and I feel completely overwhelmed by it all." Cora hated it when Erica was harsh with her. Cora knew she only did it for her own good. Deep down she knew Erica was right, seeing things from her objective viewpoint, but sometimes she wished her friend wasn't quite so blunt.

"I understand Cora, honestly I do. But you can't keep wallowing in the bad stuff. This could actually end up being a good thing. You may have a whole new family out there somewhere. You may learn stuff you never knew about your family that you'll be glad you had the chance to discover. Yes, your parents and brother are no longer here, but their death has given you an opportunity to reveal your family history, your heritage and where you really come from. Isn't that worth something?"

Cora sighed. Erica was right, but something still plagued her — a feeling — something that she couldn't put her finger on.

"As usual you're right. But I'm worried. There're some odd things going on here."

"Like what?"

Cora explained about her chat with Nick at the museum and the odd way that Sam had been acting, and the continual tussle she felt between them.

Erica snorted with laughter. "It sounds to me like both men have the hots for you and they're both trying to turn you against the other."

"Don't say that! I've had enough man trouble lately, I really don't need anymore!"

"Well it sounds like typical male behaviour to me."

"I'm not so sure. I think there's more to it. Nick thinks Sam's hiding something."

"Like what?"

"I have absolutely no idea, and I don't think he does either," she sighed. "When did life get so complicated?"

"When we became adults!" Erica laughed. "So what are you going to do? Wallow in your self-pity and come home, or let Sam continue his good work?"

"I'm still not sure. I'm going to have to think about it." Cora rubbed her temples. Her head was pounding and she needed to have a drink and take some painkillers. "I'm going to go, but I'll let you know when I've made a decision."

~

He wandered the edge of the river letting the evening activities of Luxor bustle around him unhindered. Taking a seat under a palm tree, he stared out across the swirling waters. The moon's silvery light reflected back at him from the surface and bathed the warm night with a mysterious glow. Stars massed the heavens, twinkling brightly against the inky night sky, and the hills on the opposite bank of the river loomed as dark menacing shadows on the horizon.

The day had been a long and frustrating one. Cora had finally learned where she had come from. He had watched as she ran away in tears and it had surprised him. He thought she'd be a lot stronger, more like her mother, but she'd disappointed him by falling to pieces and bolting like a frightened child. Pathetic. It seemed the fight would be easier than he thought and it was beginning to take the fun out of it. He enjoyed the chase, watching her, stalking her, hunting down his prey, but she was a blubbering mess. For the sake of face, he had become her friend, reassured and cared for her, and she had repaid him by being weak. Maybe he should just cut to the chase, forget friendship, forget earning her trust. Maybe it was time to just take what he wanted and leave her for dead in the desert. After all, who would possibly miss her?

But then again, maybe he should play on her weakness? He could spend some real time with her, take her under his wing completely, make her think that the only person that could be trusted was him. He'd make her fall for him and he'd satisfy his primal urges that were bubbling incessantly below the surface. Yes, he grinned. That was a better way to go and, once he had regained that trust he would take exactly what he wanted. Her heart, her body and her soul. They would become his, and her lifeless body would be thrown to the sand.

~

Sitting on her balcony, Cora took in the beautiful view; the rushing waters of the river, the vibrant hues of lush green vegetation, the brown dusty earth all bathed in a silvery evening glow of moon and stars. It was perfect. Sipping her tea, she allowed the warm liquid and tablets to work their magic. She was exhausted and still reeling from what she had learned earlier that day.

The tragic and captivating story she'd heard was now so much more than just a story. It was her own family history.

Cora had looked at herself in the bathroom mirror after talking to Erica and, for the first time, she saw the raven locks and deep brown eyes of Randa staring back at her. It had shocked her. How had she never noticed before? Had she really been that blind? Randa was her ancestor and part of her had descended through history, marking herself on her female descendants. She now lived on through Cora. She wondered how much of her own character was due to Randa and her Egyptian genes.

She was so upset that her mum had kept it secret. It hurt that her mum hadn't trusted her with this information. There must have been a good reason, but Cora was at a loss to know what that could be. Her mum had never talked about her side of the family. Had she been ashamed of Randa? Had she ever even known about her? It was something Cora was desperate to know and, after mulling it over for a few hours, she decided she needed Sam to translate the rest of the diary. She had no family left, but this was proof of her history. It was the only way she would ever get an answer. It was all she had left and she needed to pursue it and find out where she came from, regardless of what she found out, good or bad.

CHAPTER TWENTY

Luxor, Egypt, 2002

The humidity at the dig site was becoming unbearable. It was one of the hottest days the team had experienced and it wasn't doing any of them any good.

"Morning, Nick. You look hot and bothered." Cora said as she walked up to him and crouched next to the trench where he was working.

"Just a bit. It's unusually humid today. I feel like I need another shower to get rid of the sweaty grime already. I've a feeling there'll be a storm later."

As he spoke, she glanced around for Sam, but couldn't see him.

"No Sam? He told me to meet him here this morning."

"Sorry he's not here. I sent him to Luxor Museum to do some paperwork."

"Oh. I guess I'll have to meet with him again another time then." Cora felt frustrated. She'd been looking forward to seeing him again. She wanted to apologise properly, before getting on with reading some more of the diary. She knew Nick hadn't done it deliberately, but it irked her.

"Why don't you visit one of the temples or something?" Nick suggested.

"I suppose I could, but I don't have any maps or guidebooks on me."

Nick grinned. "Okay then. Seeing as though I've messed up your morning, let me make it up to you. Have you been to Medinet Habu?"

"No. I've never even heard of it."

"That's settled then. I'll take you."

"That's a lovely idea, Nick, but you have work to do. Your time is very precious, remember?"

"I do, and you're right it is, but they can cope without me for an hour or two. And by the time we get back, Sam should have returned."

Nick dusted down his trousers and stepped out of the trench, barking instructions to David and the rest of the team. A few minutes later he picked up his water bottle and passed a spare to Cora before guiding her back towards the gate.

"Come on, then, let's go see the temple."

They jumped into a taxi which took them as far as the Colossi of Memnon, before continuing on foot.

"So tell me about this temple," Cora said.

WIND ACROSS THE NILE

"It's a mortuary temple, and it's my favourite site in the whole of Egypt. It was built in the reign of Ramses III who was the last pharaoh of the New Kingdom era. I like it because it has some of the most detailed inscriptions of the king and his rulership. It isn't as large as Karnak, but it's still pretty impressive and gives the best idea of the intricate internal workings of Egyptian temples."

Cora laughed. "You sound like a guide book! I can't wait to see it."

"Not long now. It's that building there." Nick pointed at a large brick structure that loomed on the horizon.

"Impressive."

They walked in silence for a few minutes before Nick spoke again.

"So. Do I assume you've decided to stay in the country?"

"Yes. For the time being. I had a lot of persuasion from my best friend Erica."

"Well, that's good. I'm glad you're staying."

Cora was speechless. It wasn't something she'd ever expected to hear from him. She didn't know what to say.

"Don't look so surprised," he chuckled. "I'm glad you were able to sort things out with Sam so you can hear more about your family. It's important to know where you came from. I have a feeling that the diary is very special."

"Yes that's exactly how I feel."

"Here we are. Medinet Habu."

Cora stared up at the large imposing stone structure. A few stone steps lead to a walkway that ran through the structure. It was covered with carvings of Egyptians, holding their enemies by their heads, smiting them. As they walked under a stone lintel, a solitary black granite statue was situated to the left of the path. Nick explained that it was a depiction of Sekhmet, the goddess of war and disease. The interior was carved with yet more inscriptions and images, as if all areas of the walls had to be carved, and none were allowed to be left bare.

"This is fantastic, Nick. It's quite different from the other temples I've been to. I can understand why you love it, although it's not as big as I expected it to be."

Nick threw his head back and laughed loudly. "That's because this is just the entrance. A tiny part of the complex. Here." He grabbed her by the shoulders and swiveled her around, then propelled her forward. Passing under a stone archway into bright sunlight, they entered the complex.

Cora gazed in wonder at what lay before her. An enormous expanse of ground was scattered with the remains of buildings, and just beyond was the largest temple pylon she'd ever seen. It was similar to the one at Karnak, but almost twice the size. Realising she was doing a very good impression of a stunned goldfish, she quickly closed her mouth, searching for words.

"That's only part of it?"

WIND ACROSS THE NILE

"Yes, just wait until you see inside, you're going to love it. Come on!"

He grabbed hold of her hand and pulled her towards the imposing stone structure. As they neared it, he released her hand so he could point out the various inscriptions explaining what they were and what they meant. There were rows of hieroglyphs and large imposing figures carved into the stone on either side of the portico. Walking through it, they found themselves standing in an enclosed courtyard. Before them stood another smaller, stone pylon, while covered walkways held up by columns ran around the courtyard's interior. The roof over the walkways was still intact, protecting the walls from the sun's direct rays, and the columns were plentiful with inscriptions.

Nick explained the purpose of the courtyard as they walked along, before steering her away from the wall, and back out across the courtyard. At that point, they found themselves standing in front of a row of large statues; so large, in fact, that Cora's head only came to their shins.

"They're massive."

"Impressive, huh? They're colossal statues of Ramses III. They thought a lot of themselves in those days," he said with a chuckle.

"So it seems. It just amazes me how they built all of this."

"I know. I feel the same sometimes. They were really ahead of their time."

They left the courtyard and meandered up the ramp, through the second pylon and into the next courtyard where Nick explained its purpose. Then he steered her to the row of stone columns that ran along the wall, filling her head with more history. She took it all in, absorbing every piece of information as though her brain were a sponge soaking up excess water.

"I have to show you this set of wall carvings. I think you'll find them funny."

Cora followed him to a carved wall that was covered with row upon row of tiny Egyptian figures standing in varying stances, some with raised arms and others scribing. All faced a large carving of a seated pharaoh.

"Throughout their reign, many Egyptian pharaohs led battles into foreign lands. During one of those times this temple was in use, and a number of the battles are depicted on these walls. See this here?" Nick pointed at the wall.

"Yes. What are they?" Cora stared closely at the odd drawing.

"Piles of hands. Soldiers who went into battle were rewarded on the number of people they killed. The pharaoh instructed them to bring back one hand for each enemy they had smote, as proof of their demise. Unfortunately, as we all know, a person has two hands so this wasn't a very clever way of proving it. They tended to overestimate the figures."

Nick steered her further along the wall, pointing at a similar inscription.

"So. The pharaoh changed how it was done."

WIND ACROSS THE NILE

Cora stood and stared at the wall. It was like the other depiction, but instead of hands there were, well, she wasn't quite sure. She leaned in to try to get a clearer view of the image. To her it looked like someone had carved cinnamon swirls on the wall. She knew she was going to regret asking, but did so anyway.

"What are they?"

"I'll give you a clue." Nick's eyes were sparkling with mischief. "Only men have them and they have just one."

Cora stared at the wall as realisation hit her and her face flushed red.

"They cut off their penises?" she whispered with embarrassment, hoping that no one had heard her.

"Yep."

"Ouch! Imagine having to carry a bag of those back to the pharaoh. Poor men losing their manhood like that!"

"They wouldn't have felt it you know. They were already dead."

"I know. But still, it's a disgusting thing to do."

They sat on the edge of the stone ramp leading to the second pylon.

"There's another interesting story about this temple. It's said that a plot was hatched against Ramses here. He had a large harem and information suggests that one of the lesser queens wanted to install her own son on the throne. The conspiracy against Ramses involved a number of the harem. They got their relatives to stir up trouble in Nubia, to create a diversion, so that they could kill the king. The plot was eventually discovered, and Ramses was lucky and survived. Those involved in the plot against him weren't so lucky. They were put to death. It's just one of many tales about how devious some of these ancient people really were."

"It sounds like a dangerous time to have been alive."

"Most ordinary Egyptians died by the time they were forty. It was rare for people to live to the age we do now, and if you didn't die of old age or disease, crocodiles, scorpions any amount of other nasties were likely to get you." He paused glancing at her. "Tell me, Cora. How do you feel about learning you're part Egyptian?"

She paused thoughtfully before answering. "It was definitely a shock and I still don't understand why my family kept it a secret. When I came here, I immediately felt at home and I just couldn't explain why. It was like I had always belonged, and now it makes sense, doesn't it?"

"I have to admit, you've fitted into life in Egypt very quickly. I know I wasn't very nice about it at the beginning, but I do have to admit that you are very brave coming out here on a whim, one that looks to have paid off. I only wish I hadn't been so rude to you and had the time to help you."

"That's okay, water under the bridge. And I do feel at home here. There's nothing about Egypt that I dislike so far and I'm glad I came."

"Shall we continue?" Nick asked.

They walked up the ramp onto the terrace at the end of the second courtyard where Nick steered them to another row of columns, but with a marked difference. These were still partially covered in their original painted colour. Cora was astonished. It instantly showed how the temple would've looked in its heyday, with rich tones of blue, red, green and yellow. In some places, the pigment had faded, but in others it was really vibrant as if it had been recently painted.

Cora wandered along the walkway, absorbing as much as she possibly could. Stopping at the end, she saw an entire wall carved with inscriptions. Instead of the usual plain stone these inscriptions were painted with ancient colour. Rows of painted, brown skinned Egyptians wearing white flowing garments were standing in the typical Egyptian pose. Each row was scattered with tiny multi-hued hieroglyphs. Below the last row was a painted border, topping a scene of boats, Egyptian gods and goddesses, lotus flowers, farming activities and yet more hieroglyphs. Cora hadn't seen anything so beautiful in all her life, and Nick explained that in ancient times all the tombs and temples had all been colourfully painted, much of it had faded over time, but a few examples could still be seen. It was definitely her favourite wall relief out of all she'd seen so far. Vibrant and intense, the carvings stood out against the surrounding muted sand-coloured bricks.

As she turned to speak to Nick, she spied another of her favourites. Anubis. His body was reddish-brown, his clothing green and white and his head dress blue. His left hand was outstretched and, in his right, he clutched an ankh. Above his head was a line of cartouches, whilst hieroglyphs ran down the side and underneath.

"I love this," she breathed quietly. So quietly it was a wonder that anyone heard her. She wanted to reach out and touch it, to trace her fingers gently along the delicate carved edges, but refrained from doing so, not wanting to risk damaging the image.

Nick smiled, "It's one of my favourites, too."

"I always thought Anubis was scary, but this makes him look so majestic."

"That's because he is. Anubis wasn't the scary god everyone thinks. It's his purpose in the Egyptians belief system that gives him the reputation," Nick explained.

As they strolled back along the walkway, they passed a group of tourists who were excitedly pointing at their favourite things. Squeezing past, Nick held her arm and gently led her out into the bright sunshine of the hypostyle hall. It was very different to the one at Karnak Temple; it was fairly ruinous. Nick guided her through the narrow walkways, explaining the purpose of all the various nooks and crannies. Black granite statues stood proudly amongst the chaos. It was almost as if the temple had shaken, crumbled and fallen around them. This is what fascinated Cora the most, how some parts of temples were still standing almost as perfectly as the day they were built, whereas other parts had fallen away to almost nothing. Nick explained that this was due to a combination of things. The area was prone to earthquakes, so some buildings did unfortunately fall. Others had been taken apart by later rulers who used blocks of stone for buildings of their own. The rest was just down to buildings being abandoned and falling down of their own free will.

"Have you seen the time, Nick? We've been here for hours!"

Nick glanced at his watch in surprise. It was gone lunchtime, and they should think about getting back to the site.

"I've been enjoying myself so much I didn't even notice the time! I had better get back, though. It doesn't look good if I go off sightseeing for hours. If one of the team did it, I'd be furious with them. Come on. Time to go," he said, a little too reluctantly.

They weaved their way back through the temple and, as they reached the first courtyard, Cora stopped.

"I completely forgot I have my camera on me. I keep taking it out and then forgetting to use it. Could you take a photo of me?"

"Of course!" Once she had shown Nick how it worked, she positioned herself in front of one of the huge statues.

"Smile!"

She heard the click before stepping forward to view the picture. For once, it was a nice picture of herself. She looked quite healthy and happy. Just as she was about to put it back in her bag, a local came over to them.

"Beautiful English!" He smiled a friendly but toothless smile, before reaching out his arm. "I photograph beautiful English?" Without waiting for a response, he pried the camera from Cora's hand, motioning for the pair to get together. With an air of bemusement, Nick and Cora looked at each other and obeyed.

"I guess we're having our picture taken, then," Nick whispered as he draped his arm around her shoulder.

Her stomach somersaulted, and she tried her best to smile for the camera. Uh oh. That wasn't good. Falling for an Egyptologist definitely wasn't in the plan. The feelings had completely taken her by surprise but, despite the revelation, she was enjoying the feel of his arm around her, and his breath on her neck as he whispered in her ear.

All too quickly it was over and the local was handing the camera back. Nick pressed some dollars into his hand and he walked away shouting, "Shukran, English!"

Grabbing the camera from Nick, she looked at the photo. It was a lovely image. Both of them were smiling, and they looked happy and content. If she didn't know better, she would have thought she and Nick were a normal couple on holiday. It was a sobering thought, and not one she'd expected to have.

"Nice," Nick said peeking over her shoulder. "Come on, we should go."

She turned the camera off and stuffed it in her bag, before following him out of the temple, her mind whirling from a host of possibilities.

CHAPTER TWENTY-ONE

Luxor, Egypt, 2002

The air had become even more humid, when Cora and Nick arrived back at the site, hot and very tired, dripping with sweat.

"You're back!" Alex exclaimed. "Did you have fun?"

"I did, thanks. It was fantastic. Nick's a good tour guide. He told me so many interesting things about the temple."

Cora turned and saw Sam staring at her, a look of annoyance on his face. She instantly felt bad. She had made plans to meet Sam to go through the diary, and instead of waiting for him, she had gone off with Nick. Knowing that she should make amends, she smiled and waved in his direction. He acknowledged her and, moments later, she walked towards him.

"Hey, Sam. Sorry I wasn't here when you got back. I didn't know how long you were going to be so I took up Nick's offer of visiting Medinet Habu. It's an amazing place." She sat on the dusty ground next to his trench.

"I heard," he said. "You said you still need my help with the diary?"

"Yes. But before we go any further, I also wanted to say sorry. I overreacted. What I learned was a shock. To begin with, I was having a hard time believing it. I was also very angry with my mum for not telling me. The tale of Randa's hardship was made much worse knowing that I'm descended from her." She sighed. "But despite all of that, I've decided I want you to continue reading the diary, Sam. I've nothing left since my parents and brother died. I need to know about my family and where I came from. It's more important now than ever before. So will you help me? Please?"

"There's no need to apologise. I completely understand why you reacted the way you did. I'd probably have done the same in your shoes. Of course I'll help you. You know that."

"Thank you so much."

It was past lunchtime so the team stopped work and sat in the shade eating and chatting. Cora pulled out the diary and passed it to Sam.

"Do you mind the others hearing?" he asked.

"Not at all."

Obligingly he opened the diary to find the correct page and began to translate, as the rest of the team listened, captivated.

Southampton, England, 1908

It has been a year and my darling Albert is now a mere shadow of his former self. The doctor has seen him on several occasions, although we can scarcely afford it.

My beloved has been left with a terrible cough this winter that refuses to subside, sometimes it is so bad that he just wheezes, barely catching a breath and I can see he is in so much pain, but there is nothing anyone can do for him. He coughed up blood a few days ago which has left me frantic with worry, the doctor told him he must stop drinking but Albert refuses to. He can barely leave the house now to go his job and I fear he will lose it soon. Where will we be then without his money to keep the roof over our head and feed us? I still love him as much as the day we first met, but the years have not been kind to us and I am losing him to the vileness that is alcohol.

This is our punishment. This is my punishment. We have betrayed everyone and everything we have ever known and now we are paying for it. We have no one to blame but ourselves. Not even our love can protect us now.

~

It has been three weeks and my life has completely shattered. Egypt, and her beautiful river is a distant memory. My family are too. I feel as though life in Egypt was just a dream, a story someone once told me to make my day happier. I am no longer that woman. That woman is gone and she has left a pitiful wreck in her place.

I have lost the man I love.

Albert is dead. The doctor says his liver failed. He had no fight left in him. He ebbed away before my very eyes, and there was little I could do to help him. With his final breath he uttered his love for me and Florence and then the darkness took him from us forever. Nance was with me and held me tight as I wailed for my Albert, my sweet loving Albert, the man who loved me so much.

We had no money to bury him properly so he was assigned to a paupers grave. Not even his own parents wanted him, so he now lies in a pit with many others who ended up poor like us. This has hurt me more than his death. I have cried hopelessly since his passing, and have done little to look after myself, the only thing I do is keep Florence fed. Whilst she lives so does a piece of Albert. Nance comes in everyday to see me, but I barely notice her presence. Everyone seems so kind but all I feel is the loss and grief. It never goes away.

Hakim is dead now too. A letter arrived a week after Albert died to tell me his body gave up on him. It pains me too much. The two men who loved me, who cared for me are both lost to me forever. I am now alone. I do not know what will happen to us. I have no money to pay the landlord and he is due at the house tomorrow to collect his rent Nance got her husband to sell Albert's pocket watch for me, the money is hidden and I use it to buy food. I have nothing else left, except for two small shabti, my shawls and a few pictures. These will never be sold. They will be passed to my daughter, a small reminder of who she is and where she came from. She is Egyptian and will always be Egyptian.

~

It has been a week and you have been a comfort, diary, I read back to the first meeting with my dear Albert, and our beautiful time in Egypt. It makes my heart soar to be reminded of how we met. I miss my homeland, miss it with all my heart, but I know that I can never return.

The landlord called asking for his money, all I could do was explain. He told me in the circumstances not to worry, but I saw a look in his eye when he placed his rough hand on my arm. I know what he was trying to tell me. I do not like him. I do not trust him. I know with certainty he will return and next time he will demand payment. I dread seeing him. I know I will have to do what he wants and know that Albert would not approve, but it is for my child. I have no choice. If I have no money to pay him, then I must pay him another way. My neighbour Mrs. Meegan told me there are ways and means. Lots of women do it, but it scares me for it is a sin.

~

The Landlord returned.

Nance was with me when he arrived. I begged her to take Florence for the day. I did not want her around him. He demanded the rent, and I told him I did not have it. I begged with him to give me another chance, hoping that he would go away, but he was a brute. Much taller than my beloved Albert and much less forgiving, he seemed to fill the room. He smelt of stale alcohol and smoke. I knew what was coming, and I let it happen knowing it was the only way for Florence to have a place to live. He was lecherous and groped me with unforgiving hands, ripping my clothes and pinning my small body to the bed so that I could not struggle. He thrust at me, grunting and groaning, taking what I was reluctant to give up. All I could do was close my eyes and pray for the pain and humiliation to be over, trying my best to prevent the tears from falling.

Afterwards he grinned slyly at me, pulling up his trousers, telling me would be back the following week for further payment. As the door slammed he left me alone in the gloom, and I rolled over on the bed and sobbed my heart out. My body was only flesh and I cared not what he did with it, but my heart and soul ached with pain. I felt as though I had betrayed my beloved Albert, and this made me angry. Angry at my family for forcing us to leave, angry at Albert for leaving me.

As I collected Florence from Nance she placed a caring arm around my shoulder, telling me it would all be alright. She knew what I had done and why, and did not hate me for it. She did not have to, I hated myself enough already. Whatever happens Florence must never ever know what I have done for her.

Southampton, England, 1909

It has been six months since Albert passed away and I have managed to keep the roof over our head and Florence fed. The landlord has visited weekly to thrust and groan at me and my body is bruised and aches from his roughness. If I do not do what he says he beats me, but it is a small price to pay for keeping Florence safe. It is the only way, and I know no other.

Nance told me yesterday that she is worried about me. I have been losing weight and developed a cough like Albert had. This morning, I too coughed blood, and for the first time in my life I truly felt scared. I have put together a small parcel of things I wish Florence to have when I die. I know I am not long for this world and I must make sure she is looked after. I gave the package to Nance yesterday and made her promise to make sure Florence gets them. She will have my diary too when I am gone. I see my beautiful child sitting on the floor and I know that she will be alright. Albert has seen to that. I know he still watches over her.

This is my last entry. I know that death is coming for me and I will soon be in the arms of my beloved husband whom I love more now than the day I first met him. We will meet again once more in the dusty lane in Thebes and he will take me in his arms and tell me he loves me more than life itself, and we will once more be happy.

I too am at peace now.

Silence hung heavily in the air, and not one of the team dared speak. They had hung on Sam's every word, eager to hear what happened next. Cora wiped her face with the back of her hand. Tears had fallen fast as she had listened to the pitiful state Randa had got herself into. Her great-great-grandmother had lost everything and ended up having to prostitute herself to feed her own child and keep a roof over her head. She had lived a miserable existence at the end and Cora had no idea how she had managed to get up each day and carry on. She was distraught at the thought of what Randa had gone through, and it made her feel sick and empty inside.

Cora rose to her feet and hurriedly turned away, desperately trying to hide her tears. She needed to be alone for a while and let it all sink in.

Sam and Nick stood in unison to follow, but Alex and Lucy were too quick for them. The girls eventually caught up with her and Lucy placed an arm around Cora's shoulder, pulling her to a stop, before hugging her and holding on tightly as Cora sobbed wholeheartedly.

"It's okay," Alex said whilst gently rubbing Cora's back, trying to comfort her.

Eventually Cora lifted her head disentangled herself from the girls, and took the tissue Lucy was holding.

"I can't believe how awful her life was towards the end. It would be hard to hear a story like that normally, but when it's your ancestor it just breaks your heart."

"I can understand that." Alex linked arms with her. "Come on let's go for a walk and get away from the blokes. You need some space."

Cora nodded in agreement, allowing the girls to lead the way.

CHAPTER TWENTY-TWO

Luxor, Egypt, 2002

The distant sound of a ringing phone awoke Cora. She had slept poorly after learning of Randa's fate and the disturbance was the last thing she needed. All she wanted to do was pull the duvet over her head, shut out the world and stay in bed. But something told her she should answer it. Groaning, she reached over to lift the receiver.

"Yes?"

"It's Erica. I thought I should phone you straight away."

Cora sat bolt upright.

"What's happened?"

"Nothing bad, the flat is fine, but you've had a delivery. The solicitors sent something that belonged to your mum. They had it in a safety deposit with instructions that it only be released to you upon her death. It's a sealed box, so I've no idea what's in it."

"I never even knew she had a safety deposit box." Yet another thing her mum had failed to share. Had she ever known her parents at all? Her brain was too muddled to even think straight.

"Do you want me to open it?"

"Yes, absolutely." Cora listened as Erica set to work on the package. Her interest piqued as she held her breath and waited. The silence became lengthy, only punctuated by the occasional sound of ripping cardboard and rustling paper. The suspense was unbearable, and Cora became impatient.

"Erica! What's taking you so long?"

"I think I need to send this to you." Cora detected an undertone in Erica's voice.

"Why? What is it?"

"Hang on."

Cora's patience was wearing thin, did Erica always have to make everything into a drama? Cora was about to shout at her when Erica finally spoke.

"Just listen, Cora."

My darling Cora,
My beautiful, beautiful daughter.
If you're reading this letter, it means they've finally succeeded in killing me, too.
For years I kept a diary, as did my mother Emma, and my grandmother, Florence. I hid them

away in the only place that I knew was safe, a safety deposit box. Only two people knew the location, myself and my solicitor. Not even your father knew that I had it.

The diaries are now yours.

There was another diary belonging to your great-great-grandmother Randa. If you haven't already found it, it's in the attic in an old trunk along with some of Randa's belongings. I had to separate them and I hope you understand why. I'm not sure you'll be able to read it as it's in Arabic, but it's important you know that it exists.

I know I sound like I'm rambling Cora and I'm probably not making much sense, but there's so much to tell you and I don't know how to make you understand. Your father and Aunt Mary knew a little of what happened, and they always said I should have sat you down and told you, but I didn't want you to suffer too. Our family has been through so much. I didn't want you to always be worried, to always be looking over your shoulder, as I have.

Ours is a long and complex history which was cursed, and still is.

What I can tell you is, despite what some people think, we've done nothing wrong. Our blood may be linked to one person who committed a crime a long time ago, but it's watered down blood, and we cannot, generations later, be held responsible for the deeds of others. Even so, in some people's eyes it is blood that is at fault and we still have to pay, so we watch our backs at each and every turn and wonder if each accident we encounter may be the moment when they are trying kill us.

I pray you do not succumb to the same fate as your grandmothers', the same fate I fear I am going to soon suffer. I pray that you're able to find a way through the madness to finally piece together the truth, and live a long and happy life. For that's what I want for you the most. A long and happy life.

Whatever happens Cora, remember we are good people. We've done nothing wrong and we do not deserve to suffer the fate that others have bestowed upon us.

I will always be with you.
Your loving mum xxx

Cora dropped the receiver and ran to the bathroom and vomited violently into the toilet bowl. The dizziness she had felt at the funeral returned all too quickly and completely overwhelmed her. She lay back on the cold tiles staring at the ceiling, concentrating on calming her breathing, allowing her brain to wade through the fog to find its way back to some kind of normality. Blinking, she began to feel a little better, and sat up. The nauseous feeling was still there, but she was able to pull herself up and stagger back to bed where she lay down, feeling utterly spent.

"Cora? Are you still there?" She could hear Erica's tinny voice yelling from the phone's earpiece.

"Yes," she whispered hoarsely as she put the receiver to her ear. Her head was spinning. She'd tried her best to take in everything the letter said, but her brain was stuck on the words "*They have succeeded in killing me too.*"

Who was her mum talking about? Was she trying to tell her their deaths had actually been murder and not an accident?

"I'm sorry, Erica, but can you read it again?"

"Are you sure?"

"Yes. I need to hear it again."

She listened carefully as Erica read her mum's letter to her a second time. The words cut through her, but she refused to let her body react as violently as it had before. She engaged her brain, and forced it to listen so that she could try and make sense of it.

"What does it mean, Erica?" she asked, once she'd heard it a second time.

"I don't know. Maybe we should ring the police?"

"No. It's just a letter, there's no proof of anything. Send the box with the letter and diaries to me here, Erica. Once I get it, I'll decide what to do."

"Are you sure? The post is notoriously unreliable."

"Send it by courier, to arrive as soon as possible. I'll pay you back."

"No need. I'll parcel it up and send straight away."

Cora gave Erica the address of the hotel and said a simple, "Thanks."

"That's what I'm here for. Look after yourself. I'll try and call you later."

The line went dead and Cora shakily climbed out of bed to make a cup of tea. She needed something to take the vile taste in her mouth away.

Had her parents really been murdered? If so, who by and what for? Was this why her mum had always been so secretive and why Cora knew next to nothing about her own family? Her head was reeling and she felt like she was missing a large part of the puzzle. Maybe the answers lay in the other diaries but, until she received them, she had no way of knowing and would have to spend an anxious few days thinking it over. Maybe she should have just gone home. But no. She felt that this was where she needed to be. She finished her tea before sinking under the covers, crying until she was exhausted and sleep overtook her.

~

It was as much as Cora could do to drag herself out of bed the following day. Despite trying to sleep for most of the previous day, she was mentally and physically exhausted. Thoughts of the letter ran round her head, distressing her every waking moment, and when she did sleep she had been plagued with nightmares of her family's death, and possibly her own. She'd awoken in a cold clammy sweat, gripping the sheets so tightly her knuckles were stiff and white. She felt awful and longed to stay in bed again, but she kept to her plans of the day hoping they would distract her. The team had invited her to the site for the day to help out and learn a bit more about their work. She'd been looking forward to it before the bad news had arrived, and her enthusiasm had been stripped since hearing the news of her mum's letter, but knew it would do her good to turn her attention to something other than these stresses and turmoil. A shift of focus was definitely the right thing. When she arrived at the Valley of the Kings, the team was already hard at work and, after shouting greetings, she reported to Nick.

"Good morning!" He smiled, before tilting his head in concern. "You look tired."

"I didn't sleep very well." She had seen the dark circles under her eyes when she brushed her hair in front of the mirror that morning, and knew she looked exhausted, but she was anxious just to get on and do something so that she didn't have to think about the contents of the letter. They troubled her deeply.

"I'll be fine. Now where do you want me?"

"I thought you could start with Alex and Lucy. They're cataloguing finds. It sounds boring but it's part of what we do. After that, we'll move you to where David and I are working." Leading her across the arid desert landscape to the makeshift awning, he pulled out a chair for her at the table. On its surface sat a collection of plastic trays filled with a variety of finds. Lucy and Alex, sitting opposite, were already hard at work.

"I'll leave Cora in your capable hands, girls."

"What we're doing here is cleaning and noting what we find. It looks really boring but it's actually quite important. Without cleaning them we wouldn't be able to tell what the artefact is and without cataloguing we would lose track of what we have, where it was found and when," Alex explained, showing Cora how Lucy was gently cleaning a shard of pottery. Once Lucy had finished, Alex then took it from her, inspected it and added it to the vast spreadsheet on the computer in front of her. She then placed it in a tray alongside some other shards and gave it a reference number.

"I didn't realise how much work was involved. I thought you just dug it up and handed it over."

Alex and Lucy laughed.

"If only! Sadly it's more complex than that. Each excavation gets a special license to dig and there are many rules that apply, and rightly so. That's why we get so upset over the terrible news stories about people looting sites. When looters rob a site, they disturb the ground, they take everything out of context and only steal the items they think will make them a lot of money. Most of the time they completely destroy what's left, leaving us with little or no evidence of that site and what happened there," Lucy explained.

It made Cora sad to think that people still looted in this day and age. Now that she learned so much about the process of an excavation, she completely understood why it was so important to do it right, and why looting and illegal digging was so detrimental. She had so much respect for the team, and what they did in order to protect the country's history.

Cora was grateful when lunchtime arrived; she was starving. They all sat under the shade of the awning, taking on much needed sustenance whilst chatting. She was enjoying their company, but her mind slowly wandered back to the letter. She had been so absorbed with work that she'd forgotten about it for a few hours but, unfortunately, the respite gave her time to think again, and the confusion and worry were still there. She tried to push it aside and not let it get to her. There was nothing she could do until the courier package arrived, but she was finding it hard.

After lunch, Cora joined Nick and David in their trench. Sam, who looked more than a little put out, was excavating another trench with some local workers. She watched carefully as Nick worked and David explained the process to her. She realised that despite it being called '*digging*,' digging itself was far too extreme for the excavation of an archaeological site. Each site was an unknown entity and no one ever knew what was lurking just below the surface. Time was taken and, rather than spades, the tools of the trade for the gentle removal of earth mainly consisted of trowels, and brushes. The ground was sectioned and each area was meticulously worked.

Discovered artefacts were recorded in situ before being removed, and the ground, once exhausted, was returned to its natural state, for life to continue long after the academics had departed.

It was long, hard, backbreaking work. The sun beat down upon them; the heat almost intolerable. Dust swirled about them, coating their limbs and clothes in a fine sandy sheen. Yet, despite the hardships, they persisted. Their concentration never wavered, and excitement bubbled up on the odd occasion that a possible find peeked from the earth between stony rubble. It was fascinating and eventually Nick allowed Cora to participate with a little digging of her own under his close supervision. She was given a new section of ground in his trench and obeyed every instruction, taking her time, treating the earth as though it were precious, with gentle, careful brushstrokes. Eventually, after what seemed like hours, she was rewarded when the head of a small shabti appeared through the dusty surface of the Egyptian desert. Once photographed and documented in situ, she was finally given permission, with Nick's guidance, to fully remove it from the ground. Sadly it was broken, and only the upper part of the relic now remained. Nick indicated this was probably the reason why it was so close to the surface. But she didn't care; it was her first (and probably only) find. Laying it in her palm, it barely covered that area of her hand. Through the dust, she could see it was the brilliant colour of turquoise that screamed Egypt. With reluctance, she finally handed it over to Nick, waiting for his official verdict. Eventually he announced that it was real, before passing it to Lucy and Alex for cleaning and cataloguing. Cora was sad to see it go to the girls. She would probably never see it again, but Nick promised that on this occasion, the name of Cora Thomas would be entered into the catalogue next to the artefact. Beaming from ear to ear, she felt incredibly proud. Her very own find, and it would be recorded for posterity as part of the dig. It wasn't the most important find of the century, but it was hers.

Sitting back, Cora concluded the day by watching the masters at work, their faces a mix of concentration, contentment and pride. She knew this was where they were meant to be and what they were meant to be doing. Glancing over at Sam, she smiled and raised a hand in a wave but he turned from her as if he didn't see her. With all of the excitement of finding the shabti, she hadn't had time to speak to him. Shrugging it off, she continued watching the senior archaeologists, as they pulled more finds, albeit mostly broken pottery, from the yielding earth.

As they closed the excavation for the night, she was tired, dusty, hot and very sweaty. Her limbs ached, making walking a little uncomfortable, but it was worth it. It had been a fantastic day, and one she would never forget. Saying her goodbyes, she made her way back to the hotel for a well-earned soak in a hot bath.

CHAPTER TWENTY-THREE

Luxor, Egypt, 2002

He sat on the edge of his bed with the phone pressed to his ear. It'd been a long day and he'd endured her presence all day. It was as though she was flaunting herself in front of him, those beautiful dark locks, which today were piled high on her head, a few loose tendrils framing her face as she had scrabbled in the dirt. Her face was more prominent and at the centre were those pretty dark eyes. He had watched, drawn to her, as she occasionally brushed the back of her hand across her tanned skin to disperse droplets of sweat that fell to the ground, fleetingly darkening the dust beneath her. It had aroused him in ways it shouldn't have and he hated her for it. He hated himself.

The voice on the phone broke through his thoughts and he swiftly returned to reality, listening carefully, before replacing the receiver.

So the mother had been clever and locked away what was most precious in a safety deposit box, had she? He wondered what it contained and where it was now? He greatly enjoyed having people everywhere. It was amazing what information they would give up for a bit of money. His contact had told him that the parcel had been at the bank where he worked, but it had already been delivered to Cora's home. His contact had gone to her home to intercept it but it had been collected by someone else. He needed to discover who that someone was and get it from them as quickly as possible.

~

Erica was true to her word. A few days later a courier safely delivered the package to the hotel and into Cora's hands. It had been a hellish wait. Her mind had turned over and over, worrying that it would turn up damaged or not turn up at all, ending up on the other side of the world lost forever. But it hadn't. It was here. She locked the door to her room and sat on the bed tearing at the packaging, desperate to get inside. The contents finally fell onto the bed: an envelope with her name on it, and a light wooden box, big enough to hold three books. It must have cost Erica a fortune

WIND ACROSS THE NILE

to send and she made a mental note to reimburse her as soon as possible.

With shaking hands, she opened the envelope and removed the letter. She already knew what it said, but she needed to read it herself. The familiarity of her mum's handwriting brought tears to her eyes. The contents still upset and confused her, and she still struggled to come to terms with what her mum was so desperately trying to tell her.

After reading it, she put the letter to one side, and removed three books from the box, opening each one in turn to read the front page.

The first read, *Diary of Florence Sanders, Daughter of Randa and Albert MacKenzie.*

The second, *Diary of Emma Sanders, Daughter of Florence MacKenzie.*

The third needed no introduction. It was her mum's.

In front of her lay the proof that she was indeed Randa's great-great-granddaughter. She breathed long and deep, the reality washing over her. What on earth had happened to her family? Why had they been kept secret from her for all of these years? More importantly, why had her mum been so convinced that she was going to be murdered? The clues had to be in the diaries somewhere but where on earth to start?

The burden lay heavy upon her and as much as she wanted to read her mum's diary first — she was desperate to — she started at the beginning with Florence's. It was in English although in places the writing was scrawny and difficult to read.

Oxfordshire, England, 1921

I am Florence Sanders and I am eighteen years old. I have lived in a big old falling down crumbling house in Oxfordshire with my Grandparents since I was a child after my parents died, and today is the first day of my life.

My Grandparents are finally dead.

Even though I lived with my Grandparents for almost twelve years, the house and most of the contents have been divided up and gone to my father's brothers, leaving me with little. I have the clothes on my back, a small trunk containing the necessary, including a few personal belongings of my mother's that I had secreted under a loose floorboard and kept hidden for all of these years, and some money. I stole the money from my grandparents over the years, they never missed it, and although it is not a lot, it will help me when I move on and look for work. I have no choice but to work as no one else will support me.

But I must go back to the start.

Upon the death of my mother Randa I was sent to live with my father's parents. They were furious and did not want me, but it was my father's dying wish. My grandparents disowned my father before I was born, although for what, I do not know, they refused to talk about it, or him. Even though they wanted nothing to do with him, they reluctantly agreed to take me in, it was a legal wish and it would not have been good for them to be seen abandoning a child, but this was as far as their charity went.

They were strict, very strict and they hated the sight of me. They called me a peasant and kept me in solitude, hidden away from their friends. I was forbidden to ever speak of my parents, or the subjects of history, Egypt and archaeology. If I did, I was beaten severely. It was a lesson I learned quickly and remembered.

I could not understand why my own family treated me like this, were they not supposed to love me and care for me? I was tutored whilst young, so that I spoke properly and learned to read and write, and once old enough I was taken to the kitchen, where the staff were under instruction to turn me into whichever they thought best. Ladies maid or kitchen staff. They did not care, as long as I was out of their way, in someone else's hands and earning my keep.

The staff took pity on me and put me to work in the kitchen to keep me as far away from 'er ladyship' as possible. I think secretly they hated her as much as I did, but they would never say so as they were staff and it would not do to tell. I was still family after all. I was stuck in the middle, an above stairs below stairs, but my work did not suffer, I worked hard and they were impressed with me. I learned all there was to know about being a servant in a big house and I am glad. I now have skills and they will be useful.

So that is my history, there is not much more to tell, other than to say that I hated my grandparents as much as they hated me and I am glad they are dead. I hope they rot in hell and suffer for eternity, they deserve it for treating me so poorly.

<u>London, England, 1921</u>

It has been a few weeks since I last wrote. Upon leaving my grandparents house and my old job, I made my way to London. I was born Florence MacKenzie but changed my surname to Sanders. Other than having a reference from my grandmother's housekeeper to say I had worked for them I wanted nothing more to do with the MacKenzie name. I felt bad for my father, it was his name, but no longer being a MacKenzie made life much easier for me.

In London I walked around looking for employment in one of the big houses, and eventually found a position with a family in a place called "High House" in a very well established area in the City. I was lucky, since things in England had begun to change and servants were required less now. The First World War had seen to that. So many lives lost in such terrible circumstances and I still did not really understand why, or how it had happened? Things are still uncertain, but getting better and I hope it will settle quickly. I really want to build a life for myself.

The staff at High House are pleasant and I settled in quickly. I am so happy to be here. I rise every morning at four and change into my serving outfit before treading down the backstairs to join the staff in the servants hall. We eat breakfast washed down with strongly brewed tea, all thanks to Cook, before going about the chores of the day. It is normally midnight before I get to bed each night but I never notice how tired I am. I want more from my life but as yet I am not sure what that is, so I work hard and save my meagre salary and do my duties to the best of my ability.

High House is in an upmarket area of London, most people who live here have live in staff. The owners are Lords who occasionally dabble in Government or who had been part of the war effort. High House is no exception, the Master, Sir James, works for the Home Office, the Mistress Lady Mary takes high tea with other Ladies or attends functions. They have one child, a Son, (we call him Young Master Edward), who is three years older than I. No one really knows what Young Master Edward does, but he is often seen about town spending the family money, with pretty girls hanging off his arm. He has a reputation, but even so, I like him a lot, he is kind. He always seems to have, a smile on his face and time to talk to me.

Cora was completely absorbed. Even though Florence had been given a terrible start in life, she had landed firmly on her feet. She seemed content with her new job. Cora was proud of her. She seemed to be more like Randa than she would ever have known.

Taking a break from the heat of the balcony, she went to get a glass of water and to send a quick text message to Erica to let her know the parcel had arrived and that she was sitting in the sun reading one of the diaries. Sitting back on the balcony, positioning her chair to catch some shade, she continued reading.

London, England, 1921

It has been six months since I last wrote, things have been so busy here in the house, I have not had the time, and even though I am grateful to have a job and somewhere to live, my life is a plain one. Nothing of consequence happens, so I do not have much to write about. The Master and Mistress have been entertaining all Summer long and it has been one long house party after another. The house has been filled to the rafters with people and the sound of music, with many important guests in attendance, they have eaten fine food and drunk plenty of wine and brandy. Sometimes it puzzles me, there are people out there barely able to clothe and feed themselves and yet my Master and Mistress could feed the entire Country with the amount of money they spend on their parties. But as a servant, I should be grateful for my job, and it is not my place to question the way they live their lives.

The pace in the house has slowed a little as the Master, Mistress and Young Master Edward have gone to Paris. It is just servants here in the house, and things will be easier for the next month. I am still like my job here but wish that I had something to do with my life other than wait upon rich people. I want to do something more, but what that is, I do not know.

~

The snow fell hard and fast this Winter. It has been bitterly cold and ice froze everything in sight making it dangerous underfoot.

The Mistress fell and broke her arm, she badly bruised herself too and has been told by the doctor to rest. I have seen a different side to her since the fall, she is cantankerous and no one in the house can do anything right, she shouts, bickers and screams. We all hope and pray for her quick recovery, as no one wants to endure this for months on end. I am even busier now than I was before and my feet barely touch the floor. I am so tired that I am sure I could sleep standing.

I also got to enjoy Christmas for the first time in my life, the halls were decked in thick boughs of greenery and a large tree stood in the entrance hall, hung with beautiful glass ornaments. I was given a present from the Mistress, a beautiful scarf and I have treasured it in this cold weather. Young Master Edward bought me a necklace, it was a nice surprise but I felt it was inappropriate. I told Cook about it and she told me to put it away and not let the Master or Mistress know where it came from. I keep it hidden with my mother's belongings.

Once Christmas passed Master Edward returned to Paris and we learned he will be there indefinitely so I feel a bit happier knowing he is not about. He is a kind man and I do like talking to him, but I know my place, he forgets that I am just a servant and he is the Master, we are not supposed to have a relationship beyond that.

<u>London, England, 1922</u>
It is now Spring and the cold weather has gone and the trees have begun to bud. Flowers poke through greenery blooming quickly, and the grass has turned a bright luscious shade of green. For some reason, over the Winter months, my thoughts kept returning to my parents, I barely remember them. What little I do know was passed to me by Nance, my mother's friend. She was there the day I arrived at my Grandparents house, another wish of my father's. If it had not been for her, I would not have had a few sacred belongings of my mother's. Nance had told me my mother was Egyptian, and my father English. They met in Egypt when father was working there as a treasure seeker. She told me I had my mother's hair and eyes, and that they loved me greatly. I wish I knew more, but I was only a child back then and I must content myself with the little knowledge I have. I have my mother's diary, but I cannot read it since it is in Arabic.

One day I overheard the Master and Mistress talking about the wonderful Egyptian collection at the British Museum. It was like a sign, as though my parents were sending me a message. The first day off I got, I went for a visit there. It was just the most wonderful place with ancient relics from all over the world. But the bit that excited me the most was seeing the items from Egypt. Somehow they made me feel closer to my parents. I now spend my rare days off visiting the museum. It feels like a second home, and I wonder what my Father and Mother would think if they saw the relics? I would like to hope that they would be happy that I am learning a little about my heritage.

London, England, 1922

Another Summer has passed and it was as busy as last year. When time permits, I continue to visit the Museum. I am learning about the Country that I am related to by blood, and listen to talks when I can, about the finds that now sit in the Museum. I am even reading my historical books on Egypt, they are difficult to understand but I persevere. Even though I still hate my Grandparents with every fibre of my being, I am grateful they taught me to read. It has opened a whole new world to me. I have also met a gentleman who works at the Museum, his name is Francis and he is the son of an archaeologist, who works out in Egypt, he tells me wonderful tales and I listen eagerly, desperate to learn more.

As autumn changes to winter news of a great find comes to us from Egypt. A new tomb discovered by Howard Carter and we all wait to hear about what he finds inside. I wish I could be part of that world, digging in the ground searching for ancient finds. In reality I could never be more than a librarian, but it is something I would like to do, and so I am trying to pluck up the courage to find someone who could help me. Francis asks me all the time about my family, but it is a secret I keep from him. I don't like talking about my past, my past is mine and mine alone.

~

It is Christmas again and another year has passed so quickly. The house is once more decorated for the season and we are all looking forward to it. Young Master Edward has returned from Paris and has brought with him the most beautiful woman I have ever seen. Her name is Estelle and she is French, they are blissfully happy and have announced that they intend to marry. It was a shock. Master Edward had given me the impression that he liked me. And over the months I had grown to miss him. But why would he like me? I was just a servant, someone who was destined to serve his family not be part of it.

I still visit the Museum, and Francis and I have become firm friends and he is teaching me so much about the home of my mother's birth. He jokes that from my looks he would have sworn I was Egyptian, I feel I should be honest with him about my family, but as yet cannot bring myself to tell him, I am too ashamed with the way my grandparents treated my father and mother.

London, England, 1923

Estelle has become a regular visitor to the house and I should be happy about the marriage which is due to take place in the height of Summer, only one month away. But my heart is heavy. Young Master Edward has been so nice to me again; upon his return from Paris, he gave me a beautiful brooch. It glittered with precious stone and the silver shone. I hid it away with the necklace knowing I couldn't show it to anyone. I like him and I miss him so much when he was away, but he confuses me. He talks to me with a sparkle in his eye and a smile on his face; it is as though he likes me. He has started bringing me gifts every time he goes into town, secret little offerings that he shares with me when no one else it looking, but he never tells me how he really feels. I know I am risking my reputation but I do not care. He means too much to me, and I refuse to admit that a life as a serving girl is all there is. I know that I am destined for more.

I am still visiting the museum and Francis and I have continued our friendship. I have finally told him about my family. He was so kind and so patient as I told him everything. He shows no signs of love towards me and for that I am grateful, I am confused enough as it is. I am glad that I have a friend, even if it might be frowned upon, since he is a man who is not a relative.

London, England, 1923

I feel sick. I am so ashamed. On my day off, I returned early from the Museum and the house was deathly quiet. Most of the staff were out, the Mistress and Estelle had gone for afternoon tea and Sir James was at work.

Young Master Edward caught me unawares, in my room. I knew it was wrong. I knew he shouldn't be there, but I love him so much and thought that he loved me. His piercing dark eyes bore into mine and I averted my gaze for a moment before looking back at him. He smiled and hungrily kissed my lips and neck. I knew then that I would give myself to him, and I did, accidentally tearing my clothes in the process. After we had made love we lay there on the floor. I stared at the ceiling smiling, visions of myself in fine dresses attending the ball, being escorted to Paris or Rome to dine on fine food and view the sights. Turning over I had stroked his cheek and whispered I love you. He had turned and stared at me before standing and quickly dressing. Leaning down he kissed the top of my head before whispering in my ear, "Our secret Florence, no one must ever know."

"But you love me. I thought we would be together now?"

Young Master Edward had laughed, and shaken his head. "How can I love you? You're a serving girl! I can never marry you. It was fun whilst it lasted and we both got what we wanted. As much as I like you, you were just a bit of fun to pass the time until I marry Estelle."

I had stared at him in shock as he left the room. I had been used, I thought he had loved me but he tricked me into sharing a bed with him. But not even a bed had been good enough for me, we had used the floor. I was such a fool. I felt sick, I felt used and most of all I felt betrayed. I have no idea how long I sat there, but knew I could not remain forever. I cleaned myself up, and wiped the tears from my face, trying as best as I could to mend my torn garments. By the time I returned downstairs life had returned to normal and no one knew anything was wrong.

CHAPTER TWENTY-FOUR

Luxor, Egypt, 2002

Cora was shocked, she lifted her glass to drink some water. Edward had treated Florence appallingly. He had pretended to like her and then just used her. What a bastard! The glass slipped from her hand, splintering into tiny pieces as it struck the balcony floor. A stray shard sliced across her foot, instantly drawing blood. Hastily she jumped out of the chair and ran to the bathroom to stem the flow, rinse and cover with a small adhesive bandage. She returned to the balcony to carefully gather up the remaining pieces before throwing them into the bin.

After pouring a fresh glass of water, Cora walked back out to her balcony and sat down. She stared out across the Nile lost in thought. She couldn't even begin to imagine what Florence had gone through. Men like Edward were despicable, thinking nothing of others, manipulating her like that. Her poor great-grandmother. It seemed to be a family trait that the women in her family suffered badly at the hands of men, but it was never their fault. They just ended up being unlucky, or in the wrong place at the wrong time. Cora felt sad for Florence. With such a bad start in her life she had tried so hard to put her grandparents horrid past behind her, to make her life better.

Steeling herself, Cora lifted Florence's diary. She was determined to read on.

London, England, 1923

A few months passed and Young Master Edward and Estelle's wedding finally arrived. I had done my best to avoid him, and thankfully he had kept out of my way, something I was very grateful for. I was annoyed with myself, I was still in love with him, but he no longer cared and wanted little to do with me. The wedding was a lavish affair, it seemed that the whole world had been invited and Sir James and the Mistress were so very happy. But I could not understand it. I was shocked that they still got married when Young Master Edward had treated me so badly. I just could not understand who would do that sort of thing to someone and pretend nothing had happened. To those on the outside Young Master Edward and Estelle were the perfect couple, but I knew better. He was shady and underhanded and I felt nothing but sorrow for his new bride. How many other girls had he used and abused the way he had me? I wished I could tell her, try and prevent her from marrying him, but it was not my place to say anything, and I wouldn't be believed anyway, so I just stayed in the shadows, doing my job hoping it would all be over very soon. Thankfully they left for their honeymoon straight after, and it was a welcome relief. I could finally go about my daily life without living in fear.

Barely a week later I awoke feeling ill. Rushing out of bed I vomited heavily and felt poorly for the rest of the day. I was given the day off, so that I could stay in bed and get better, but the sickness continued coming over me in waves without warning. Finally the doctor was called and with him came a bombshell that blew apart the household.

I was with child.

I was stunned. This could not be happening.

The Mistress screamed at me for bringing shame upon her household, the other girls glared at me as they were bearing the brunt of the wrath and Cook barely spoke to me. I was surprised when Lillian the housekeeper called me to her office. She said she wanted to help me and asked me who the father was. I could hear his words echo though my head, and told her it was just a man I had met only once and I could not remember his name. She knew I was lying, she told me she could see it in my eyes, but I stayed true to my lie. I was not going to tell anyone, and in that moment sitting there with Lillian glaring down at me seeking an answer, I knew my time at High House was limited and that night when I returned to my room tired and weary, I made preparations to leave.

<u>London, England, 1923</u>

Three months later my time at High House was behind me, and I found myself moving from rented house to rented house, my savings dwindling quickly. I had no more jewellery to sell. Young Master Edward's unwanted gifts were all gone now. I was over six months gone and it was the start of another cold, harsh winter, I prayed that my baby would be born safely and I would still have somewhere to live.

I visited the British Museum as often as I could and spent time with Francis who had become a great friend. One day, tired and feeling so lonely, I sat there and cried, telling him about Young Master Edward, and everything that had happened. Francis was so kind. He told me I could rent a room in his house in return for helping him with Saturday reading lessons at the library. I was so grateful and moved in straight away, I knew some people would gossip if they knew, but I did not care. All that mattered was that I had somewhere safe and reliable to stay where my baby could live when it was born.

All too soon my darling daughter was born into the world and I was so happy, she was healthy and I named her Emma. Francis loved her and even offered to marry me, but even though I loved him as a friend, I could not ever feel that way about him. He would always be special to me but as a friend only. I was grateful to him and if he had not come along I do not know what would have happened. Francis had appeared in my life when I needed him the most.

I shall always be grateful to him, Francis Anderson my beloved and wonderful friend.

An ice-cold shiver crawled up Cora's spine and she felt bile rise in her throat. Francis Anderson.

Anderson.

Wasn't Anderson Sam's surname? It's funny she couldn't fully remember since it had only been said that one time when they met. She was sure it was Anderson, though. Her stomach filled with butterflies, and she hurriedly turned the page to read on, but it was blank save for a few hurried lines. She knew Florence hadn't been much of a writer, but the short sentence followed by blank pages was unexpected.

<u>*London, England, 1924*</u>

I have always trusted the wrong people in my life. I thought he was my friend, but he was nothing more than an enemy to me. My daughter Emma is safe. For now. But I fear so much for my own life.

So much so, that I know that by this time tomorrow I shall probably be dead.

With mounting dread, Cora ploughed through the remaining pages of the book for an answer but none came. They were all blank. It was beyond frustrating. She had no idea what had become of

Florence, but it sounded as though bad luck may have befallen her too. Back in her room, Cora paced back and forth. No wonder her own mum had kept all of this a secret from her. It seemed as though the women in her family were destined for a life of misery and bad luck. Deciding to take a break from it all, she locked the diaries in her safe in the closet and went in search of food.

Sitting poolside, she eased her nervous rumbling stomach with some food, but she couldn't shake those two words from her mind.

Francis Anderson.

CHAPTER TWENTY-FIVE

Luxor, Egypt, 2002

Cora needed answers, and she needed them quickly. Her brain was working overtime and the more she thought about what she'd learned, the more confused she became. After eating, her mind had begun to race even more and she couldn't sit still. Instead of returning to her room, Cora hailed a taxi and ordered the driver to drop her at the Valley of the Kings. She needed to allay her fears. Perhaps her brain was just making assumptions and she had it all wrong.

The taxi arrived at the Valley of the Kings and she paid the driver before stepping out into the heat, pushing her way through the tourists until she reached the team. She breathed deeply and planted a smile on her face. *'Just act normal,'* she thought to herself.

"Hello!" she shouted, waving her arm in the air. The smiling but, nonetheless, hot and bothered Egyptologists raised their heads and waved back.

Nick stepped from the trench and made his way over to her.

"Hi, what brings you here?"

"I was bored and thought I'd pop by to say hello," she responded. She scanned the site for Sam, but couldn't see him.

"No Sam?"

"No, he's just gone over to the museum to drop off some paperwork."

"Oh!"

"Is something wrong?"

She gently grabbed hold of Nick's arm pulling him out of earshot of the others. With a bemused look he followed her.

"Is everything okay, Cora?"

"Yes. No." She was trying to find the right words. "I need to ask you something, but I need to know that I can trust you."

"Okay." He steered her to a nearby outcrop, where they perched on a rock.

"Can I trust you, Nick?" She looked up at him searching his eyes for an answer, she needed to see his response as well as hear it. His eyes were open and honest, and Cora knew then that she would trust him with her life.

"Yes. You can trust me Cora. What's this about?"

"It's going to sound really weird. You have to promise that you won't say anything to anyone. I can't tell you why, I just need you to promise me."

"Alright, I promise," Nick said.

"What's Sam's surname?"

He smiled, bemused at her question. "It's Anderson. I thought you knew that?"

Cora's brain went into overdrive, she had been right. Her mind hadn't been playing tricks.

Francis Anderson.

Sam Anderson.

Were the two related?

"Anderson," she barely whispered, as though she was almost afraid to utter the name. "I have another question Nick. He mentioned his family worked in archaeology and history. Is it just his parents or does it go back further?"

"As far as I'm aware, it goes back generations. I think some of them worked at the British Museum. Why do you ask?"

She felt the cold wash of fear spread throughout her body. Her heart leapt into her mouth. History was repeating itself and she knew now that she was in danger. It all made sense now. Why Sam was so desperate to help her. But what was it that he wanted from her? What was it that connected her family to his? What had happened to make the Andersons hate her family so much that they would kill for it?

Cora stood, desperate to leave the Valley before Sam returned. She wasn't sure she'd be able to contain herself. He hadn't helped her because he was being nice. He had helped her because he wanted something from her, something to do with her family. He'd been devious and underhanded and she hated that.

"Cora?"

"It's nothing. I just needed to know. Thanks, Nick. And please remember: don't tell anyone that I asked you."

"Is there something I need to know, Cora? You look unnerved."

"No!" she replied a little too quickly. Smiling as best she could, she placed a hand on his arm in an effort to both reassure him and get away. "It's nothing and I'm sorry for the questions. I'm all over the place at the moment. Sorry, I'd better let you get back to work."

She backed away, ready to make a swift getaway, but he was too quick for her. He grabbed her arm again, and turned her to face him, before releasing his grip.

"Whatever it is, you *can* trust me. I promise faithfully, Cora. Whatever is bothering you, please tell me and let me help you." He reached into his back pocket and took out a small notebook and pen. Tearing out a page he scribbled on it and passed it to her. "You're not alone. That's my mobile phone number if you ever need anything."

She looked up at him, directly into those beautiful blue eyes of his and she knew right then

WIND ACROSS THE NILE

he would keep his promise, always. She knew she could trust him, and that telling him would be the right thing. He would protect her and he would come to her aid if she ever needed him. She took the piece of paper and smiled stuffing it into her jeans pocket.

"Hello! What are you doing here? I wasn't expecting to see you today." Sam sauntered towards them, and the moment was broken. She'd lost her chance. Turning to Sam, she breathed deeply trying her damnedest to smile.

Nick gave her a supportive *"I'm here, don't worry"* look, before walking away and leaving her alone with Sam. She wished Nick had stayed, she didn't want to be alone with Sam, but the last thing she could do was beg Nick to stay. Her heart pounded in her chest and she felt her palms go clammy. She wanted to turn and run from Sam, but her feet refused to move. So she remained staring at him, with a fake smile planted on her face whilst she fell to pieces inside.

"I wish we hadn't finished translating the book. I'm intrigued to know what happened to Hakim's letters. Randa seemed quite worried about him," Sam said.

Cora dug deep, determined to be strong. "I'm surprised Randa's diary survived. So many things get thrown away by people over the years. The letters probably weren't important."

"It's a shame. I think they would've been really interesting."

"Maybe," Cora shrugged before waving to the team. "I think Nick wants you."

Sam turned to look at his colleagues. "Okay. Well it's nice to see you, as always. I better get back to work. You know what *he* can be like." Sam nodded in Nick's direction.

"Yeah."

Cora watched as he walked towards the rest of the team. Content that he was settling down to work, Cora turned her back on the Egyptologists and trod the path as quickly as she could, desperate to find a taxi and get back to the sanctuary of her hotel.

~

He watched her leave. Something was very, very wrong. He needed to work out what it was before the news got back to his father. This wasn't how things were supposed to go. He was in charge, not her.

~

Grateful to be back in the safe haven of her air-conditioned room, Cora changed out of her dusty clothes and had a refreshing shower. Pouring a tall, cold glass of water, she knew what she had to do. She couldn't let her brain run wild. She needed to follow this through and read the other diaries. She opened her room safe and carefully removed the next diary. Opening the balcony door, she stepped outside and pulled the chair into the shade before sitting and turning to the first page of the small book. The writing was very different, and the spelling terrible but she was still able to decipher it. Pulling down her shades, she decided to find out what her grandmother, Emma, had to say for herself.

London, England, 1941

Me names Emma Sanders. Im seventeen, I have little to me name but I been luckee to be taken in by a womin called Missus Smith or Lillian as she now tells me to call er. She new me mum when she werr younger, they werked together in some posh place called Hi House. Lillian, used to be the howskeeper there but shes retired an lives in a small house in south London.

I dont remember me mum, she died when I was a babe, Lillian never told me wat happinnd. We bin lucky, Lillians house is one of the few houses left standing after the destrukshin of the bombs. Life is filled with fear an death an I hate it.

The worlds at war ya see, and they say it aint over yet. Londons suffered an many people av died at the hands of the enemee, that damm Jerry. Night is the worst, the streets are dark an those unluckee to not av homes huddel togethr in the safest places thay can find, under briges or if luckee in the tunnels of the undergrownd trayn sistem. Sirens screem in darkest hours an we all hide listenin for that wyne an buzz of them bloody doodlebugs. Before I lived with Lillian I werr homeless. I lived under them briges and in them trayn tunnels. Sometimes I only made it to a doreway. I seen homes an busnisses blowed apart, men wiv clothes on fire, or bleedin, slowly dyin from ware the shrapnul ripped through thayr flesh. One of em missin a limb died in me arms one night, I never new his name but I cried so many tears as his blud stained me already filthy clothes. There werent nuthin I could do for him. Its a horrible thing an yet we still live it every day.

The war goes on forever but the speerit of the people dont fail. They stay strong.

Twas on me sixteen birthday Lillian found me. She had bin serchin for me. I still aint got no idea how she found me but then she aint like me, shes posh and nose people who woodint even spit on me in the street if I was on fire. She said she ad somethin that belonged to me. She sat me down an pulled out a woodin trunk an opened it. She showed me me muthers diary an some other things wat belonged to me grandmuther some lady called Randa. She told me she looked after the stuff not long after me muther left er job in disgrace. Lillian said she spent years lookin for me, she knew I were sent as an orphen sumware by me muther, an she wanted to make shor I got it. She told me I had the same eyes and hair as me muther, all black locks an dark eyes. It was nice lernin about me muther from her. It made her real agenn, and nice to know someone cared about her. Lillian told me me days livin under briges werr over. Lillian took me to live wiv er.

Once I were better dressed, clean and fed and got used to sleepin in a bed Lillian started to read me mums diary to me an then used it to teech me to read so that I could understand it better an I read it back to myself wenever I wanted. She then got a tutor in to school me as best they could. I overheard the tutor tell Lillian one day that I was a quick lerner. I aint got a clue what that means but Im happy, Im doing everythin right an that Im finally making me muther proud. Im graytful Lillian cares an shes a nice person to live with. I still av no idea how she found me, I av asked her. But that dont matter. Its good she cares.

Im intrestid to learn about me family an where I come from. Me life aint been grayt so far an I dont remember me muther. I werr just a baby when she went missing. Lillian said she herd tell me muther ad killed erself by throwing erself in the Temz river. It panes me to hear that, an I hope it aint true but if it is she must av been very unhappy with her life. Maybe it ment she didnt love me? Or maybe she loved me to much to stay. I wish I new the answer but I probably wont never find out.

London, England, 1944

It has been many years since I first wrote anything down. I found this book I had forgotten about, buried in a box of my things and felt inspired to write. The war became vicious and unforgiving and still rages on. I have spent all my time helping Lillian and our neighbours and it gave me little time to concentrate on myself or anything I wanted to do. One thing that was constant for a while was my Tutor, who worked hard on me and managed to get me to write and spell properly. It's like I have changed as a person. I have gone from being a grubby little urchin into something more of a young lady, and to Miss Lillian I'm very grateful. She was so nice and life with her was so very happy, despite the war that is always at our door. Sadly she passed away a few days ago, her heart failed they say, probably brought on by all the stress of the war.

I'm not quite twenty-one years old yet and I am alone again. I have been told by her solicitor that she left what possessions and money she had saved to me as she had no other family. I'm able to stay in the small house she owned too, it's a home, and it means that I'm able to try and make something of my life.

Cora broke off reading to take a drink. She was frustrated that her family was so erratic in their diary keeping. They seemed to forget about it for months or years at a time and she felt like she was missing out on so much. But she was being hard on them. Emma certainly hadn't had an easy life. Living through the war must have been awful, not knowing when it was going to end, or when the next bombs would fall. Diary keeping must have been the last thing on her mind.

One thing she had learned from Emma's sporadic and short entries was that she had the same looks as the rest of the women. The Egyptian blood. Dark hair and eyes seemed to dominate itself through the generations to the next child, and they all seemed to have the same strong willed character. Cora was glad Emma had learned to write properly and that Lillian had given her such a good start in life. She deserved it.

Putting down her glass, Cora plowed on.

London, England, 1945

It's been a year since I last wrote and things have been so busy and my life has changed so much! I barely have the time to breathe let alone write. The war is fading away now and they say it will be over soon. Many times they have said this, but this time I would like to believe it is true. The wireless says that the allies are making advances and the Germans are on the run.

I used Lillian's money wisely and only spent what I needed to. She had given me such a good start with the tutor that I felt I should put my skills to good use. My old Tutor also helped me get a secretarial job last year in one of the Government offices. I enjoy working, I get to meet interesting people and it gives me a purpose and a decent income.

~

It's almost Christmas, and what a Christmas it will be! The war is finally over, everyone is so happy. People line the streets and we don't have to worry about bombs falling on us any more. Sadly I have lost my job at the Government office, but my boss knew someone who needed help so I now have another job. I help out at the British Museum. It feels like some kind of twisted fate. It seems like my family are due to be part of the Museum regardless of what happened in the past. What happened to my mother happened years ago. That was her life, mine is different and now I will have the opportunity to learn about the history of my ancestors, just like she did.

The job was meant to be mine.

Every day I start at nine in the morning, and finish at four in the afternoon, I do my job well and have learned a lot about the Museum, its history and its treasures. Things are getting back to normal, and the Museum has been lucky that most of its collection had been moved to safety during the war. The Museum suffered some damage, being set alight by an incendiary shower, which set the roof and the rear of the building alight, but unlike others they were very lucky. Parts of London are nothing but rubble, and the City will take a long time to heal from the sustained attacks.

I use every snatched moment I have at work to read the history books, and visit the collections. My reading and learning is getting better every day and I have completely fallen in love with History and everything to do with Egypt. It really is the perfect job.

I met someone today who knew my mother! I'm so excited! His name is Francis Anderson, he used to work at the Museum and was there showing his own son Henry around, who is about my age. Henry is very handsome and is training to become an Egyptologist! They've been so nice to me and Francis has told me so much about my mother, how she used to visit the Museum and how they became close friends. He told me that he and my mother were close and it was nice to talk to someone who knew her and could tell me things about her that I had not heard before.

I think Francis and Henry will become my new friends and I am glad that I have found them. I'm so very happy!

Cora let out a long unsteady breath.

The Andersons featured far too heavily in her history. It couldn't just be a coincidence that she had suddenly met up with Sam Anderson? Was Henry his grandfather? Her stomach was filled with a thousand tiny butterflies and her hands had become sweaty. She didn't like where this was heading. Nervousness and anger intertwined into a growing canker in Cora's soul.

She had risen and was pacing, the nervous energy winding her up like a coiled spring. She wanted to go and find Sam, confront him, and have it out with him. She needed to know what the hell was going on. She needed to know why her family had been targeted. But she couldn't. Reality set in and she sank back into the chair. She had little to go on, a few rambling old diaries, and the coincidence of a name. He would laugh in her face.

She couldn't read any more of the diary today. She was just too tired and her brain was buzzing, turning everything over and over, leading her down impossible avenues and dead ends; a useless jumble of thoughts that made no sense at all.

Returning to the coolness of her room, she took the wooden box from the safe, placed Emma's book safely inside, and locked it once more.

It would keep. For now.

CHAPTER TWENTY-SIX

Luxor, Egypt, 2002

Cora lay in the dark, staring at the ceiling. She was having a fitful night and just couldn't sleep. Every time she drifted off, she fell into horrible nightmares where she was being chased through the ancient, crumbling ruins of Egypt by the entire Anderson family. All of them had evil twisted faces and bayed for her blood. As fast she tried to run, her legs just wouldn't respond and they eventually caught up to her, coming at her, wielding weapons of pure hatred. Just as she was about to die, she would wake in terror, clutching sweat soaked sheets.

The dreams petrified her, completely eradicating any chance of restful sleep. With a sigh, she rose from the bed, turned on the light and made a cup of tea. The air was thick with the promise of a storm. She could feel the humidity rub against her skin, drenching it with each movement. Opening the balcony door, she stared out into the blackness, watching as the fast approaching thunderstorm began to make itself known. The hills were suddenly illuminated; great hulking masses, appearing briefly from the darkness as the sky turned into a battling mixture of sheet and forked lightning. It was swiftly followed by great earth shaking cracks of thunder, which grew closer with each passing minute. As the storm arrived in all its glory, she sat on the balcony, watching as nature's sound and light show went round and round, putting on a spectacular air-sizzling performance, outdoing any she'd witnessed before.

~

Sam stood at the window of his room staring out at the storm. The night was humid, and the storm wrapped itself around him like a comforting blanket. He loved weather like this, the drama and uncertainty of it, the violence of it. It suited his mood. Egypt very rarely had rainfall with a storm and it made the crashing thunder and bright lightning all the more spectacular.

His thoughts returned to Cora and their meeting at the site earlier. What had she been doing there? Why had she been with Nick? It made him feel uneasy. She was his friend, not

Nick's. Seeing her with Nick had made the jealousy rise in him and he'd had trouble keeping it down. Cora invaded his thoughts and dreams constantly and he just couldn't shake her from his mind. It made him want her more than he'd ever wanted any other woman in his life, and that scared him. As a large rumble of thunder shook the small apartment, he stared out at the buildings that surrounded him. He was lucky to be able to see over them towards the Nile. As another flash of lightning lit up Luxor, he caught sight of the looming mountains and inky black river that sliced its way through the town. He wanted to seek her out, and comfort her in the storm, take her in his arms and reassure her. But he knew that was a fleeting fantasy. For Sam, life was never straightforward and he wished that he could be normal, but he knew that would never happen. He would just have to be content to watch the tempest alone, content with his own lonely company.

~

Cora took a break from watching the spectacular storm that still raged over Luxor. She padded across the room, stopped at the safe and removed the box. She couldn't sleep and, as fun as it was to watch the elements, she may as well do something productive with her time. Holding the wooden box close, she shut her eyes, feeling the history and turmoil within flow through her body. It was as though blood had connected her to the writing locked inside. She knew there was more upset to come, and that she would have to continue reading, so persevere she must. It was what she was meant to do.

Carefully placing the box on the table, she opened it and removed each book, placing them on the table one by one. Turning her attention to the box, she studied it. It was an odd little thing, made of the lightest wood she'd ever seen, making it incredibly delicate. The interior was lined with thick purple velvet, and reminded her of one of the gifts her mum used to make. Cora wondered if this was one of her creations. The inside base of the box caught her attention. The lining was coming away and a corner protruded upwards. She would need to re-glue it at some point but for now she pulled it straight, trying to tuck it back in, but instead of fixing it the whole bottom came away in her hand.

"Shit! Exactly what I didn't want to do."

Holding it up to the light to get a better look, surprise caught her as a bundle of papers fell from a hidden compartment. Picking them up, Cora placed the box on the table before going through the sheaf of papers. There were photos of two women she'd never seen before. But both had a familiar air about them. She read the back of the first, *"Florence, High House, Christmas."*

Her great-grandmother. Cora smiled at the beautiful face of Randa's daughter who had, so suddenly, disappeared without a trace. The second said, *"Emma. A summers day."*

Her grandmother. She hadn't yet found out what had happened to her but she looked so happy. Putting them to one side, she lifted two sheaves of paper. They were old with faint writing on the front, opening them she was unable to make out what was written there, as it was in Arabic.

Excitement rose within her. Was it possible? Were they Hakim's missing letters? She would have to get them translated as soon as possible. Should she risk asking Sam or bypass him completely and ask Nick? With everything she had learned recently she no longer knew who to trust. She needed to think very carefully about her next move. The last piece of paper was large and seemed to be part of a map. Unfortunately, the writing was also in Arabic. It would have to be translated along with the letters. Lastly there was another envelope containing a petite wedding band, the piece of paper with it simply read *Randa's wedding ring*. Without even thinking she slipped it onto her finger, and tears filled her eyes.

It fit her perfectly.

CHAPTER TWENTY-SEVEN

Luxor, Egypt, 2002

As the night progressed, the storm passed, allowing Cora to finally fall asleep on the bed, surrounded by family heirlooms.

A beautiful blue sky greeted her as she awoke early the next morning, and stretched her sleepiness away. The glint of Randa's ring still on her finger caught her attention and she smiled, twisting it gently, lost in thought, before removing it. She placed it back in the box along with the other items, before locking the box in the safe. She made herself a cup of tea and began to make a plan. She knew she had to get the papers she found translated, and until she did, she knew they would nag at her. But who to ask?

She knew that Alex and Lucy's grasp of Arabic was minimal, and she didn't know David well enough to ask him, so it had to be Sam or Nick. It was a difficult decision, but she knew after what she had read in the diaries that she couldn't ask Sam. It had to be Nick. She grabbed her purse, and rummaged through it, finding the scrap of paper with Nick's number on it. Without hesitation she sat on the bed, lifted the receiver and dialed.

~

Cora peered through the spyhole before opening the door to Nick. Once he was inside, she shut the door, motioning for him to sit.

"Is everything okay?" he asked with a look of concern.

"Yes...No...I don't know...but thanks for coming. I've a favour to ask, and I can't ask Sam. I know you're really busy and don't have time for dealing with crap that isn't your job, but I really need your help, Nick. I need you to look at some documents and tell me what's in them."

"Okay," he said curiously. "I can give you an hour."

"Thanks. I appreciate it."

"Before we start, though, I need to ask: why didn't you ask Sam?"

"It's related to the diary. But I can't explain why I don't want Sam to be involved at the moment. My brain's running wild, and it's all just supposition. I promise you'll be the first to know once I've worked it all out."

"Okay. You'd better show me these documents."

She sat at the table and Nick sat next to her. Pulling the box towards her, she opened it and withdrew the contents one by one, explaining them to Nick and how she came to have them in her possession.

"And Sam has no idea you have these?"

"No. Erica, my best friend, is the only other person I've told. I want it to remain that way for now."

"Of course."

"It's these two that are most important. Randa's diary mentioned letters from her brother, but they weren't with the diary. I'm wondering if these are the missing letters."

Cora passed them to Nick, and he studied the writing carefully, silently reading for a few minutes.

"They're from someone named Hakim."

"That's Randa's brother!"

"Are you sure you want me to read them to you Cora? Some of it may upset you."

"I need to hear it Nick, however bad it may be."

Nick took a deep breath, and began to read the first letter.

To my dear Sister Randa,

For so long I have wanted to write to you, but Father strictly forbade it. I am now only able to send you this letter as I no longer live under fathers roof. Something terrible happened, something so disgraceful that I can no longer live with the burden. I have brought such shame on our family, that leaving home in the middle of the night without saying goodbye was my only option.

I now know how you felt when they turned you away from their door, but your only crime was to fall in love with Albert, and I am glad you did. He is a great man and I know he loves you deeply. I know he will look after and cherish you and the baby for the rest of your lives and to him I am grateful. You found true love Randa and that is not a sin.

As for me, my sin is too great to even begin to explain, but I will try my best to. Unlike you I have committed a crime. You must remember the Farsi brothers, they worked at the excavation site. They and I have broken laws Randa, and at this moment the brothers are in custody receiving their punishment. I managed to escape and I am hiding in Southern Egypt.

It is so hard to explain, I feel like such a coward. Please do not think badly of me sister. I hate myself enough already for what I am putting the family through. But I must explain my actions to you, so that you know the truth.

The Farsi brothers and I have been stealing artefacts from archaeological excavations for years. How long it has gone on for I do not know, the years have melded into one long horrible period of time. I did not want to do it, but I could not say no to them. They threatened me. We dug illegally as well as stealing from the open site, hiding our tracks as best as we could. For years we kept the artefacts hidden away with the hopes of selling them.

I only wanted a better life for the family, sister, but the eldest Farsi brother was greedy and he got caught. It was not long before he gave my name to the authorities. It is how it is here, and I am fearful I will be severely punished.

After their arrest I moved some of the artefacts to a safer place. I cannot tell you where, sister, as I cannot implicate you, but they will be protected until I am able to return them to their rightful owners. That is how I will make amends, I will not sell them, I will return them all.

I know what I did was wrong, this is my way of putting things right.

Please forgive me sister. That is all I ask of you.
Your loving brother
Hakim

Cora was stunned. Randa had already been through such pain already only to learn her brother had been a thief who had been on the run from the authorities. It must have been such a terrible burden for her. Her family seemed to have fallen apart at the seams and she had lost everyone she'd ever loved. So sad and yet familiar, too.

Cora's own life had cracked apart, leaving her without those she loved. Was this what her and her ancestors were destined for, battling against a life of hurt pain and loss?

"Cora?"

Nick's voice brought her out of her reverie.

"Sorry, Nick I was miles away. I think you should read the second one. Get it over with."

"Are you sure?"

"Yes. I'm sure."

Without hesitation he began.

To my dear sister Randa,

This is my second and last letter to you, for you see I am soon to be taken from this world. My body is being ravaged by disease, and it fails more and more each day. I know it has been so long since I last wrote to you, I hope you received it. I am sorry but it must have worried you greatly.

I hope life has been good to you. I have missed you throughout the years and our beautiful Egypt seems too big and empty without you.

I never told you the full story in my last letter. We did not just steal the artefacts. We actually got caught on site one night by one of the archaeologists, Jeremiah Anderson. You may remember him Randa. He was friends with Albert and our father. The Farsi's stopped him from going to the police but in the worst possible way. They killed him Randa. They killed Jeremiah Anderson and left him there to die in the desert. He had a wife and a child, a young boy called Francis.

I feel the guilt every day as though it was me that used the knife, even though I did not. You must undo my bad deed, sister, and return the artefacts to the Egyptian Government when I have gone. I am too frail and too ill to do it myself and I do not trust anyone else. There is a map with this letter that will help you. If you travel south to Aswan and cross the river to the East bank, you will find a rock outcrop in the hills there. It is about an hour's walk from the monastery of St. Simeon. You will find the artefacts buried in that area. Trust your instinct and you will find them. Do this for me, sister.

I love you very much, and will always watch over you, even in the next life.

Until we meet again.
Your ever-loving brother
Hakim

CHAPTER TWENTY-EIGHT

Luxor, Egypt, 2002

Cora was up and pacing the room, no longer able to sit still. It went all the way back to Albert and Randa. A feud started over the theft of a few artefacts and the death of an innocent man. Jeremiah Anderson. At every corner it was an Anderson. It was about revenge. It had to be.

"Jeremiah Anderson. Francis Anderson. Henry Anderson. Sam Anderson." She whispered, beside herself, wringing her hands, her heart thudding in her chest. "Bloody Andersons, always there, always in the shadows," she muttered as she whirled around, seeing Nick's concerned face through the tears that were falling. As the fear and dread washed through her, her knees buckled and she sank to the floor. Nick pushed back his chair and rushed over to her, crouching next to her.

She looked directly into Nick's eyes and whispered, "I'm next, Nick. They're going to kill me. *He's* going to kill me."

Nick sat next to her and scooped her into his arms rocking her gently.

"Talk to me. Tell me what's going on, Cora."

"I can't, Nick. I just can't. If I tell you, they'll kill you, too." She sobbed uncontrollably.

"Yes, you can." He brushed a stray hair from her face. Slowly, as their eyes locked, Nick took her face in his hands. He lowered his lips to hers and she responded without hesitation. Emotions overwhelming them, they surrendered to each other, lost in the kiss. Suddenly, Nick broke away and ran his hands through his hair.

"Shit. I'm so sorry, Cora. I shouldn't have done that."

"It's okay." She slid from his arms and leaned against the bed, staring at the table littered with clues from her past.

The room was still and silent for a few minutes. Nick stood and walked over to the window to stare out across the Nile.

Cora spoke.

"Hakim was there when Jeremiah Anderson was murdered. All the way through my history, it seems an Anderson has been involved with my family. They keep coming up in my family's diaries. Suddenly, after losing my family, another Anderson appears in my life. Sam. What if they're all related and they've been watching us all this time? There was no reason for Sam to help me, Nick, but he did. I've always wondered why. Maybe now I have the answer. Maybe he deliberately sought me out because it's his turn. Maybe he's only helping me to get what he wants, some kind of revenge?"

Nick turned his back on the window to look at her.

"I don't understand, Cora. What am I missing?"

She reached up to get her mum's letter from the table, before passing it to Nick.

"Read it. They killed my mum, Nick. How many of my family have died at their hands?" She tried her best to stay calm, but it was too late. The tidal wave crashed over her again picking up all of the grief and hurt, enveloping her.

Nick read the letter and, the further he read, the more shocked his expression became. "Your mum thought she was going to be murdered?"

"Yes and I'm next, aren't I?" she wailed. Tears of loss escaped for Randa, Florence, Emma, her parents and brother, and finally herself.

Throwing the letter to one side, Nick only had one thought on his mind.

Cora.

He lifted her from the carpet and into his arms, holding her tightly, allowing her to cry, allowing all the pent-up grief and emotion to spill from her.

"I promise I won't let anyone hurt you, Cora. I'll do everything I can to protect you."

"I can't ask you to do that for me, Nick."

"Yes, you can." He placed her on the edge of the bed and sat next to her, taking her hands in his.

"I can't. This is my burden and mine alone," she whispered. "And besides, we barely know each other. You hated me when we first met."

"I never hated you, Cora. I was just miserable, and had been through a lot, with the cheating and divorce. I know I told you parts of it...but, well, I always thought that Anna was the one for me. We met at university and she had been there for me, understood me, been by my side as my career grew.

"But something had changed. I can't pinpoint when exactly, but Anna suddenly became distant, snappy and no longer supportive. One day my world crumbled into tiny pieces. I was at work, and someone had delivered an envelope. Tearing it open, my heart almost stopped as I saw the photos. The images were of Anna naked in the arms of another man. Each photograph made it obvious that it wasn't a one-time thing." Nick paused and picked at the bed cover as if he was unsure how to continue.

"Take your time, Nick." Cora smiled sympathetically and placed her hand on his, giving him the courage to continue.

"Everything suddenly made sense, and in that moment, I knew my marriage was over. I left work and went straight home. Anna was there and I confronted her. I'm ashamed of how I dealt with it. I've always been a calm person, but she had pushed me over the edge. I threw the photographs at her, demanding to know what had happened. And do you know what she did?"

Cora shook her head seeing the hurt in his eyes.

"Anna told me she hated me. I made her feel trapped, she felt left behind by my career, and accused me of putting it before her. She felt she had no other choice than find someone else! I demanded to know who he was but she refused. We argued like cat and dog, screaming and shouting at each other, but she refused to tell me. It was the last time I saw her."

"Oh Nick, I'm so sorry. I can understand why you have been so miserable. To go through all that must have been awful. Damon cheated on me, but we didn't have the long history that you both had, so I can't even begin to imagine. Knowing your divorce had come through must have brought everything back."

"Yes it did, and I was a bastard to everyone around me, including you. I'm so sorry."

"You have nothing to apologise for."

"Thank you. I'm glad you walked into my life, Cora. Since getting to know you I'm no longer miserable. Meeting you was the best thing that's happened to me in such a long time."

She turned to face him and looked up into his handsome face, falling deeply into his beautiful blue eyes.

"I have feelings for you, Cora. It's crept up on me. You've got under my skin and I want to be with you and be part of your life," he barely breathed. As his lips met hers for the second time, she knew in that moment that she had feelings for him, too, a surprise that completely overwhelmed her. She hadn't expected to feel like this, especially as they had started out hating each other. But now that she knew him, she liked him a lot, and wanted to spend time with him. She felt happy when she was around him. She surrendered to his kiss, wanting to be close to him, and suddenly so many things felt right.

The grief of her family's death. Damon's betrayal. The hurt and deceit that had befallen her family. It all became a distant memory, and all she could see before her was Nick. Nick was her future. She knew that in a heartbeat. He would love her, protect her and be a friend to her, and that was all that mattered. The rest were mere obstacles to be overcome. Her future was right here in front of her.

Cora couldn't remember who had pulled who onto the bed, but it's where they ended up. As clothes were removed, they were replaced by gentle butterfly kisses on bare skin. The sun streamed through the open balcony door making their already hot limbs damp and slick. As she allowed him to take her, all she felt was complete peace and happiness.

~

They had lain naked in each other's arms, dozing, content with each other's company, until the sound of Nick's phone ringing disturbed them. Reluctantly, he answered it.

After he clicked the phone off, he said, "I'm sorry, Cora, I'm going to have to go. I told the team I would only be an hour and I've been gone nearly four. I hate to run and leave you like this. We still have so much to talk about."

"It's fine. I know you have a job to do."

"I meant what I said though," he said as he pulled his clothes on. "I'm here for you and I will look after you. You mean so much to me."

He leaned forward and kissed her again.

"I love you, Cora Thomas."

The words pleasantly surprised her.

"I think I love you, too, Nick Foster."

Then he was gone, and she lay back on the bed, replaying everything in her head, before falling into a much needed, contented dreamless sleep.

CHAPTER TWENTY-NINE

Luxor, Egypt, 2002

Sunlight streamed into the room. It was early in the morning and Cora had slept right through, having the best nights sleep she'd had in months. She was naked and wrapped in twisted sheets, a pleasant reminder of the few hours spent with Nick. She sighed with contentment, and reached for her phone. The display showed a single text message and she opened it, her heart flying the moment she read the message. Three simple loving words from Nick and she returned the sentiment immediately. Scrolling through the phone, she found Erica's number and hit 'dial.'

"Thank goodness you're there, Erica."

Before her friend could get a word in, Cora spilled her heart out about everything: the diaries, the letters, the map, the possible connection with Sam's family.

"Oh, Cora. Are you sure?"

"I think so," she groaned, as she walked around the room, putting away the family heirlooms that she had left out overnight. "So much has happened. I'm exhausted with it all."

"I can imagine. What are you going to do?"

"No idea. Take each day at a time I suppose, and hope I don't end up dead like my parents," she replied with a hollow laugh.

"That's not funny. I'm really worried about you!"

"I know. I am too, but there's nothing I can do, Erica. I can't go to the police. I have no proof. I just have to let it play out."

"Come home, Cora. Please," Erica begged.

"You know I can't do that."

"Why not?"

"I have to keep at this for a while longer. I know I probably sound irrational, but I'm not ready to leave Egypt yet, and if the Andersons are involved and they did kill my family, I have to try and get some justice."

"But you could be risking your life, Cora. Maybe this sounds selfish but you're my best friend. I don't want to lose you! Come home and tell the police here everything, let them handle it."

"You won't lose me, I promise. Please understand, Erica, I have to see this through, whatever *this* turns out to be. I just can't leave now."

Erica sighed. "Alright, but if anything happens to you I will personally hunt this Sam person down and make him pay!"

For the first time since getting on the phone, Cora laughed. She knew Erica was worried, more than worried. She had heard the fear in hear voice. If the roles were reversed, she would feel the same.

"I'll check in regularly. Don't worry, I'll be fine."

"You'd better be. Please call me or text me every day so I know you're okay."

Cora laughed. "I will. Speak soon." As she hung up, a knock at the door startled her. She made her way across the room and peered through the spyhole, before flinging the door open, grinning widely.

"Good morning, Professor Foster," she purred with a cheeky twinkle in her eyes.

Nick grinned and kicked the door closed behind him as he propelled her towards the bathroom.

"You've exactly ten minutes to shower, change and meet us downstairs."

"Why? What's going on?"

"We've been given special permission to look at a royal tomb, and you're invited, too. So get in there and get yourself ready," he laughed.

"Are you sure you don't want to join me?" she teased, gently fingering the buttons on his shirt.

He groaned. "As much as I would love to, we haven't time, but keep that idea in your mind. I'm definitely taking you up on it later." He kissed her passionately before exiting the room, leaving her leaning breathlessly against the bathroom door frame.

~

Fifteen minutes later Cora joined the team, freshly showered and dressed and was seated in the front passenger seat of the van. She chatted with the others as they sped through the streets of Luxor towards Luxor Bridge. Sam had been invited, and Cora did her best to be as polite and friendly to him as she could. But things had changed. She no longer trusted him. He was no longer her friend and she didn't like being around him.

It wasn't long before they were in the Valley of the Queens. After piling out of the vehicle, Nick stepped forward to greet an official from the Supreme Council of Antiquities. Cora smiled to herself. It would seem that Sam Anderson wasn't the only one with friends in high places. Nick then gathered them together to announce that they'd been given special permission to enter Queen Nefertari's tomb, but there were ground rules. No photography and no touching any walls. The tomb was extremely fragile. Alex and Lucy squealed in delight and David stepped forward to thank the SCA representative.

Excitedly, they all stood and watched as the official unlocked the gate and allowed them to step inside the ancient monument. First through the door was Nick, closely followed by Sam and David, with the three women at the rear.

It wasn't long before they had made their way down the steps into the modern vault-like entrance, passing under a lintel painted with the winged goddess Maat. She sat serenely, arms outstretched, spreading her beautiful feathered wings across the entire door span. The team found themselves in the square, decorated antechamber. From this point, they all went their separate ways, gazing in wonder at the white walls, decorated with countless brightly-coloured depictions of the famous queen, hieroglyphs, gods, and other ancient deities. In places, the tomb was badly damaged with chunks of painted relief missing, lost forever to inclement conditions. The SCA representative explained that the tomb had been carved out of poor quality limestone, causing rain to seep through cracks. The liquid caused salts to grow and crystalize behind the layers of painted plaster, pushing them outwards, eventually making them fall. It was sad to see such damage, but it didn't detract from the tomb's startling beauty.

In the main burial chamber, large pillars broke up the space. Each one was decorated with portraits of the queen, as well as Isis, Horus and Anubis. Cora was captivated; it was the best tomb she'd seen. So much detail and colour had gone into the preparation and finishing of the tomb. Nefertari must have truly been loved and adored by her people.

"What do you think?" Nick whispered softly into her ear, so quietly she could barely hear him. Glancing around, she saw that everyone was lost in their own world, lost with their own thoughts, so she pulled him behind the pillar for a stolen kiss.

"I can barely...Nick, it's...I'm speechless."

"Amazing, isn't it."

She nodded in return, completely dumbfounded by the beauty of the hidden room. Sam stepped behind the pillar, breaking the moment, and placed his hand on Cora's arm. She jumped, and momentarily flinched at Sam's touch. She caught the look of confusion on his face, and Cora remembered her promise to herself.

"Hey, Sam. You made me jump! It must be something about these old dark tombs," she said.

"Sorry, I didn't mean to frighten you. I've seen something you will just love, Cora. Come with me." Too quickly for her to protest, he dragged her off to the other side of the tomb. Feeling helpless, all she could do was go with him. Taking a quick backward glance at Nick, she saw him shoot her a protective look, as if to say, *"It's okay. I'm here if you need me. Just shout."*

"Look at this. It's a seated Anubis, portrayed as a jackal. I know how much you love Anubis. This one's really interesting. He has a flagellum. That's the gold coloured whip by his rear flank, and he has a red band around his neck too. I don't think I've ever seen one like this before."

She listened as best she could and, in a way, he was right. Anubis had been her favourite and it was a truly stunning depiction. But a slow realisation had hit her. Sam was like Anubis, an evil jackal, holding all of the cards, dealing out everyone's fate. He was admired by so many and yet he could never truly be trusted. Like Anubis, Sam dealt in death and already had too much blood on his hands.

"It's great, Sam. Thanks for showing me." She didn't know what else to say. She was so confused. Why was he still being so nice to her? Had she got it all wrong?

"Is everything alright, Cora?" he asked. "You've been awfully quiet these last few days."

"Yes. I'm fine. Just a bit tired is all. I haven't been sleeping well. The diary has made me think about my family and I've been missing them."

"You don't have to keep it all to yourself. You have a friend in me if you need one." Sam leaned in to hug her. Inwardly she flinched, as though his very touch had burned her. Awkwardly she tried her best to hug him back. Eventually he released her and walked away to study the opposite wall, leaving Cora to stare in disgust at the ever-present jackal.

All too soon, their tour of the tomb was over. In the glare of bright sunshine, the team climbed back into the van whilst Nick said his goodbyes to the SCA official, thanking him for his time. Minutes later, he was back in the vehicle and they made the short journey to the dig site. The van came to a stop in a cloud of dust.

"Right, then. Back to work everyone," Nick said as he locked the vehicle and turned to make his way to his trench.

Cora stood, perplexed, not quite sure what to do next.

"Don't just stand there, Cora. You're working today, too. I'm putting you with Alex and Lucy, unless you have anything better to do that is?" Nick asked, grinning.

Cora smiled widely, "No, nothing!" She ran over to the awning and settled herself next to the girls, following their instructions for the task in hand. Glancing up, she caught Nick's eye and the twinkle in it as he winked at her. Her heart somersaulted instantly and she realised there and then that she was as much in love with him as he was with her. When had it happened, she wondered? She had no idea, but she had fallen deeply. It wasn't so long ago that her life had been so bleak, loveless and empty. It only seemed like yesterday, when she'd been sitting huddled in a blanket at the manor in Scotland, watching the rain fall, suffering from heartbreaking grief and loss. Now she had discovered an entire family history stretching back generations, a new country that she could call home and a man who wanted to support and encourage her, who would love her for who she was and who, she hoped, would never let her down.

Pulled from her thoughts, she turned her attention to Alex and Lucy. It was time to stop daydreaming and help with the cataloguing.

CHAPTER THIRTY

Luxor, Egypt, 2002

It was that magical time of day in Egypt when the sun began its fiery descent behind the hills in a blaze of riotous colour, paving the way for the stars and moon. Cora sat on the balcony enjoying the spectacle. The safe was open and the box and its precious contents were spread across the bed. In her lap lay Emma's diary. She re-read a few lines leading up to where she'd left off, before continuing.

<u>London, England, 1946</u>
I have been spending time with Francis and Henry Anderson. I like them a lot, they are nice people, and I am learning so much about this

beautiful Museum that I work in. I am lucky to have my job and I am very settled.

I have my own home and a life. Things are so much better for women now. The war and the suffragettes saw to that. I have come so far from where I started, so much so that sometimes I wake and wonder if it is all a dream?

I met with Henry again the other day. He is such a nice man, I think he likes me, but he is not someone I wish to court. He stares at me sometimes with a look that I cannot understand. It is almost a fleeting glance of hatred, fear, the unknown, and it worries me. Maybe he fears that his father will be cross for us meeting without his father chaperoning? I just don't know.

My favourite place in the museum is the Egyptian gallery. There are large statues that tower over the heads of the visitors, of long dead Kings and strange gods. I never imagined there was more than one god, not that I believe in religion, but the Egyptians had gods in the shapes of animals as well as humans! Henry told me that Egypt is a complex land and the Ancients had a civilization that went back for thousands of years. Much of what they built still stands and is being re-discovered to this day. He has learned so much from his father and hopes to visit it one day.

I think I would like it in Egypt, I would walk around the old sites that Henry describes to me, and I would pretend to be an Ancient Queen. Yes I would like that very much.

London, England, 1946

I am so excited! I have met a gentleman, and he is so handsome. He came to the Museum to talk about donating some finds he had inherited from his family. Some Scottish coins and other interesting historical artefacts. I watched him as he waited to see the curator, his handsome profile, looking strong and manly. He was dressed in a fine suit and had travelled all the way from Edinburgh to meet with friends and called by during a spare hour.

I talked to him about the Museum and my job and he was very friendly, and on his way out, he left me his card telling me he would be honoured if I'd go to dinner with him. His name is Robert Hillingdon, Esquire. I liked the name, but as much as I wanted to accept his offer, I just couldn't. It wasn't appropriate. He was persistent, however, and I was surprised to return from my tea break to a formal invitation from Mr. Hillingdon, Esq., inviting me to dinner at the Savoy that evening. My fellow secretaries said it would be rude not to accept, so after much consternation I did the polite thing. I accepted.

I had never been to such an expensive restaurant before, and two of my work colleagues helped me with suitable clothes and make-up. I felt foolish getting all dressed up for a man. But it was worth it. He was everything I remembered from our fleeting meeting, and he treated me like a Princess. I have never eaten such fancy food before and as I sat amongst the fur and jewel covered diners I couldn't believe my luck. Robert was a complete gentleman, and kissed my hand as he bade me a good evening, with promises of taking me to dinner again soon.

~

It has been a few weeks since I last saw Robert. He had to return to Scotland but has kept in touch with me, sending me letters of affection and the occasional bouquet of flowers. He even sent me a brooch which I wear on my coat. I think I may be in love!

My fellow secretaries are over the moon for me, they are living my life with me, and are convinced that I will one day marry him and become Mrs. Robert Hillingdon. I dare not even begin to dream. Life can be taken so quickly. I must live in the moment.

<u>London, England, 1946</u>
Robert has returned to London a few times now and it has been four months since I officially began courting him. He makes me laugh so much and has the funniest stories to tell. I long to see Scotland and the great house he lives in called Craigloch Manor, it sounds so very grand. All my friends are so happy for me, and are predicting wedding bells soon. I am not so sure. Why would such a grand man like him be interested in me? I am nothing and I came from nothing.

I saw Henry Anderson today and he ignored me. I wonder what I have done to upset him so? Francis also blanked me the other day too. I miss their friendship and wonder why they have become distant with me? I think Francis may have heard about Robert and I. I think he secretly hoped Henry and I would marry, but Henry is just a friend and I just do not see him in that way. I am giving them the space they need to get past their hurt and anger, in the hopes that one day we can all resume our friendship. I do miss them so.

London, England, 1947

Robert has proposed! I can barely contain myself! I am to become Mrs. Robert Hillingdon! I am to leave my job and move to Scotland to live at Craigloch Manor with him and will finally become his wife, friend and confidante. Secretly I dared to dream and that dream came true. Maybe luck can change after all? I will miss my job at the Museum and the hustle and bustle of London, but I love Robert more, and am looking forward to my new life in Scotland.

The weeks have become a whirl of dress fittings and wedding preparations, and I am due to travel to Scotland for the ceremony tomorrow. My meagre belongings are packed and I have said farewell to my friends and work colleagues, taking one last walk around my beloved Museum. I tried to see Francis and Henry but they refused to talk with me, both were angry and distant. I don't know why they are being like this, and it upsets me. I wished with all my heart that they could have supported me, but it wasn't to be.

CHRISSIE PARKER

<u>Craigloch, Scotland, 1947</u>

Yesterday I was plain old Emma Sanders, today I am Mrs. Emma Hillingdon! My wedding was so very beautiful. Garlands of flowers hung throughout the church and my dress flowed clean and white behind me as I walked the long aisle. So many people were there and I knew barely anyone in the sea of faces. Robert wore the smartest suit I have ever seen and he looked so handsome.

After both saying 'I do', we celebrated with his family and friends, before climbing the sweeping staircase to the bedroom. I have never been with a man before, but he was gentle and tender and everything I hoped it would be. The love in his eyes was all I needed to see, to know that he was the man for me.

I love him more than words can describe and I am so glad that we found each other.

<u>Craigloch, Scotland, 1948</u>

Married life with Robert has been wonderful and the last year has been the best time of my life. I wish I had more time to write everything down, but life needs so much attention, that I just do not have the time. I adore the Manor and the beauty of the countryside that surrounds it. There is always something happening and I truly am Lady of the Manor. I assist Robert with his work dealings and play hostess to his dinner parties. I still miss my friends in London and my job at the Museum, but the longing has begun to subside a little. My days are too full of my new life to worry about what has been lost, and now that I am expecting a child, my life will be fuller and richer. I want my child to have everything, parents who love her, a life where they do not have to want for anything. Good things can happen to good people and I am proof of that and my child will get the best start possible in life.

<u>*Craigloch, Scotland, 1949*</u>
Our baby girl was born healthy and happy and we have named her Elizabeth. I like to call her Lizzie, but Robert prefers her full name, he is funny like that. She is beautiful and has my dark eyes and hair and is so very loved. I will always call her Lizzie when her father is not around. She is so very precious to me and I love her more than life itself.

Cora smiled to herself, placing the diary in her lap, as she gazed at the night sky. Elizabeth. Her mum. Cora knew very little about her mum. She had always been so guarded about her past. Whenever Cora had tried asking her dad, he had told her they loved her and that was all Cora had needed to know. Now she knew why. Cora's mum had wanted her and Alastair to have a life free from the curse of the past. Free from pain, anguish and suffering. Cora now understood, but wished her mum had confided in her. She would rather have heard it from her, than learnt about it now, when she was alone still mourning their loss. Cora remonstrated with herself. She had to stop thinking like that. She was no longer alone. She had a best friend in Erica, and now she had Nick too.

Turning back to the diary, excitement grew. She may now be able to finally learn something about her mum from her grandmother's diary. The hour was getting late, but she couldn't stop. She had to press on.

Lizzie has begun to crawl and tried to stand the other day, it was such a lovely sight to see. She is a happy child and is always laughing and smiling. Robert loves her dearly and he tells me every day that Lizzie and I are his world. I am going give her all the things I never had in life, she will be happy and healthy and bring joy to us all our lives.

<u>*Craigloch, Scotland, 1950*</u>
I am upset. More than upset, I am completely distraught. Robert had gone to London for a week and I was alone at the Manor with Lizzie. Yesterday the front door bell rang and on the step stood Francis and Henry. It was a shock as I had not heard from them in such a long time, so long in fact that I never expected to see them again. The staff were out on half day and I was alone in the house, but I knew them, they were friends, so I let them in. Seated in the drawing room, it was uncomfortable, as both seemed reluctant to talk. I was confused as to why they had come to see me. But eventually they spoke. They demanded I give them everything I had relating to Randa and my family. They said it was of historical importance for the Museum, but

something about their demeanor made me wary, so I lied to them. I told them I didn't know what they were talking about.

They said I was lying, but I persisted telling them that I really didn't know.

Suddenly Francis sprang like a gazelle from across the room, his hands encompassing my throat leaving me gasping for breath. I kicked out with my legs, but Henry grabbed them holding me down. I was unable to move, their grip too strong, too powerful. I couldn't scream, I couldn't even speak. I felt Francis's breath on my neck as he called me a liar. He told me I was nothing but a whore like my mother.

Tears fell from my eyes as he ranted and raved about how my mother had made the mistake of lying to him and how she had paid for it. How he had held her down giving her one last chance to obey him and when she had refused he had used his hands to crush her throat, before tossing her lifeless body into the Thames. As his grip about my throat tightened, I saw stars and began to feel weak and breathless. I tried to claw and scratch at his hands to pry them from my throat, but his grip was too strong. I could feel myself getting more lightheaded as he continued to squeeze. I reached the point of unconsciousness, and was left with nothing but images of my beloved baby and husband passing before my eyes, knowing the end was near. It was then through the haze that I heard a terrific crash and muffled voices. As suddenly as he had grabbed me the grip released.

Through gasping, gulping breaths and falling tears, I saw Harold the gardener holding Francis in a vice-like grip. Edward the gamekeeper, shotgun aimed high, was bellowing for them to back away from me. With fear and anger written across their faces the Anderson's hurriedly turned and ran.

Harold and Edward were kind and phoned the doctor to make sure I wasn't hurt and they stayed with me until the housekeeper returned, and she sat with me until Robert was able to get home.

I couldn't tell Robert the truth and for the first and only time in my life I lied to him. I told him the men were thieves looking for jewels. My only saving grace was that Lizzie was unharmed. I felt so guilty and wondered why I just didn't tell him. I had thought Francis and Henry were my friends but it turned out Francis was nothing more than a murderer. He killed my mother. So why was I protecting him? Why had I begged the staff not to call the police? I still have no idea, but the guilt of what I had done ate me up from the inside out. Guilt that I would end up having to live with forever.

<u>*London, England, 1950*</u>

Robert is going to London, and I have decided to go with him, the fear of what had happened has lingered and he refused to let Lizzie and I remain in the Manor on our own. I am looking forward to getting away and seeing old friends, and also looking forward to going to the Savoy for dinner. I will leave Lizzie with the nanny for the evening. It will be nice for Robert and I to re-visit the place where we first courted.

Cora turned the page. It was blank. As was the next page and the next.

There was nothing more in the diary. A familiar feeling of fear and dread gripped her stomach. What had happened that had stopped her grandmother from writing? She hoped she hadn't suffered a similar fate to *her* mum. To be sure she flicked through the book again but there were no further entries. Moving from the chair, she returned Emma's diary to the box before taking out her mum's. She paused a moment before opening to the first page. She was greeted with her mum's familiar scrawl and a thousand memories flooded over her the instant she began to read.

CHAPTER THIRTY-ONE

Craigloch, Scotland, 1970

My name is Lizzie (Elizabeth) Hillingdon and it is my twenty-first birthday. My dear father, whom I love so much, is dying. The cancer has taken hold of him and he no longer has strength to fight it. It's such a sad time.

Today, he gave me a small wooden trunk, which was full of strange items and diaries I'd never seen before. He told me it was time to learn about my family and where I came from, he said he'd thought long and hard and knew that what I learned may upset me greatly, but sometimes life is hard and the truth hurts.

I left my father to sleep, with his nurse by his side, and returned to my room to open the trunk and read what I could. My father was right, it did upset me. All I could do was flee to his bedside to hold his frail body in my arms, but the hurt wasn't over. He had one last thing to tell me. Hunched over his bed I listened, allowing my tears to stain my face and the bedclothes as I learned of my mother's final days, and why I never knew her growing up.

~

I was barely two years old and whilst we were on a trip to London, my parents had left me in the care of my nanny so that father could take mother for dinner at the restaurant where they'd had their first date. They'd had a wonderful evening and it was here that my mother announced she was due to have another baby! Father said they were so happy and she really was the love of his life. They left the restaurant and walked down towards the river, to enjoy a moonlit walk. Suddenly without warning, the evening ended in chaos and tragedy. Two men had appeared, one held a knife to my mother's neck, the other held my father, pinning his arms to stop him from helping. My father told me of my mother's shock at finding Henry, an old colleague from the British Museum, threatening her so violently. Father said the incident was a confusing nightmare. My parents had been out walking enjoying the night air, as they turned a corner there was Henry, with another man. A little surprised, mother had introduced father to Henry but he had turned on her. He screamed at them insisting my mother hand over 'Randa's' things. My father had been confused, he had never known a Randa, and thought the men must have mistaken them for someone else and he desperately tried calling for help but no one came. Henry had screamed at my mother calling her a whore demanding she give up what was rightfully theirs but she stoically refused.

My father watched on helpless as Henry grabbed my mother and slit her throat leaving her to bleed out on the pavement, the other man turned and stabbed my father before they both ran away. My father dragged himself over to my mother, pulling her into his arms and cried a thousand tears as his beloved wife and unborn child died in his arms.

I couldn't take it all in. My mother had been ruthlessly murdered, and despite much searching her killers had never been caught.

~

My father died not long after telling me. I think waiting to tell me the truth was the only thing that had kept him alive. His breath ebbed away as I held his hand, cradling him as best as I could in my own arms telling him that I loved him and he wasn't to blame.

I could never have blamed him. He was my father. He meant the world to me and I loved him so very much.

CHRISSIE PARKER

<u>Craigloch, Scotland, 1970</u>

This last six months, after the death of my father, have been the hardest of my life. I have wanted to live a happy life like he begged of me, but the past has plagued me. What I learned about my mother and read in the other diaries have scared me and I have felt like I have been pulled into something that will haunt me and my family for the rest of our days.

This morning when I awoke, I sat and looked at the photos on the mantelpiece in the living room, and I knew then that I was the only one that could make a change. Maybe if I did things differently I could break the cycle and stop the past from returning and threatening me? So I'm putting a stop to it all. The old artefacts and diary of my great grandmother have been resigned to a locked trunk in Craigloch's attic, a reminder that she is always with me, even though I can't read what she wrote. Randa was the first and it all started with her, she will watch over me and protect me. The rest of the diaries along with the letters I also cannot read, will be locked in a safety deposit box that only I and my solicitor will know about. It is best to split them up, then they will never be whole and hopefully the curse that has lain on our family for decades will be broken.

No one will ever learn of the hurt and destruction that has befallen my family, and I don't even want to know why it happened. All I know is, I will never tell my children about it, and no one with the name of Anderson will ever become part of my life. I will make damn sure of that. I will live my days out in the comfort and safety of Craigloch Manor for that is where I truly belong. No one can ever touch me here.

The diary slipped through Cora's fingers and landed on the floor next to the chair. She had begun to cry upon learning of her grandmother's death. Her mum's strength had been incredible. She tried in vain to wipe the tears from her face, but they refused to stop falling, so she just let them. It broke her heart to hear that her grandmother had been murdered along with an uncle or aunt who had never been given the chance to be born, and that her grandfather had died of cancer despite surviving a stab wound inflicted by the Andersons.

Why had they wanted the diaries so desperately, why had they stooped to murder? It just didn't make sense. They could have just stolen them and no one would have been the wiser. She completely understood her mum's actions. She now knew that her mum felt she was protecting herself and her family, but it seemed that the Andersons were determined, a determination that had spanned generations, and they would stop at nothing.

It had come back to them again. The Andersons. Had her parents and Alastair suffered at their hands, too? They seemed to have a vile history of violence and murder. Did Sam have that same streak? She shuddered at the thought, and pushed it away unable to deal with it.

A knock at the door disturbed her train of thought. She looked at the clock. It was almost midnight. Who could it possibly be at this time of night? The fear contained within the diary's pages still gripped her, and it wafted about the room. She stayed put on the balcony, silhouetted in weak light emanating from the outside light, content with the darkness that had wrapped itself around her like a comforting blanket. Whoever it was would give up and leave soon. All she had to do was stay quiet. The knock became more insistent and a voice shouted her name. Nick? Standing, she put the diary on the chair and ran to the door. She peered through the spyhole, and her heart leapt as she saw a slightly disheveled version of her man standing on the other side. Flinging open the door, she threw herself into his arms, clinging on for dear life. After walking into the room, Nick kicked the door closed, then pulled back from her momentarily to stare at her tear stained face.

"Hey, what's up?"

Cora recounted everything to him as she gathered up all the family heirlooms and securely locked them in the safe. Once done, she took a seat on the bed next to him.

"It's all such a bloody mess, Nick. From the minute Randa met Albert, my entire family has been stalked and wiped out by the Anderson family. It scares the hell out of me. It looks like the Andersons killed every single one of them and I'm next. I think Sam is after me. He wants the diaries and maps. He wants the treasure. He's going to kill me, Nick!"

She curled up on the bed and sobbed, tears staining the cover. Nick put his arms around her and held her tightly, letting her cry and soothing her until, finally, she ceased. She turned to face him and lay there allowing him to gently wipe her tears. Stray hairs had fallen forward across her face, and Nick gently tucked them behind her ears.

"I promise, Cora, I will not let him hurt you. I love you too much to lose you." Leaning forward, he brushed his lips to hers and she surrendered to his kiss; passionate, loving and caring. Moments later, hands fumbled and met with naked skin as clothing fell, or was thrown, to the floor, both surrendering to the passion and love they so desperately needed.

~

Cora sat on the lounger by the pool, deep in thought. Her knees were pulled up to her chest, and she was nervously chewing her thumbnail. Nick had left early that morning to go to the site. Staring out across the Nile at the view she adored so much, her mind wandered. Recent events had unsettled her greatly. She had learned some distressing things about her family, and it made her question everything about her life, and left her feeling terrified.

Her journey was nearing its end and she had begun spending her money like water. She knew she should start thinking about going home soon. Now that she had discovered all there was to know about the diaries, it was almost time to move on. It was time to start living her life, a life that took her away from her past and steered her towards a bright new future.

But would Sam stay in the past and let her move on?

Leaving Egypt would be incredibly difficult. She had fallen in love with the country — the sights, the colours, the sounds and the culture — and leaving it would be the hardest thing she ever had to do.

And then there was Nick.

She had only just met him, but she knew that knew she loved him, and he said he loved her too, but would they survive the distance and time apart? Distance and separation had been the death knell of his marriage to Anna. What made her relationship with him any different? They had only just begun to know each other, and so much could go wrong.

It was not a decision to make lightly, but it was one she had to face.

~

As she stepped from the shower that evening, Cora heard a knock at the door. As was her habit, she peered through the spy hole, even though she already knew it would be Nick. She grinned as she opened the door, pulling him to her and kissing him, before closing the door.

"Good evening, Professor," she said, running her fingers through his hair. "I'm glad you came to see me."

"I thought you might like dinner, but I see you're very unsuitably dressed. I don't think short towels are acceptable in the restaurant," he laughed.

"Well if you give me two minutes, I'll change." She scooted under his arm and pulled on her clothes whilst he took a seat on the bed. She was just brushing her hair and wrapping a shawl around her shoulders, when there was a knock at her door.

"Expecting someone?" Nick raised an eyebrow.

"No. It's probably just hotel staff. I rang earlier for some extra towels." Forgetting to look through the spy hole, she threw open the door to be greeted by Sam and another man, who was older and yet not unlike him. Before Cora could speak, they had barged their way into the room and slammed the door behind them. Each man held a gun, the elders trained on Nick, Sam's on Cora. Nick went to stand, but Sam spoke quickly.

"I wouldn't if I were you, Nick." He glared at Cora and shook his head. "I have no idea what you see in this one, Cora. I assume you *are* sleeping together? A shame really as I was hoping for that honour myself. Win some, lose some I guess."

"Enough, Samuel!" barked the man at his side. "We have come for Randa's things and the rest of the diaries that were sent to you from England. This has gone on long enough."

"I assume you're an Anderson. Sam's father, judging from the attitude and looks," Cora said with bravado she didn't feel. Inside she was shaking like a leaf. History was repeating itself once again and, like her ancestors, she was completely helpless.

"You guessed right," he grinned slyly. "The name is Andrew. I need no introduction to who *you* are. The family resemblance is uncanny. I would say it's nice to meet you, but there's nothing nice about your family. You're all liars and thieves, and like your mother and grandmothers before you, you're a nothing more than a whore."

"Don't talk to her like that!" Nick rose and took a step towards him.

"Or what, Foster? What exactly will *you* do?"

Nick shook his head, "You're a phony, Andrew. You're nothing more than a failed Egyptologist who rides off the back of the discoveries of others and takes the glory for himself. Everyone knows you're nothing more than a black-market thief!"

"Sit down, Foster, before I put a hole in your head!" he yelled.

Nick did as he was told. He knew it was a futile situation, two armed men against the two of them. They were defenseless. The menacing gleam in Andrew's eye told Nick everything he needed to know. Neither man would hesitate to kill them. They were just looking for an excuse. The situation was grave indeed. Maybe Cora should just give in and let them have the diaries?

"Randa's stuff, Cora, and whatever else was in that safety deposit box," Sam growled menacingly. "Now!"

"How did you know about them?" Cora shook her head. Were the Andersons really that devious that they'd had people watching her every move? She refused to give in. "The answer is no, Sam. They don't belong to you. What happened in the past is the past. They are not yours to take." Her response was defiant.

Stepping forward, Sam grabbed her by the throat, pressing cold steel to her face. His icy, vengeful eyes bored into hers, filling her with grief, pain and the fear of death.

"All it would take is one tiny squeeze of the trigger and you'd die, Cora," Sam whispered, menacingly. "I'd hate to spoil that pretty little face of yours."

"You don't have the guts," she choked, barely able to breathe, her bravado evaporating.

"Haven't I? I wonder if you'd like to really know how your family died?" He was smiling like one possessed, and kept stroking her face with the length of moulded steel. "You see, your parents wouldn't give up the information either. I did feel sorry for your Father and brother. They just happened to be in the wrong place at the wrong time. A bit like you, Foster." Sam glanced at his boss, and was pleased to see the fear that had gripped his face.

He turned his gaze back to Cora and those eyes, those beautiful eyes. "Now, your mother, well she was a fighter, it must run in the family. Father and I made your parents watch as we tortured your baby brother. Ah the pain we inflicted on him, but would she give us what we wanted? No. She refused, so I squeezed his throat and watched as life slowly left him, poor Alastair. I hoped your mother would crack, but she just sat in silence, like the heartless bitch that she was. So we moved on to dear old daddy. She had every opportunity to give us what we wanted but she refused again and again, so I snapped daddy's neck like a twig, right in front of your mother, but did she shed a tear? No. She just continued to sit there. The callous whore just allowed it to happen!" Sam bellowed, like a madman, unleashing a tornado of wrath into the room.

Sam's wild and crazy eyes burned into Cora's. He tightened the grip on her throat a little and she began to see stars. Trying her best not to panic, she calmed her breathing. She would not die like this! Not at his hands! This time it would end differently. She had to think that way, she couldn't just give up.

"Your mother killed them both, Cora, and still she refused to give us what we wanted! I had no choice. She'd witnessed the deaths of your brother and father and still she refused. In the end we knew we still had you, and we've been tracking you for a long time. We had spies everywhere, sometimes where you least expected them. Kindly old men who helped you at a railway stations, an ex-fiancé who was so willing to marry you for a slice of the money, colleagues at the British and Egyptian museums who would do anything for a bit of extra cash," Sam sneered. "So in the end it didn't matter that your mother refused to talk, we still had you, so I put her out of her misery. I strangled your mother with my own hands, just like this." His grip momentarily tightened again, and Cora felt the dizziness wash over her. For a moment everything blurred, and she thought the end was coming. If she did have to die out here, like this, tonight, she hoped he would just make it quick. She couldn't stand the horror of what happened in the past and the evil taunts any longer.

"I hate her for that. She made me do it. Her lifeless eyes are the last thing I see at night before I sleep. She never leaves me and I hate the fucking bitch for it." Completely spent, Sam threw Cora roughly to the ground and she lay there gasping huge lungs full of welcome air. She had survived this round, but knew that it wasn't over yet.

Nick bent down to check if Cora was okay. The situation had gotten completely out of hand and neither of them knew what to do. One false move and they would die. However hard they tried, they just couldn't see a way out.

"Cora. Just give them what they want. You've no choice. They're not worth dying over," he whispered.

Cora knew he was right. She didn't want to lose her life, too, but the diaries were all she had left of her family and its history. It took all the strength she had to relent. Indicating where they were, Cora watched as Sam stepped over to the wardrobe, demanding the code for the safe.

Once open, Sam removed the box, opened the lid and rummaged through it, before nodding at his father. "Four diaries, two letters and what looks like a map," he scanned the letters. "It's here, the location. We have it!"

Andrew Anderson smiled and nodded at his son.

"Well done, Son. Now bind their wrists. We can't risk leaving them here. We can use them to help us dig, before we kill them. You two do as we say and keep your mouths shut."

The pair realised with horror that the situation had just moved up a notch and they were about to become hostages. Nick watched helplessly as Sam used anything he could to tightly tie Cora's wrists together in front of her body, before doing the same to Nick. Andrew opened the door motioning to two men dressed in hotel uniforms, who wheeled large laundry carts into the room. Andrew watched as Nick and Cora were bundled inside, before they were covered with towels and bed sheets

Shaking with fear, Cora wept silently. Her neck hurt and she could still feel the imprint of Sam's fingers. She thought he was going to kill her there and then. At least the whole sorry mess would have been over with and she'd be with her family again. But then there was Nick. Stupidly she'd got Nick involved, and it looked like he was now going die, too. She loved him too much for that to happen, and she didn't want to lose anyone else she loved.

They were on the move. The swaying and jolting motion of the cart rattled her around as it traversed corridors and lifts, taking her farther and farther away from safety. Cora listened carefully, trying to work out what was happening, but there was nothing except for the veiled mumblings of her captors. Eventually she realised they were outside. The laundry was lifted and she was roughly pulled from the cart, where she found herself standing in front of open doors of a small truck. Before she could speak, she felt a sharp pain to the back of the head. Everything turned black and she lapsed into unconsciousness.

CHAPTER THIRTY-TWO

Southern Egypt, 2002

Cora finally came to. She was groggy and disoriented, and her head was pounding. She tried to move, but her neck was stiff and painful; her body battered and bruised. The bindings on her hands were too tight and were really painful; they had cut her skin, causing small trickles of blood to run down her arms staining her skin. She was lying on her side and could feel the swaying bumpy motion of being inside a moving vehicle. Fully opening her eyes, she blinked to adjust to the gloom that surrounded her. She could make out shadows but little more.

How long had she been there and where was she being taken?

Shuffling sounds to her right caught her attention and she tried to turn but couldn't. The shuffling increased and moments later she heard a whisper through the darkness.

"Cora? Are you there?"

"Nick?"

"Yes. Are you injured?"

"My neck hurts and I've a banging headache. The bindings on my wrists are really painful but other than that I think I'm alright."

"My head hurts, too. I think they knocked us out. My wrists hurt, but I can't get them undone, they're just too tight".

They lay in the darkness turning everything over in their minds. It was almost impossible to believe that Sam had done this to them. God only knew where they were heading and, to top it all, no one even knew they were missing. It was a terrifying situation to be in.

Cora had hoped the diaries would have been enough for the Andersons, but she knew it was more than that. It was about revenge. They didn't just want to find the artefacts. They wanted her. They wanted to toy with her, like a cat would an injured bird. They wanted her dead. They wanted her entire family dead and buried for all eternity and that scared the hell out of her.

Cora felt Nick move as he tried his best to sit up, but the jolting of the vehicle made it hard to do so. Their eyes were becoming more accustomed to the gloom now and they could finally make out the silhouette of each other.

"I'm so scared, Nick." She was trying hard not to cry. She'd had shed enough tears to last a lifetime. But the realisation was just too much to bear. Her mum's words ran through her head. Over and over again.

"It means that they have succeeded in killing me, too. I pray that you do not succumb to the same fate and are able to find a way through."

Well, she was suffering that same fate now, wasn't she. Sam was an Anderson. He had only become friends with her to get hold of the information left by Randa. Her fate would probably end up being the same as her mum's.

Death by Anderson.

Killed in revenge for the death of one of his ancestors a hundred years before.

How deranged were he and his family to have pursued this their entire lives? In a way it was quite sad. To let something that had happened so long ago rule your very existence.

Cora's curse was her family living in fear of being killed. Sam's was that he lived in fear of being forced to do the killing. She had seen that fear in the back of his eyes, as he had gripped her throat. It had been masked by pure pleasure and he had seemed to enjoy it. Yet the fear had remained and she hadn't missed that, so maybe there was hope for him?

What turmoil he must live in.

She almost felt sorry for him. But then she remembered.

He had killed her dad, mum, and brother. It made her sick to the stomach, and she would never forgive him for that.

She kicked out at the side of the vehicle in sheer anger and frustration. Kicked and kicked and kicked. Yelling, she heaved great gasping sobs of nothingness that echoed around the van, her anger and frustration spilling out in great waves.

"Cora! Don't. Please stop! I know you're angry and upset, but don't let them see it. It's what they want."

She stopped, as Nick's voice calmed her. The fury abated slightly, but only slightly. It still simmered beneath the surface ready to explode at any moment.

"I know you're right, Nick, but I'm angry. Angry at them for what they've done. Angry with their damn ancestors. Angry with myself for getting you involved. I just wish I could wind the clock back and change everything. But I can't!"

"You wouldn't be able to if you tried. Your families have always seemed destined to cross paths. They would always have come after you, Cora, and I'm glad it's here in Egypt with me rather than you being alone in England."

She knew he was right, but it didn't make her feel any better.

"What are we going to do, Nick?"

"I've no idea. No idea at all."

Sam studied the map. It wouldn't be much longer before they reached Aswan. He was angry that Nick had become involved. His suspicions had been right, though. There was definitely something going on between him and Cora. They looked far too close and comfortable. It meant he would now have to deal with Nick, too.

Sam glanced out into the blackness of Egypt. She'd changed the game, something Sam hadn't expected, and now she would be forced to help them.

Then she would die.

During the journey south, Sam had mulled over ways of killing her. He had already decided he would force Nick to watch. It would make it more fun and serve the bastard right for getting involved. His choices were numerous but his favourite was strangling her, finishing off what he'd started in the hotel room. He wanted a chance to stare into those beautiful eyes one last time, force her to look at him whilst he drained the last breath of life from her body.

Yes, he liked that.

Nick's death would be easy; he'd just shoot him and leave him for dead.

Looking over at his father, Sam sighed. It was a shame his own father didn't trust him enough to finish the job alone but, as with the generations before, nothing could be left to chance, and maybe he could kill his father at the same time?

Yes. Killing his father would be a nice end to it all.

~

The journey was long and uncomfortable. By the time they arrived at their destination, everyone was tired and irritable. With guns raised and ready to use if necessary, Sam and Andrew watched as their two henchmen dragged their captives from the vehicle, and bundled them into a small room in a nondescript house, and firmly locked the door.

Cora sat on the small bed, watching Nick as he paced back and forth.

She knew he was angry with himself for not being able to do anything to stop what had happened. It wasn't his fault though. There was nothing either could have done.

"Please sit down, Nick," she begged. She was exhausted and his pacing was getting to her. She wished she could get some sleep, but she was too frightened.

Rubbing his bound hands awkwardly against his forehead to alleviate an itch, he stopped and smiled weakly at her. He had taken a quick look around as they'd left the vehicle. Judging by the length of the journey, or at least the part where they were conscious, they were on the outskirts of Aswan.

"I'm sorry, Cora. I feel completely helpless. I should be able to do something and I can't. They're psychopaths. Whatever I say or do will only make them overreact and do something stupid. I promised to protect you and all I've done is get us kidnapped."

Cora rose, her legs leaden and unsteady. Stumbling towards him, she still felt groggy from her head wound. When she reached him, she leaned her head against his shoulder.

"It's not your fault. It's mine. It's me they want. But I'd rather have you here, Nick, than be on my own. I'm sorry if that sounds selfish but I love you so much. I'd rather die with you by my side than die alone."

Nick kissed the top of her head.

"I love you, too. We'll get through this somehow. We have to. I won't let them hurt you."

Nick stared over her head at the squalid room as they listened to the low murmur of voices the other side of the door.

Cora hoped he was right, but she wasn't so sure.

~

Sam and Andrew sat in the small main room of the rented house.

The contents of the box lay before them and they pawed through diaries, letters and maps looking for further clues, re-living Cora's family's misery. They already knew most of it, but it piqued their interest to see it told from her family's side and they relished every sordid detail.

Dawn had risen by the time they'd finished, and they had formulated a plan.

Sam flung open the bedroom door, finding Nick and Cora asleep on the bed, cuddled together. Storming over, he roughly shook them awake, using their wrist binds to drag them from bed. Sam motioned them from the room, and into the main living space.

Sam ordered them to sit, and then set about removing their wrist binds before placing bread, cheese and water in front of them. The same two henchmen from the night before stood by the door.

Nick and Cora ate ravenously.

"What do you want with us, Andrew?" Nick asked without looking at the younger Anderson.

"It's simple, Foster. We have most of the information we need to find the missing artefacts stolen by Cora's family. They're buried in the desert and we'll need to dig for them but, as you know, permission is needed for all excavations in Egypt. We don't have time for all that bureaucratic crap, but an eminent Egyptologist like you will be of great use in case we do run into any trouble. You're good with the authorities and locals. She'll come with us and help dig."

"And if I refuse?" Nick asked.

"Then I'll shoot you in the head and bury you in the desert and she'll be left to our mercy." Andrew gave an evil grin.

Despite being snubbed by the archaeologist, Sam was rather enjoying all of this. He was well aware that his father thought he was useless but this time, with Sam's help, they had come up trumps. It was true that his father had insisted on no deaths this time around; but death and destruction seemed to act like a drug with Sam, and he enjoyed it.

Eventually his father had relented and let Sam do things his own way, and he had to admit the thrill of watching Cora's family die had even begun to excite him. Maybe it was in the Anderson blood and they had no choice? Now he relished the thought of watching Cora and Nick die and couldn't wait for that time to arrive. Until then, there were more important things at stake and his concentration was needed to ensure that they found what they had been seeking for so long.

"Well?" Andrew said of Nick, pulling Sam back to the present.

" I guess I have no choice, but Cora goes everywhere I go. You are not to separate us," Nick replied adamantly.

"Agreed, but it's the only demand you get to make, Foster. Don't even think of trying to cause trouble or escape. There will be a gun trained on you at all times. One false move and you both die."

Nick nodded gratefully.

Cora sat in silence throughout the exchange, looking exhausted.

Sam stared at her, his face twisted, pure malevolence emanating from every pore. He had been so nice to her when they'd first met, and she had been classically duped. His face was now a mask, the smile faded and worn with an edge of desperate menace to it. His eyes were untrusting and filled with hatred. If they were left alone, he wouldn't hesitate to kill her, and Cora seemed to understand that perfectly well. Andrew stood and holstered his gun, hiding it under his jacket so it was handy but not visible. He motioned to Sam and his henchmen to do the same.

"Remember what I said," he warned his captives. "Come along, we've work to do."

Andrew grabbed hold of Nick's arm, propelling him out of the room. Sam followed suit with Cora. Moments later, the bright morning light washed over them, as Andrew unlocked a jeep parked alongside the house. There was no sign of the van that had transported them the night before. Andrew directed Cora to the front passenger seat, whilst instructing Nick to climb in the back with Sam. Both obeyed.

They set off traversing the roads of Aswan, to a happy, wealthy, deadly end.

~

It wasn't long before they reached the ferry crossing point. Andrew parked up and ordered everyone to leave the vehicle.

"We're taking the ferry from here. We're tourists heading to the tombs to sightsee. Sam, you take Nick and, Cora, you're with me. No heroics from either of you!"

Obediently, Cora and Nick did as they asked. They climbed onto the boat and sat next to each other. As she leaned back, Cora saw Andrew's hand slip under his jacket and then she felt the gun poking in her ribs. Sam mirrored his father's move. Escape seemed impossible. They'd be dead or seriously injured in seconds.

Cora glanced around the boat, but none of the other passengers seemed to notice, as they were all focused on other things. It wasn't long before the ferry had crossed the river and docked. After getting off the boat, they found themselves staring at a large mountainous expanse of arid desert. In the heat of the advancing day, the two hostages and their captors slowly climbed up to the ancient tombs that dotted the landscape. To any outsider, they looked just like any other tourists. Sam occasionally threatened Nick, digging him in the ribs with his gun, reminding him that he was in control. Andrew held Cora's hand ensuring she wasn't able to run.

Cora hated feeling the grasp of the elder Anderson. It made her nauseous to know that someone who had helped kill her family was holding her hand when she wanted nothing to do with him, but Nick just nodded, reassuring her that it was the right thing to do. Even if they had been given the chance to do so, neither would have bolted, for fear the other would suffer the consequences.

Upwards they climbed, the exertion taking its toll on Cora's and Nick's already tired and hungry bodies until, finally, they reached the top. Sam consulted the map and the letters, trying to make sense of Hakim's instructions. Staring out across the expanse of beige and brown dust, he realized the futility of the task ahead. How many times had archaeologists dug believing they were in the right area only to find nothing?

"This is a bloody waste of time!" Sam yelled angrily. "How the hell are we going to find anything? That bastard Hakim could have hidden it anywhere, and what if he lied and didn't hide it here at all?"

"Calm down, boy. Nothing is a waste of time. We're closer than any of our ancestors ever got. I know we are in the right place. I feel it. All we need to do is figure out the instructions. We then mark the area and come back at night and dig." Andrew was busy studying the map he'd snatched from his son. After a few minutes he spoke, but only to issue instructions.

"This way."

They all set off, following him across the baking sand, heading for a less busy area, where the landscape eventually fell away to nothing but endless flat desert. With habitation and the river behind them, it was quiet and the four were left to the elements; two frightened prisoners being led into the bleakness of the harsh Egyptian desert by their ruthless, unstable captors.

CHAPTER THIRTY-THREE

Luxor, Egypt, 2002

Cora and Nick sat on a rock, taking a welcome break. Both were in pain, terrified and exhausted. They slugged back some water and watched Andrew and Sam consulting the map and letter once again, whilst surveying the landscape before them. The sun beat down, overheating them, and they were beginning to feel the effects.

"They're not going to let us go once they find what they're looking for, are they?" Cora whispered nervously.

"Don't think like that. You have to try and stay positive. We'll get through this."

Cora looked up at him, that handsome face. Her clever, kind, gorgeous man. She knew he was trying to make her feel better, but she wasn't an idiot. She knew the situation was dire. She had no idea how they were going to get out of this alive.

"No need to shelter me from the truth, Nick. You know as well as I do that one false move and we're dead. Generations of my family have been cut down in their prime because of *them*. It never ends well. Someone *always* dies."

"You're strong, Cora. You have a kind and beautiful heart and it's why I love you. Now that I've found you, I refuse to lose you. Not to them. Not to anyone." He reached forward and briefly stroked her face. Just feeling his touch, and seeing the love radiating from his eyes, was enough to calm her. She had to be strong. He was right. They would get through this. As long as she was with Nick, nothing else mattered.

"I'm trying. I just hope you're right."

"If it helps, there is one person we can rely on. David. He'll have realised that Sam and I are missing from work today and will be looking for us," Nick said.

The thought gave Cora hope and she smiled at Nick.

"Thank you. I needed that."

"We know where to dig now." Andrew's voice made them jump. "Collect some rocks and follow Sam, we need to leave markers." He ordered Cora, she looked at Nick and he nodded in agreement. She did as she was told, collecting as many rocks as she could. Under Sam's direction, and keeping an eye on Nick, who was watching her every move, she piled them up as directed, so they were easy to spot amongst the sameness of the never-ending desert.

Once done she stood and used her trousers to wipe the excess sand from her hands.

Sam grabbed her roughly, steering her back to the others.

It was time to leave.

~

Back at the house, Nick and Cora were pushed roughly back into the bedroom, and given some food and water.

"You can't get out of this room. We're leaving your wrists untied this time, but you make one wrong move and we'll tie you up again," Andrew warned before slamming the door.

Grateful to have some freedom of movement, Nick and Cora agreed to behave and watched as the door was closed and locked. Cora sat on the bed and buried her head in her hands. Exhausted, hungry and feeling more than a little dehydrated, she was desperate for sleep. But she knew that even if she lay down, sleep would not come. Nick sat next to her, forcing her to drink and eat something. He then placed his arm around her shoulder, pulled her close and wrapped her in his arms.

Gently, he kissed the top of her head before resting his cheek on it.

"You need to get some rest. They'll be back by nightfall to drag us back to the desert to dig. Get some sleep."

Cora nodded, and closed her eyes, relaxing into his arms, breathing in his smell, happy just to be safe in his arms. As he gently rocked her, she felt her eyelids droop. Carefully, as if she were a fragile artefact, Nick laid her on the bed and threw a blanket over her, before joining her. Eventually her body and mind surrendered and she drifted off, with Nick lying wide awake on the bed next to her.

~

Andrew pushed open the door, allowing Sam to carry a tray of food into the bedroom. Nick sat up like a shot, and shook Cora awake. She opened her eyes and took in the room. Despite dozing off Cora hadn't slept much and was exhausted. She had known it wouldn't be long before their captors returned. She turned over and begged for sleep to come again, she was so tired.

Sam set the plates on the small wooden cabinet next to the bed, before ordering them to eat. The door slammed and Nick gently shook Cora again. She turned over and looked at him and smiled weakly. She wished they were in her comfortable hotel room in Luxor; instead they were prisoners in a filthy room somewhere in southern Egypt.

"They brought us food. You should eat something," Nick said as he handed her a plate, which was thankfully filled with more than just bread and cheese this time.

"Thank you. Did you sleep?" she asked, as she shoveled food faster than she could eat it.

"Slow down! You'll give yourself indigestion! Yes. I managed to sleep,"

She could tell he was lying but allowed him the small untruth.

"That's good. Do you think the others have realised we're missing?"

"If I know David, he'll have searched high and low for us by now and is calling the police as we speak. I wouldn't mention it to the Andersons, though. If they knew a rescue party was on its way, they'd kill us without hesitation and be damned with the consequences. We need to stay alive so that we *can* be rescued."

Cora just nodded. He looked so tired. Tired and frustrated. He was even more disheveled than normal and the stubble had begun to show on his face. She liked it, it suited him, and made him even more attractive, if that were possible. She never thought she would be able to love or trust another man again after what had happened with Damon, but Nick had changed all that. Even if they didn't make it out of this mess, she was glad she had met and fallen in love with him.

"What?" he asked with an unexpected smile

Placing the plate on the bed, she took his face in her hands and kissed him deeply. Eventually pulling back, she gazed into his eyes, eyes that would forever remind her of Egyptian sky.

"Whatever happens, I will always love you, Nick Foster."

Pulling her back to him, he kissed her passionately, urgently, desperately, to show her how he felt, but footsteps outside the door parted them, and they watched with fear and dread as it opened.

"It's time." Andrew turned, leaving the door open, and they stood and obediently followed him.

They repeated the journey, but this time it was dark. Bribing a local, they crossed the river with ease. On the other side, it was hard going and it took them over an hour to find the right place again. Out of the shadows, not far behind them, stepped four local Egyptian men, armed with shovels. Andrew barked instructions at them, ordering everyone to start digging.

Cora could see the horror on Nick's face as the ground was attacked with fervor, and random holes opened up quickly. The landscape became pockmarked, with no thought for what may lay beneath; with no regard for the fact that they may be destroying something remarkable that could be hidden. Nick's reluctance to dig showed, but a sharp jab in the ribs from Sam's gun forced him to put shovel to earth.

They dug for hours, only stopping for a short break two hours in to take on some much needed water. Nothing had been found, and the Anderson's impatience was showing. As every hour passed, they became more annoyed, shouting and cursing at those digging for not finding what they so desperately sought.

As dawn arrived, they still hadn't found what they were looking for and the holes had been refilled. Tired and aggravated, the Andersons paid the Egyptian workers. Accompanied by their henchmen they returned to the house with their hostages to get some food and rest.

CHAPTER THIRTY-FOUR

Aswan, Egypt, 2002

Cora and Nick were so exhausted they could barely eat, but knew they had to. They forced down the food as best they could, before falling onto the narrow bed to curl up in each other's arms. Cora slept but was plagued with vivid dreams that turned nightmarish. In one, Damon refused to let her go and forced her into marrying him at gunpoint whilst the Andersons looked on, leering and jeering. In another, her mum and grandmothers sought revenge slashing their way through the world, killing anyone called Anderson. In the last one, she sat in a dark room watching as Sam, his eyes wild and chaotic, tied Nick to a chair before holding a knife at Nick's throat, taunting her. She screamed herself awake as Sam slowly sliced the knife across Nick's skin, killing him in an instant.

Nick was jarred awake by her scream and he quickly wrapped his arms around her as she cried in anguish. She was clammy and shaking like a leaf. It was a long time before the images finally disappeared.

"It's okay," he whispered, wishing he could do something to help her, but they were trapped in a waking nightmare. There was no waking up and breathing easy this time. They were forced to live it, every second of every hour. Cora took comfort in his embrace, letting him rock her gently and she eventually closed her eyes, drifting back to sleep to rest easy for the remainder of the day.

~

Dusk had fallen and Cora's eyes fluttered open. Sam's face was inches from hers and spite radiated from it. Instinctively she grabbed for Nick. He was awake in an instant and pushed Sam away, giving him a cold dark stare. The younger Anderson backed off, muttering to himself.

The strain was starting to show.

Sam left them some food and backed out of the room, shutting and locking the door behind him. Cora sat up and rubbed her eyes.

"How much longer will they keep us here, Nick? I hate this. I had no idea it would all come to this and I'm so scared. Every time they come through that door, I think that's it. I think that will be the moment they'll kill me. Kill us. I don't have any fight left in me. I've lost track of the days. I'm desperate for a shower. I can't do this anymore!" She knew she was rambling, but she'd had enough of being kept prisoner, at someone else's mercy. She just wanted it all to be over. One way or the other, even if she was to go the way of her mum and grandmothers before her, then so be it, but she wanted it over with now.

"Don't give up on me, Cora. I'm sure David's on the case. He'll have half the country looking for us by now."

"Really?" She wasn't convinced.

"Really. Now eat. They'll work us hard again tonight, so you need as much food as possible to keep up your strength."

She knew he was right and ate as much she could before attempting to clean herself in the small bathroom. Her clothes were filthy and smelled of sweat. Sand from the desert was everywhere and, no matter how hard she tried, she couldn't get rid of it, and she had a tear in her trousers. Staring at herself in a small cracked mirror that was firmly stuck to the wall, she saw an extremely tanned face staring back. With her inherited eyes and hair colouring she could almost pass for a local. In that one fleeting moment, she saw the faces of Elizabeth, Emma, Florence and Randa all staring back at her. Strong, powerful women who had always fought in the face of adversity, even to their deaths, and she wasn't just a part of them, she was them.

It was time to stop being frightened. It was time to be brave. Gathering all the strength she could, she made herself a promise there and then. She would avenge her family. This time the Andersons would not succeed. They would suffer for everything that they and their family had done. She would see to it that Elizabeth, Emma, Florence and Randa were honoured for the brave women they were and if she, too, had to go down fighting, then she bloody well would.

It was her heritage and her heritage was too important.

As Nick opened the door, he caught Cora staring at herself in the mirror. Instead of fear there was a renewed determination and courage etched across her face, as though a mask she'd been wearing had fallen to reveal the real her. Seeing him behind her in the reflection, she turned and smiled. Taking him in her arms, she pulled him close and whispered in his ear.

"As long as you're with me, and love me, it will always be okay."

CHAPTER THIRTY-FIVE

Aswan, Egypt, 2002

The jeep trundled its way through the dark streets of Aswan. Andrew and Sam were growing desperate. Even though they had only been in the southern town for a few days, they had grown impatient. When his father had inherited the secret from his grandfather, Sam learned that Andrew had been brought alive. His father had told him that he'd been excited by the thrill of the chase and had been happy to watch the Thomas family, stepping in where necessary. But as he had gotten older, Andrew told Sam that it had become a burden. He wasn't a murderer like Sam's grandfather. Yes, he dealt in theft and other black market crime, but never murder.

Sam knew that Andrew now hated this burden and wanted it all to be over and Sam had been only too glad to take the mantle from his father. Sam knew his father would have been happy just to live out his days with the company of his mother, seeing through secret deals, handling stolen artefacts every now and again, but it was not to be.

This was his destiny and he had to finish what was started so long ago.

He just hoped for a swift end to all of the madness.

~

The locals were patiently waiting on the arid desert plain. Their tools lay on the ground, but they picked them up and readied themselves for work as soon as they saw Andrew, Sam, their henchmen and captives approaching. As they reached the locals, Cora caught glimmers of lightning in the distance, followed by a far off rumble of thunder. She hoped the storm would stay away, but the increasing humidity was a sure sign it was likely heading in their direction and would pass overhead in the next few hours.

Sam barked orders as he threw shovels at her and Nick. Reluctantly they lifted them, and began to dig where instructed. The humidity made it harder work than the previous night and Cora's muscles screamed with pain from the harsh physical punishment. She was feeling the effects of lack of sleep, the stress of being kidnapped and not enough food. All she wanted to do was throw the shovel on the ground, lie down and sleep. As the time dragged on, she became slower, and lifted less. The only thing that kept her going was knowing that if she gave up, Nick would stop work to help her and that would put him in danger, so she struggled on.

Three hours later, a shout arose, making them all stop. Andrew and Sam ran over to one of the diggers and stared into his pit. Nick and Cora, thankful for the break, dropped their tools and followed to see what the fuss was about.

Andrew shone a torch into the hole and yelped with surprise.

"I think we've found it!" He instructed everyone to train their torches on the area whilst two of the men widened the hole. Finally, at the bottom, they saw it. Some timber, similar to a crate lid. Feverishly, Andrew pushed the men away and took over flinging shovels of sand every which way, until finally the crate was uncovered.

Carefully, under instruction, the local workers lifted the old wooden storage crate from its resting place, and set it down on the desert floor. It was hastily pried open to reveal the contents.

Nick couldn't bear to look and turned away, unable to watch the wanton destruction, but Sam had other ideas. He was forced to assist, as the men grabbed what they wanted, throwing ancient relics to each other in whoops of delight.

"Enough!" Andrew bellowed. The men ceased, placing the items back where they had come from.

One by one, Andrew lifted them, passing them to Nick to identify. Under the increasing threat of the fast approaching storm, Nick sat on the sand and did his best to establish what they were. The artefacts were exquisite. A mixture of fine jewellery made from precious, ancient beads. Statues of Egyptian gods and other deities that were too priceless to even contemplate. A few gold items, from an unknown tomb burial, sparkled in the lightning that flashed across the heavens. With them were other lesser pieces of pottery and stele.

Everyone stared in awe at the incredible haul.

As Nick continued to examine the pieces, Cora crouched next to him.

"They want them to sell, don't they?" Cora whispered.

"Yes." Nick seemed rightly wary of the men overhearing, but continued anyway. "Some of these pieces are incredibly rare. If they sell them on the black market, they'll become very rich men."

Nick sat on the sand and watched the Andersons and their men whoop and holler some more, and he put his head in his hands. Cora could see how angry he was and it made her angry too. All they had wanted was their thirty pieces of silver. Was this what they had killed her family for? Ruined lives for? Kidnapped them for? It was sick.

The anger bubbled inside of her, on the verge of unleashing its wrath, just as the storm brewing above their head was threatening to do. Suddenly

Cora sprung like a panther and rushed at Sam, who was kissing a golden statue.

"You bastard! You selfish bloody bastard! You killed my mum for this?" Her hands were pummeling him, her nails scratching him, blindly lashing out. With every glancing blow, she wanted to inflict as much damage as possible, wanted to get revenge. She felt the hurt and pain for her family spilling out and enveloping them all.

Throwing the statue to the ground, Sam grabbed for her, but missed. They circled each other like two lions facing off over the last available hunk of meat. The storm that had warned of its arrival hours before was closer now and the lightning flashed wildly, hauntingly illuminating the desert. The thunder crashed, shaking the earth, threatening to send them all tumbling.

"Yes, I killed your fucking mother!" Sam screamed. "I enjoyed every moment of it, too, and now I'm going to kill you, you pathetic little bitch!" He pulled the gun from his pocket and pointed it at her, the tiny click of the safety catch barely audible amongst the cacophony of the storm.

Nick rushed forward, but two of the Egyptians were too quick and they grabbed him and held him back. He struggled in vain, reluctant to give in, but he had no choice. Their grip was too tight. He was forced to stand and watch as the woman he loved faced down certain death.

"I love you, Cora!" he yelled, so desperate to be heard above the din.

"I love you too, Nick!" she cried. Fleetingly she glanced at him, seeing him doing his best to struggle to help her, but unable to. She really did love him and, if she had to die here right now, at the hands of a psychopath, at least she'd go knowing she was loved by a man who would fight to the end for her.

"Shut up, you bitch!"

Cora felt her face smart and her brain rattle within her skull as Sam's hand met her face with full force.

"You shut up, too, Foster! You're nothing but a loser. You already lost one woman, and I'm going to make sure you lose another. You never did find out who was screwing that tart of a wife of yours, did you? Well, let me tell you. It was me! Me!" Sam screamed, his eyes wide and deranged. Momentarily he lost his focus, waving the gun at Nick. It was the chance Cora needed and she took it. Rushing Sam, she put the full weight of her body into the lunge and pushed him to the ground.

In the confusion, the gun went off, causing panic. Lightning illuminated the chaotic scene as the men scattered into the night, leaving captives and prisoners alone, uncertain.

A scream rose into the air. Andrew had stepped forward to help his son, but now lay on the sand, a pool of dark red liquid pouring from the bullet wound in his side, staining the ground. Sam blindly rushed to his father's side, and held him in his arms, not knowing what to do to help.

He pulled him closer, crying and rocking like a child.

Free from the grip of the men who had now disappeared, Nick rushed forward to lift Andrew's gun. He held it firmly on father and son. As Andrew breathed his last breath, Sam looked up at Cora and Nick. His mask fell and his face twisted with suffering.

"Tell my mother and sister that I love them."

Nick and Cora could only watch in shock as Sam turned his gun upon himself. The shot echoed in a brief lull between cracks of thunder and his lifeless body fell across Andrew's, as father and son's blood merged on the ground.

As the storm continued, gathering pace, Nick and Cora held each other tightly, thankful that the worst was now over, and that they were, by some miracle, still alive.

CHAPTER THIRTY-SIX

Aswan, Egypt, 2002

As the sun rose in Aswan, heralding a new day, Cora and Nick found themselves sitting in the police station going over everything that had happened. They had exhaustingly managed to find their way back to the ferry at the river Nile, then walked to the centre of Aswan and into the local police to report what had happened. In the police station Nick called David to let him know where they were and that they were okay.

The storm had blown itself out and the sun was now shining again. They were beyond worn-out, and wished they could go back to Luxor to shower and change and get some much-needed sleep. But the police had other ideas. Wary of their story, they made them go back out to the site and explain exactly what had happened. Statements were taken and they were kept waiting whilst stories, papers and identities were checked and verified.

Eventually the police accepted their version and they were allowed to leave.

On the way out, Cora was given a plastic bag. Opening it, she saw the box containing her family heirlooms. She never thought she'd see them again.

Smiling at the policeman, she gratefully thanked him in Arabic.

"Thank god you're okay! We've been worried sick!" David, Alex and Lucy had been pacing anxiously outside, waiting to see them, after getting the first available flight from Luxor. David shook Nick's hand and threw his arms around Cora.

"Let's get you somewhere where you can change. I hate to be rude but you two stink!"

Nick laughed. "It's good to see you, too!"

They climbed into the jeep and allowed David to drive them a short distance to a small hotel on the bank of the Nile.

"We took the liberty of borrowing a room so you could both change and shower and stay the night if you don't want to travel back today. The girls got you some fresh clothes, too."

Cora nodded her thanks. Gratefully, she took the clothes from Alex who smiled kindly. It had been a tense few days and all of the emotions

WIND ACROSS THE NILE

seemed to be overwhelming her at once, like an immense tidal wave, threatening to engulf her.

Silently, she stepped into the bathroom and locked the door behind her. Placing the clean clothes next to the sink, she stripped and put her old, soiled clothes straight into the bin. Stepping under the heat of the shower, the wave finally crashed, fully consuming her. She sank to the floor of the shower, sobbing her heart out, the pain and anguish of all that she had learned about her family and the final act of the Andersons just too much to cope with.

~

It was half an hour before she finally emerged from the shower, having cried herself out. She felt better for having been able to wash her hair and clean her teeth properly. She smiled at Nick as he passed her to take his turn. Once both were clean and dressed, they sat on the hotel terrace and ate a hearty meal with David, Alex and Lucy. Sam's behaviour had stunned them all, and none of them could find the right words to convey just how they felt. It all seemed so surreal.

David told them the artefacts had been collected by a Supreme Council of Antiquities official and were on their way to the Cairo Museum for cataloguing. They were all happy to know that they'd end up where they belonged, in a museum as part of a collection, ultimately belonging to the people of Egypt. The shocking news was learning that Andrew Anderson and his son had been on the Egyptian police's radar for a long time. They had been suspicious of their activities in the country and suspected them of looting and selling illegal artefacts. The Anderson name had been well and truly tarnished.

Later that night, as Nick and David talked work, the three women walked along the banks of the Nile, chatting.

"So what will you do now, Cora?" Alex asked.

"I'm going home. I can't stay here. Too much has happened."

"What about Nick!"

"What about Nick?" Cora repeated.

She'd been turning that very question over and over in her mind ever since the death of the Andersons. There was nothing else to keep her in Egypt. She'd done what she'd set out to do. She'd discovered her family history and was now able to move on with her life. She did love Nick. But too much had happened and every time she looked at him, it would only remind her of that awful night.

She needed to get away. She needed a fresh start and time to think.

If she and Nick were meant to be, then it would happen, but for now she needed to look after herself.

Lucy stopped Cora and stared at her, crossing her arms defensively. "You're going to dump him, aren't you? After everything you've been through." She was incredulous.

"I...," Cora sighed, looking out across the water. It always amazed her that even when no air seemed to move in Egypt, there was always wind across the Nile.

"It's complicated, Lucy."

"Do you love him or not? That isn't too complicated."

"Yes! You know I do, but so much has happened. We nearly died out there, and it was my fault. If it hadn't been for me and my bloody family diary he would never have been involved. Us staying together would just be a reminder of all of the bad stuff. I can't do it to him, or to myself."

Alex and Lucy could only shake their heads. In silence, they all strolled back to the hotel and, when they arrived, went their separate ways.

~

Cora opened the door to see Nick pacing back and forth.

"Just when were you going to tell *me*?"

She sighed, leaving the door open and crossed the room, trying to put some distance between them. It took every ounce of strength she had not to run into his arms and kiss him. Instead she lowered her eyes and stared at her feet. She just didn't know what to say.

"You told me you loved me, Cora. Were you lying?" She knew he was angry and understood why.

"Look at me! Please." He walked to her and she raised her head. The sight of him took her breath away and before she knew what was happening her back was against the wall and his fingers were running through her hair. He caressed her cheeks as his lips desperately searched for hers. Unable to fight feelings she had tried so hard to forget, she surrendered. It was hopeless, she loved him too much. Eventually, he pulled back and stared deeply into her eyes, searching for an answer.

"Talk to me."

"I have lost so much in my life, Nick. I seem to attract trouble at every turn, and this time you were caught up in it and nearly died. I can't do that to you again."

"Why? Is there another maniacal family after you that we don't know about?"

She laughed. It was good that she could still do that.

"No. But my life is a mess...," she trailed off.

"Then let me help you tidy it up." He paused, a serious look passing over his face. "I love you, Cora Thomas, so much so that those three little words could never even begin to convey how much. I know you love me, too. Let me love you the way you deserve. Please."

She wanted him as much as he did her and she couldn't leave him now. She never really wanted to. She had just thought it was the right thing to do for the both of them.

"I love you so much, Nick."

WIND ACROSS THE NILE

"So you'll stay?"

"Yes, I'll stay," she smiled, finally caving.

"I thought maybe I could show you around the country properly for a few months. We could explore everything; tombs, temples, museums. I also thought we could even try that felucca thing one night like your great-great-grandparents did. It sounded like a lot of fun!" he joked, the twinkle back in his eyes.

"Nick!" She liked the sound of staying in the country a bit longer. "But what about the excavation?"

"David and the others can handle that, and Josh Caplin is coming back out to replace Sam After everything we have been through, I think I deserve some time off."

"It sounds like fun. Let's do it!"

"Great! Now about that felucca thing?"

"Don't push your luck, Professor Foster!" she laughed.

EPILOGUE

Cairo, Egypt, 2002

Cora stood with her hand shielding her eyes, trying her best to block out some of the sun's glare so that she could better experience the vista.

It was truly breathtaking.

After a strenuous climb on precariously jutting stones of varying sizes and shapes, she now found herself standing at the summit of the great pyramid of Khufu on the Giza Plateau. She hadn't believed Nick when he had told her he'd been given special permission to climb it. But it was true. Tourists had jealously watched their ascent, wishing they could be in her shoes and, despite the climb, which had been hot and hard going in places, she'd enjoyed every moment.

She surveyed Cairo in all its sprawling glory, taking in every part of the panoramic view: the chaos of the city in one direction, encroaching on the ancient site, and endless miles of desert in the other. She felt on top of the world and couldn't be happier. Standing beside her, Nick pointed out the sphinx and funerary buildings at the end of the pyramid causeway far below them. They looked so small from this height although no less magnificent. It really gave her an idea of how large the plateau was and how much more there was to it than just pyramids. Watching the tourists below being hassled by locals, they sat on one of the large stones to drink some deliciously cold water.

"It really pays to know you, doesn't it?" Cora teased.

"Maybe." He winked.

"I think this view will live with me forever. It's been an amazing few months."

Nick had been true to his word and they had toured the length and breadth of Egypt, taking in the sights. They had been to Abu Simbel, the Island of Philae, Abydos, Dendera, Alexandria and now Cairo. It had been fantastic.

"Apart from almost being killed by a couple of psychopaths."

She let out a burst of laughter, feeling lucky that she could finally now begin to laugh about the whole ordeal.

"Yes, apart from that."

"I have a surprise for you later."

"Another one? You really are spoiling me, Professor Foster."

"Professor? I thought we were well past that now!"

"I may be in love with you, but I can still call you professor every now and again, can't I?" A cheeky grin spread across her face, illuminating it.

"You can call me anything you want." He leaned in and kissed her gently on the lips, feeling her respond. Finally parting from him, she laid her head on his shoulder and breathed a contented sigh.

"So, back to this surprise. I know I may be spoiling you, but you're worth it and I think you will love it," Nick said.

"Even more than climbing one of the great Pyramids of Giza?"

"Oh, so much more."

"Now I'm intrigued. Can you give me a clue?"

"No."

"Not even a small one?"

"No."

"Now that's just unfair."

"Maybe. But it wouldn't be a surprise if I told you would it."

"I guess not," she sulked.

They sat in contented silence once more, staring out across the plateau as life below them continued as normal.

"Do you still have Randa's ring?" Nick asked.

"Yes. I wanted to wear it, so it's around my neck on a chain I bought from the market."

"May I see it?" he asked holding out his hand.

"Of course." She removed it, taking care to slide it off the chain into his hand and not drop it down the side of the pyramid.

"It's beautiful. Quite plain, but very beautiful. It has so much history to it," he said, holding it closely and watching it glint the sunlight.

"It is. I'm so glad I have it. Randa and Albert may not have had the happiest of lives once they'd been disowned and returned to England, but I do believe from her diary that they truly were in love with each other. I like to think that the ring symbolises their happiness and love."

"I'm glad I chose it then, as it will have even more importance to you." A grin crept across his face, lighting up his eyes. Eyes that were filled with nothing but love. Very carefully, he knelt on the jutting stone next to her.

"I love you, Cora Thomas. So much so that I would have died if they had succeeded in killing you. I don't ever want to lose you. So, to that end, will you marry me?"

Tears of joy sprang from her eyes as she looked at him holding Randa's ring to the tip of her wedding finger, she could barely speak and nodded frantically trying to make up for her dumb silence.

"Is that a yes?"

"Yes! It's most definitely a yes," she breathed, watching as he slid the band onto her finger, before sitting beside her and kissing her.

"I'm so glad you said yes."

"Why? Because otherwise you would have looked a fool?"

"No. I'm glad you said yes because proposing to you at the summit of Khufu's pyramid is just about the coolest proposal story in the world!" he said laughing.

"So I take it this was my surprise then?"

"This? Oh no, that's yet to come," he teased. "Right. Come on, it's boiling up here and there's more to see on the ground. Be careful climbing down, I don't want you to break your neck!" Nick stood and held his hand out so he could help her to her feet. As she stood, he pulled her to him again gently brushing his lips to her and she closed her eyes surrendering fully to his kiss. It was probably the only time she'd ever get to kiss a man on top of a pyramid so she made the most of it.

~

Cairo's streets were exceptionally busy, and traffic was jostling for any and every available space, each vehicle beeping their horn loudly at the other. It made her smile, reminding her of her first day in the country. It was less than a year ago, but seemed like a lifetime. She felt as though she was a completely different person now, and she was no longer angry with her family. She understood them, and was very proud of them. Nick pulled the car off the road onto the forecourt of a local restaurant. He turned the engine off and opened the door to climb out.

"Hungry?"

Cora nodded. She was famished. All that climbing and exploring had given her a hearty appetite. Following suit, she got out, slammed the door shut, and entered the restaurant behind him. It was unusually quiet. A small group of locals were gathered at a table in the corner, and she looked around her with interest as Nick spoke quickly with the owner in Arabic. It had a homely feel about it and was pleasantly decorated as well as being clean and tidy. A few minutes later, they were sitting at a table discussing what they were going to eat.

Nick placed his menu on the table and looked up at her. "So what do you think of this place, then?"

Looking around her again, she nodded. "It's nice. I like it and the smell coming from the kitchen is delicious."

"Good. At least you won't offend the owner then."

"Is there any reason I would?" she asked, puzzled. Nick had an odd look on his face and, if she wasn't mistaken, the locals in the corner were staring a bit too much.

She, too, placed her menu on the table.

"Right. What's going on, Nick Foster?"

"Here." He stood, beckoning her to do the same. She shrugged and played along, following him as he walked over to the locals at the nearby table. She stood timidly behind him, not sure what to expect.

"Cora. I'd like to introduce you to some very important people. They're the owners of this restaurant."

She smiled at the family, customarily greeting them in their native Arabic. The eldest, a weathered Egyptian woman stood and took Cora's face in her hands before turning to Nick to speak. Cora couldn't understand what she was saying, but she did seem ecstatically happy. Nick responded and, as he finished, the woman released Cora's face before taking her in her arms hugging Cora tightly.

Mystified, she turned to Nick for an explanation.

"This is your surprise. This family is directly descended from Randa's brother, Ishaq. They're your Egyptian relatives, Cora, albeit distant."

She looked at the smiling woman.

"My family?" she asked, in barely a whisper.

"Yes." Nick smiled and put his arm around her. "I found your family for you."

Looking from one to the other, with tears in her eyes, she finally realised she'd come home, and her family was once more complete. She had come to Egypt with a heavy heart filled with grief. Once the grief had subsided, she'd discovered her history, fallen in love and gained a whole new family. Now, she had her life back. Nick had made it all possible and she would be forever in his debt.

Cora hugged the old woman back, and said hello to the rest of her new family.

Glancing over her shoulder, she looked at Nick, mouthing *"Thank you."* All he could do was nod his head, as his unspoken words of devotion floated across the room to embrace her.

Acknowledgements

Huge thanks as always to my incredible team, without them it wouldn't be possible to do what I do. Dale Cassidy, my wonderful editor who kicks me into shape when I need it and makes me a better writer for it and Paul Francis, my proofreader who's done an amazing job, thank you for your hard work. You've both helped me make this book what it is and I couldn't have done it without either of you. Rachel Lawston, thanks for our patience and for designing such a wonderful book cover, I love it.

To my friends, there are many and I wish that I could thank each and every one of you, but that would end up being another book! Dee Thompson, who's always at the end of a message and continues to push me on, your support is amazing, thank you. To my girls, Katerina Tsekouras, Louise

CHRISSIE PARKER

Inzk and Julie Ann Mystriotis, where do I even begin? Thanks for being there for me, but especially for the vidcalls, and funny messages that keep me sane. You're truly brilliant friends and your support means the world to me; με πολύ αγάπη και αγκαλιές.

I must say a special thank you to the many people who've helped with my research. Nanette de Ville, The British Museum, The Petrie Museum and the Egyptian Exploration Society. Many hours have been spent online, on the telephone and walking round exhibits for help and inspiration, and it's been invaluable. I'd also like to thank Lucia Gahlin my Egyptology course tutor at Exeter University, I've learned so much, and my love of Egyptology has only grown throughout these courses.

To my loyal readers in the *Chrissie Parker Book Group* on Facebook, as well as my brilliant admins Rose James and Sylvia Stein. Your support has been truly overwhelming, and without you I wouldn't be here, so thank you for sharing this journey with me, there's so much more to come and I'm looking forward to sharing it with you.

Finally, to my husband T and my family. Thank you for your continued support, I love you all very much.

About the Author

Chrissie Parker lives in Devon in the UK, with her husband.
Web - www.chrissieparker.com
Blog - https://chrissieparkerauthor.wordpress.com
Facebook Group - https://www.facebook.com/groups/chrissieparkersbookgroup/
Facebook Page - https://www.facebook.com/ChrissieParkerAuthor
Twitter - https://twitter.com/Chrissie_author
Instagram - https://www.instagram.com/chrissieparkerauthor/